high note 4

Workbook

Pearson
KAO TWO
KAO Park
Hockham Way
Harlow, Essex
CM17 9SR
England
and Associated Companies throughout the world

www.english.com/highnote

First published 2020
Eighth impression 2024

ISBN: 978-1-292-20979-1
Set in Akko Pro

Printed and bound by CPI Group (UK) Ltd, Croydon, CR0 4YY

Acknowledgements
The publishers would like to thank Halina Lewandowska for writing the Active Pronunciation sections.

Image Credit(s)
The publisher would like to thank the following for their kind permisson to reproduce their photographs:

123RF.com: canrail 45; **Alamy Stock Photo**: age fotostock 44, Art Collection 3 7, chombosan 93, ClassicStock 115, Cory Seamer 106, dpa picture alliance 68, Gregg Vignal 118, Historic Collection 7, imageBROKER 112, Lev Dolgachov 9, Luca Oleastri 99, Marc Tielemans 123, Michael Siluk 85, michaelklok/Stockimo 41, Nunnicha Supagrit 43, pawita warasiri 17, Peter Chan 64, Phanie 100, Rafal Olkis 117, The Picture Art Collection 81, Tony Smith 68, 69, Trevor Collens 93; **Getty Images**: 3DSculptor 16, A-Digit 76, adventtr 45, Alex Pantling 105, alvarez 88, Anna Quaglia/EyeEm 53, Brooke Whatnall 52, Busà Photography 109, Caiaimage/Martin Barraud 46, Cavan Images 41, cookelma 5, Dean Mouhtaropoulos 105, Dgwildlife 53, DisobeyArt 77, Dougal Waters 54, FatCamera 32, 33, fizkes 75, Flashpop 60, Forgem 89, Francesco Riccardo Iacomino 7, Geri Lavrov 63, gorodenkoff 81, Graham Oliver 111, Hero Images 23, ilbusca 28, Indeed 61, janulla 57, jhillphotography 30, Josef Kubes/EyeEm 113, Kuleshin 101, martinedoucet 78, Mike Point 33, MileA 89, Mint Images 117, Mirko Vitali/EyeEm 22, Monica Schipper 31, Oliver Furrer 103, PeopleImages 95, poba 59, RapidEye 11, Ryan McVay 22, 114, SDI Productions 8, Siwat Charoenkit/EyeEm 71, Stan Honda 69, Thomas Barwick 35, tomazl 29, Troy Aossey 39, vgajic 65, Xsandra 82, yongyuan 102; **Shutterstock.com**: Alex Staroseltsev 21, D. Kucharski K. Kucharska 20, GraphEGO 71, Hans Engbers 21, Johan Swanepoel 21, Kev Williams 67, M.Stasy 25, Nneirda 45, Ollyy 57, Tatiana Popova 42

Cover Image: *Front:* **Getty Images**: Chris Ryan

All other images © Pearson Education

Text Credit(s):
p105, **Telegraph Media Group**: Ellie Simmonds

Illustration Acknowledgements
Illustrated by Sean (KJA Artists) p58, p90; Sarah (KJA Artists) p121.

Every effort has been made to trace the copyright holders and we apologise in advance for any unintentional omissions. We would be pleased to insert the appropriate acknowledgement in any subsequent edition of this publication.

CONTENTS

01 Get the message

1A GRAMMAR AND VOCABULARY

Present and past tenses

1 ⭐ Match sentences 1–11 with their meanings a–k.

1. ☐ He's been writing thank-you letters all morning.
2. ☐ I wrote an English essay last night.
3. ☐ She's writing a text message right now.
4. ☐ Young people are writing by hand less often these days.
5. ☐ I was writing to Eleanor when she called me.
6. ☐ They've written several very long essays.
7. ☐ We were writing to each other regularly back then.
8. ☐ I've written down everything she's said so far.
9. ☐ Carl writes at least ten texts every day.
10. ☐ I'd already talked to that police officer about the burglary, so he knew I was innocent.
11. ☐ Teenagers rarely write emails.

Present Simple
a routines and habits/things that happen repeatedly
b facts and things that are generally true
Present Continuous
c things happening now or around now
d situations which are changing during the present time
Past Simple
e actions that started and finished at a specific time in the past
Past Continuous
f actions in progress at a specific time in the past
g a long activity interrupted by a shorter one
Present Perfect Simple
h actions and states which began in the past and continue until now
i finished actions in the past when we don't say exactly when they happened
Present Perfect Continuous
j an action in progress or repeated over a period of time up until now
Past Perfect
k an action in the past that was completed before another action or time in the past

2 ⭐ Choose the correct time expressions to complete the sentences.

1. I usually take a break from my screen *right now / from time to time* to give my eyes a rest.
2. According to my phone, I've spent sixty-seven minutes online *since nine o'clock / ever since*.
3. We've been learning about ancient methods of communication at school *recently / last week*.
4. I forgot my password and blocked my email account *the day before yesterday / in recent weeks*.
5. It's getting more and more difficult to maintain face-to-face communication *nowadays / at the time*.
6. We were walking on the beach *earlier today / once in a while* when we found a message in a bottle.

3 ⭐⭐ Complete the sentences with the forms from the box. There are two extra forms.

---
are becoming   are you using   do you have
do you know   don't usually send   'm talking
never writes   ~~prefer~~   writes
---

1. Most teenagers *prefer* texting to calling.
2. My friends and I _____ emails.
3. Once in a while, my grandfather _____ a letter.
4. _____ your laptop right now? I'd like to borrow it.
5. Can I call you back? I _____ to someone else at the moment.
6. Landline telephones _____ less and less common these days.
7. _____ how much credit you've got left on your phone?

4 ⭐⭐ Complete the pairs of sentences with the correct endings in bold.

1. **ALL MORNING / THREE TIMES TODAY**
   a I've been texting Jackie _____.
   b I've texted Jackie _____.

2. **TWO ESSAYS TODAY / THAT ESSAY SINCE THIS MORNING**
   a Kay's been writing _____.
   b Kay has written _____.

3. **ENGLISH FOR VERY LONG / HOW TO WRITE IN ENGLISH YET**
   a Amal hasn't learned _____.
   b Amal hasn't been learning _____.

5 ⭐⭐ **Complete the story with the correct forms of the verbs from the box.**

concentrate ~~drop~~ go happen leave lose not be not hear sit steal

Leon was riding his bike when he **¹***dropped* his phone. He **²**_____ on the road, so he **³**_____ it fall. He arrived at school and **⁴**_____ straight to his first lesson. He **⁵**_____ in English class when he realised that he **⁶**_____ it. He thought he **⁷**_____ it at home, but when he got back at the end of the day, it **⁸**_____ there. He never found out what **⁹**_____ to it and assumed that someone **¹⁰**_____ it.

6 ⭐⭐ **Use the prompts to write questions.**

1 you / receive / any hand-written letters / recently?
Have you received any hand-written letters recently?

2 social media / change / the meaning of friendship?
_____

3 you / watch / the documentary / about communication through the ages / yesterday?
_____

4 Grandma / know / how to switch on the computer?
_____

5 you / see / her photos on Instagram / before you met her?
_____

6 you / have a bad dream / when / I / wake / you up?
_____

7 ⭐⭐ **Complete the news story with the correct forms of the verbs in brackets.**

Members of an Australian family **¹***found* (find) the world's oldest message in a bottle over 100 years after German researchers **²**_____ (throw) it into the Indian Ocean.

The Illman family **³**_____ (walk) on the beach in Perth in Australia, when they **⁴**_____ (come across) a bottle lying in the sand. Tonya Illman **⁵**_____ (pick it up) and **⁶**_____ (discover) a note inside asking the finders to contact the German authorities. Researchers **⁷**_____ (write) the note 132 years earlier.

8 ⭐⭐ **Choose the correct forms to complete the sentences. Sometimes more than one form is possible.**

1 I ___ a message to you when you phoned!
  a was just writing
  b have just been writing
  c am just writing

2 You ___ on your project all morning. Haven't you finished yet?
  a were working
  b had worked
  c have been working

3 What ___ of my new keyboard? It's specially designed so it's comfortable to type with.
  a are you thinking
  b have you thought
  c do you think

4 When I got up, my dad ___ coffee.
  a has made
  b made
  c was making

5 Internet connections ___ faster and faster all the time.
  a have got
  b are getting
  c get

6 When I got home from school, I ___.
  a was falling asleep
  b had fallen asleep
  c fell asleep

7 Sadly, I ___ in touch with anyone from my old school.
  a haven't stayed
  b am not staying
  c wasn't staying

8 When I checked my email, the results ___.
  a were already arriving
  b had already arrived
  c arrived already

9 ON A HIGH NOTE **Write a short paragraph about writing by hand. When do you use a pen and paper to write? When do you use an electronic device? Why? What things did people write with a pen and paper which they now use electronic devices for?**

1B READING AND VOCABULARY

1 Read the article quickly and look at the photos. Tick the ones which contain the objects mentioned in the text and write their names.

- ☐ Photo A _____
- ☐ Photo B _____
- ☐ Photo C _____

2 Read the article again and choose the correct answers.

1 How can the author's opinion of the Rosetta Stone in Paragraph 1 best be summarised?

- **a** Its popularity as a museum exhibit is difficult to explain.
- **b** It is far more significant than it looks.
- **c** It is a disappointment for most museum visitors.
- **d** It is a dull administrative document.

2 Which statement is true about the Rosetta Stone?

- **a** It was made for a child ruler.
- **b** It was the only one of its kind.
- **c** Its sole aim was to declare the pharaoh a god.
- **d** It contains a multilingual message.

3 What does 'decipher' mean in line 51?

- **a** interpret
- **b** reproduce
- **c** pronounce
- **d** imagine

4 What does the author say about Rongorongo?

- **a** It may not actually be writing.
- **b** It is a kind of calendar.
- **c** It is a kind of decoration.
- **d** It tells stories of the natural world.

5 Which object does the author say has become a part of popular culture?

- **a** the Rosetta Stone
- **b** the Rongorongo carvings
- **c** the Voynich Manuscript
- **d** the Tartaria Tablets

6 What does the author believe about mysterious texts from the past?

- **a** There are some texts we will never be able to work out.
- **b** We should only try to understand written languages, not symbols.
- **c** It's impossible for experts to agree about any texts from the past.
- **d** People will always try to make sense of them.

Vocabulary extension

3 Look at the highlighted verb–noun collocations in the text and complete the sentences with one word in each gap.

1 The true identity of the infamous killer 'Jack the Ripper' remains a *mystery* to this day.

2 Documentary makers go to great lengths to satisfy our _____ about the mysteries of the natural world.

3 Historians have made a _____ in understanding how the Egyptian pyramids were built.

4 The prince has been waiting decades to inherit the _____ from his mother, the queen.

5 Alan Turing saved millions of lives by cracking the _____ that Germany was using to send military communications during WW2.

6 Violence continues as various groups fight for _____ of this magnificent city.

ACTIVE VOCABULARY
Adjectives formed with a suffix and a prefix

Some adjectives are formed by adding a suffix to a verb (e.g. -**able**: solve – solv**able**).

Sometimes you need to make changes to the spelling (e.g. forget – forgett**able**).

You can also add a prefix to an adjective to make it negative (e.g. **un**-: solvable – **un**solvable, forgettable – **un**forgettable).

---

4 Write the negative adjective forms of these verbs.

1 accept	*unacceptable*	**5** deny	_____
2 afford	_____	**6** predict	_____
3 believe	_____	**7** suit	_____
4 break	_____		

5 Complete the sentences with the adjectives from Exercise 4.

1 This film contains violent scenes and is *unsuitable* for young children.

2 The exhibition entry fees are _____ for many school pupils and their families.

3 It's _____ that social media have contributed to a huge increase in the amount of contact among people around the world.

4 'The theft of objects from Egyptian pyramids is absolutely _____,' says the president.

5 In tests, we managed to crack the _____ screen on this phone in less than two minutes.

6 Mountain weather is _____, so you should always carry warm clothes while hiking.

7 I found his explanation of the broken window completely _____.

6 ON A HIGH NOTE Write a short paragraph about a famous historical site or object in your country.

A

B

C

COMMUNICATING *with* THE PAST

Unlike many of Egypt's ancient treasures, the world-famous Rosetta Stone is nothing much to look at. Nevertheless, visitors to the British Museum flow endlessly past the large piece of rock, despite being unable to read what is written on it. If they could, they might be disappointed to discover that it is a kind of bureaucratic tax document. However, as the museum guides explain each day, the Rosetta Stone is the star of an incredible true story about cracking codes and communicating with the past.

The tale begins over 2000 years ago in Egypt and the city of Alexandria. When Pharaoh Ptolemy IV died, his throne was inherited by a six-year-old son. This was the start of years of chaos as rival groups fought for control of the child and his kingdom. Eventually though, the boy-pharaoh grew up and, with the assistance of powerful priests, he became an influential leader. In 196 BC, like all the other pharaohs before him, he wished to announce to the world his status as a living god. The Rosetta Stone is one of eighteen similar stones that were put up in temples around Egypt; their purpose was both to spread this message and to bring into law some very generous tax breaks for the priests who had helped him. The stone is of particular historical importance because the 'memo' it contains is written in three languages: classical Greek, an everyday Egyptian language called Demotic, and hieroglyphics like those found on statues, tombs and monuments throughout Egypt.

The Rosetta Stone remained in Egypt throughout 2000 years of its troubled and often violent history. Then in 1801, it was captured by the British army and taken to London. There, academics set to work analysing the text in order to decipher what was written on it. Scholars of ancient Greek could understand the Greek version, but the hieroglyphics remained a mystery. That was, until an English researcher named Thomas Young made a major breakthrough by recognising a group of symbols that spelled out the name 'Ptolemy'. His work was continued by Frenchman Jean-Francois Champollion who finally figured out how to read the mysterious text in 1882. Young and Champollion's work opened a channel of communication with the past that has allowed us to work out exactly what is written on all the great objects and monuments of Egypt.

However, despite the best efforts of linguists and code breakers, a number of unexplained manuscripts and mysterious languages have proved unsolvable to this day. A notable example is Rongorongo, which scholars believe may be a written language from Easter Island. It was found in the nineteenth century on various wooden objects and is made up of symbols showing animals, humans and plants. There have been many attempts to work out what meaning it conveys, but only one has met with partial success. This suggested that it may be related to the cycles of the moon. It is also possible that Rongorongo is not written text at all, but is in fact an early kind of memory aid or even simply decoration.

Then there's the beautiful Voynich Manuscript, a large illustrated book which has been dated to the early fifteenth century. It is thought to be written in a European language – though not a familiar one – and contains strange pictures of plants and animals that don't actually exist. Some researchers have suggested it is a fake and others a guide to medieval medicine, but no one is sure. Perhaps because it remains so mysterious, it has inspired many contemporary films and books.

One final puzzle could be the oldest of them all. According to some estimates, the Tartaria Tablets, which were unearthed in Romania in 1961, are over 7000 years old. This would make the symbols on these small round discs the earliest known form of writing. However, similarly to Rongorongo, whether or not they are actually a written language is still open to question.

As with many messages from the past, opinions differ and even the experts can be sure of almost nothing. It is not easy to satisfy human curiosity however, and where mystery remains, investigation will surely follow. Driven by incredible success stories like that of the deciphering of hieroglyphics through analysis of the Rosetta Stone, scholars, experts and historians will no doubt continue their code-cracking efforts to communicate with the past.

1C **VOCABULARY** | Idioms and phrases related to communication

1 ★ Match the two parts of the sentences.

1 ☐ Sharing a house creates a strong
2 ☐ My tutor and I really hit it
3 ☐ My friends and I always have
4 ☐ I met our new neighbours and I took
5 ☐ I'm not good at making
6 ☐ Although I may come across
7 ☐ Thankfully, Jenna made
8 ☐ I always try to strike up
9 ☐ If someone pays you

a to them immediately.
b a favourable impression on her new tutor.
c bond between young people at university.
d small talk and I often end up saying silly things.
e off, so I'm looking forward to our lessons together.
f as a confident person, I'm actually quite shy.
g a compliment, smile and say 'thank you'.
h a laugh when we get together.
i a conversation when I meet someone new.

2 ★ Choose the correct words to complete the idioms.

1 *throw* / *fire* questions at someone
2 insist on having the last *say* / *word*
3 put somebody *on* / *in* the spot
4 jump down somebody's *neck* / *throat*
5 not get a word in *edgeways* / *sideways*
6 refuse to let something *drop* / *stop*

3 ★ Match situations a–f with idioms 1–6 from Exercise 2.

a ☐ Then the boss asked me to say who I thought was to blame. It was so embarrassing!
b ☐ You always have to be the last one to speak, don't you?
c ☐ I told him I didn't want to talk about it anymore, but he wouldn't stop.
d ☐ He just kept asking me one thing after another for what seemed like ages.
e ☐ When I told her I was going to be a few minutes late, she got really angry!
f ☐ She talked so much that I didn't manage to say anything at all during lunch.

4 ★★ Complete the conversation with the words from the box.

across   bond   compliment   ~~hit~~   impression   laugh
small   strike   take

Rory   So how did your evening go, Kate? Did you and Lottie ¹*hit* it off?

Kate   I'm not sure. I tried to ²_____ up a conversation by paying her a ³_____, but I have a feeling that I came ⁴_____ as a bit over-enthusiastic.

Rory   Oh, I wouldn't worry. I'm sure you made a favourable ⁵_____. People usually ⁶_____ to you, right? Perhaps you were just trying a bit too hard.

Kate   Maybe, I mean – there was quite a lot of ⁷_____ talk, but we had a ⁸_____. She's got a good sense of humour.

Rory   Well, there you go. I mean … you can't expect to create a strong ⁹_____ after just one evening out. I think it went better than you imagine.

5 ★★★ Complete the letter to a problem page with one verb in each gap.

ASK MARIANNA:

Marianna gives advice on readers' personal problems

Dear Marianna,

I have a real problem with one of my classmates at school. He's the captain of our debate team, but basically he's a bully who enjoys ¹*putting* his peers on the spot and often ²_____ impossible questions at them. Whenever someone gets something wrong, he immediately loses his temper and ³_____ down their throat. I once gave a bit of a silly answer to one of his questions and he ⁴_____ to let it drop, teasing me about it every time I saw him. He loves the sound of his own voice and unless he's pressuring us to answer one of his endless questions, we can't ⁵_____ a word in edgeways. As you might guess, he's also the kind of person that always has to ⁶_____ the last word. I'm thinking of quitting the debate team because of him.

What, if anything, can I do?

Regards,

Kylie

6 ON A HIGH NOTE Write about a time you met and talked to someone new. Use some of the phrases and idioms from this lesson to say how you and the other person behaved.

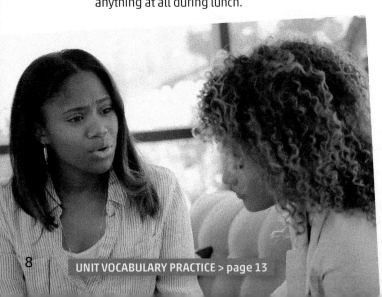

1D **GRAMMAR**

Question tags and echo questions

1 ⭐ Match sentences 1–6 with responses a–f.

1 ☐ I'm having a great time.

2 ☐ I met a really nice guy last week.

3 ☐ George and Ola have arrived!

4 ☐ Ray didn't want to dance.

5 ☐ Abi was wearing some beautiful shoes.

6 ☐ I can't understand what he's saying.

a Can't you? Why don't you ask him to speak more slowly?

b Was she? She's always so stylish.

c Have they? OK, I'll be there in two minutes.

d Are you? I'm glad you could make it.

e Didn't he? Maybe he doesn't know how.

f Did you? What was his name?

2 ⭐⭐ Choose the correct words to complete the question tags. Then add an echo question to complete the mini-conversations.

Ann Oh, dear. I'm talking too much, **1**_don't / aren't_ I? I get nervous in new situations.

Sam **2**_Do you_? I hadn't noticed. You seem quite self-confident to me.

Aaron Everybody likes chocolate **3**_aren't / don't_ they? I'm planning to make a chocolate cake for the party.

Noah **4**_____? Well, I certainly do, so please go ahead!

Paul You haven't met Alice, **5**_have / haven't_ you? She moved in next door recently.

Mike **6**_____? Hi, Alice. Welcome to the neighbourhood. I'm Mike.

Vicky Choose some more music, **7**_will / should_ you, Joey? My tablet is on the table.

Joey **8**_____? Oh, yeah. Right, let's get this party started!

Emma This is a great party, isn't **9**_it / this_? Ours wasn't nearly as much fun.

Kate **10**_____? I had a great time at our party.

Sarah Everything went wrong, **11**_didn't / wasn't_ it? I don't know what to do now.

Robert **12**_____? Well, perhaps I can help.

3 ⭐⭐⭐ Complete two conversations at a party with question tags or echo questions.

Becky Hi there. Love your dress. We haven't met, **1**_have we_?

Caitlin No, I don't think so. I'm Caitlin – Martin's cousin.

Becky **2**_____? Well, it's nice to meet you. I'm Becky and I'm in Martin's year at school, though I don't really know him very well. This is a great party, **3**_____? So, is Martin a nice guy?

Caitlin Actually, I find him a bit annoying, but don't tell him, **4**_____?

Becky Ha! I won't. I guess you're allowed to say that because you're family. And that's his sister, **5**_____? The girl with the black hair?

Caitlin Who, Amal? No, they're just friends. Martin hasn't got a sister.

Becky Oh! **6**_____?

Martin Change the music, **7**_____, Amal?

Amal Let's put on some hip-hop, **8**_____?

Martin Whatever you fancy. Do you know that girl who's talking to Caitlin? She goes to our school, **9**_____?

Amal Yeah, I think so. Her name's Becky. I don't really know her.

Martin She's looks like a nice girl.

Amal Well, we can go and say hello, **10**_____?

Martin Wait a minute! We can't just walk up and say hello.

Amal Of course we can! It's a party after all. It'll be fine.

Martin **11**_____? Hmm, I guess so. Do the talking though, **12**_____?

Amal Oh, come on Martin. Confidence is the key to success!

4 ON A HIGH NOTE Write a conversation at the party between two of the characters from Exercise 3. Include questions tags and echo questions.

1E LISTENING AND VOCABULARY

1 🔊 **2 Listen to a radio interview about language and choose the correct answers.**

1 What is the main topic of this week's programme?
a scientific English
b translating and interpreting
c words and phrases describing happiness

2 The guest on the programme has
a written a book.
b reviewed a book.
c translated a book.

2 🔊 **2 Listen again and complete the sentences with a word, a phrase or a number in each gap.**

1 There are estimated to be approximately *one million* words in the English language.

2 Words for emotions in other languages are often _____.

3 The Danish word 'morgenfrisk' describes how people feel after _____.

4 The _____ word 'mbuki-mvuki' refers to a desire to dance in an ecstatic way.

5 Dr Tim Lomas is a _____ at a university in London.

6 According to Dr Lomas, our _____ can increase thanks to understanding emotion words in other languages.

Vocabulary extension

3 Complete the collocations in bold with the correct forms of the words from the box. Use the information in brackets to help you.

arouse express genuine high mixed ~~stir up~~

1 Politicians have been accused of trying to *stir up* **people's emotions** (deliberately make them feel anger or hatred) before the election.

2 I felt _____ (positive and negative) **emotions** on my final day at secondary school.

3 My grandfather has difficulty _____ (showing or talking about) **his emotions**.

4 Whitney Houston sang with _____ (real or true) **emotion** and fans adored her for it.

5 Hunting is a topic that _____ (causes people to feel) **strong emotions**.

6 **Emotions are running** _____ (people have very strong feelings about a particular situation; there could even be violence) after another night of protests on the streets of Paris.

4 ON A HIGH NOTE What are your favourite words or phrases in English? Write a short paragraph, giving reasons.

Pronunciation

5 🔊 **3 Listen and complete the sentences from the interview in Exercise 1 with a question tag in each gap.**

1 It is, _____?
2 Now, these examples come from a book, _____?
3 Well, that covers rather a lot of us, _____?

6 🔊 **3 Listen to the sentences from Exercise 5 again. What do you notice about the way the speakers pronounce the sound /t/ at the end of the first word in each question tag (*isn't, don't, doesn't*)? Choose the correct answer.**

a The sound /t/ is very clearly pronounced.
b The sound /t/ disappears.

ACTIVE PRONUNCIATION
Omitting /t/ in question tags

In fast speech, the sound /t/ at the end of the first word in question tags can be omitted. English speakers do it quite often (e.g. *isn't it* – /'ɪz(ə)nɪt/, *doesn't she* – /'dʌz(ə)nʃɪ/).

7 🔊 **4 Listen and tick the question tags where the sound /t/ is omitted.**

1 ☐ Weren't we?
2 ☑ Hasn't he?
3 ☐ Can't I?
4 ☐ Hadn't they?
5 ☐ Doesn't it?
6 ☐ Wasn't he?

8 🔊 **5 Listen and practise saying the sentences.**

1 The world has become a different place, hasn't it?
2 Ben gets on your nerves, doesn't he?
3 I should release the negative emotions, shouldn't I?
4 The idea of making contact with aliens is ridiculous, isn't it?
5 We could at least try to break the ice, couldn't we?

9 🔊 **6 Complete the sentences with question tags. Listen and check. Then practise saying the sentences.**

1 Vanessa likes people paying her compliments, *doesn't she*?
2 David has been firing questions at you all day, _____?
3 Our boss is completely fed up with all the paperwork, _____?
4 Diane was bewildered by her nephew's behaviour, _____?
5 He could try to work on his emotional intelligence, _____?

1 🔊 *7* **Listen and repeat the phrases. How do you say them in your language?**

SPEAKING | Expressing emotions

EXPRESSING ANXIETY

It's been keeping me up at night.

I'm worried sick about my sister's surgery.

EXPRESSING RELIEF

I can breathe a sigh of relief now.

That's a weight off my mind.

Thank goodness.

EXPRESSING ANNOYANCE AND FRUSTRATION

That beeping noise **is driving me up the wall!**

His loud laugh **really gets on my nerves.**

I've had it up to here with your constant complaints.

EXPRESSING SURPRISE OR DISBELIEF

You've got to be kidding me!

Get out of here!

Who would have thought it?

EXPRESSING SADNESS

I'm feeling a bit down in the dumps.

I'm feeling a bit blue.

I'm heartbroken.

EXPRESSING ENJOYMENT OR HAPPINESS

I'm walking on air!

I can't stop smiling!

---

2 **Choose the correct words to complete the sentences.**

1 Get *out / off* of here!
2 I'm worried *sick / ill*.
3 That's a weight off my *brain / mind*.
4 Now I can *breathe / blow* a sigh of relief.
5 You've got to be *kidding / joking* me!
6 It's been keeping me *out / up* at night.
7 Who would have *understood / thought* it?
8 Thank *goodness / happiness*.

3 **What do these phrases express? Choose *A* for annoyance, *S* for sadness or *H* for happiness.**

1 I'm heartbroken. A / S / H
2 This computer is driving me up the wall! A / S / H
3 I'm walking on air! A / S / H
4 I'm feeling a bit down in the dumps. A / S / H
5 I'm feeling a bit blue. A / S / H
6 I can't stop smiling! A / S / H
7 I've had it up to here with the traffic in this city. A / S / H
8 Her voice really gets on my nerves. A / S / H

4 **Choose the correct phrases to complete the mini-conversations. Ignore the gaps for now.**

John What's the matter with you?

Celia The neighbours are playing their music at full volume again. ¹*It's driving me up the wall! / I'm walking on air!*

John ª*What a pain!*!

Celia Maybe I should go and talk to them again.

John I think you should. I mean – ᵇ_____

Tony My aunt's dog died. ²*She's heartbroken. / It really gets on her nerves.*

Gilly Oh no! Poor thing. ᶜ_____

Aisha How did it go?

Kim I got the job – summer in Italy! ³*I'm feeling a bit blue. / I can't stop smiling!*

Aisha That's awesome! ᵈ_____

Piet Just calm down!

Milo Calm down? My phone is broken again! ⁴*I'm feeling a bit down in the dumps. / I've had it up to here with the stupid thing!* I want my money back!

Piet ᵉ_____ That's the third time this month.

Milo ᶠ_____

5 🔊 *8* **Now complete gaps a–f in Exercise 4 with the phrases from the box. Listen and check.**

I don't blame you.
I know, right?
I'm really pleased for you.
I'm so sorry to hear that.
~~What a pain!~~
what's the worst that could happen?

1G WRITING | An informal email

Start with a friendly greeting.

Mention your last contact with the other person.

Mention any news from your friend.

Cover each topic in a separate paragraph.

Finish with a friendly, informal goodbye.

Hi Tim,

How are things? **1**___ in ages. Have you settled in to your new school? **2**___ that you passed your driving test! Congratulations! How did it feel to drive on your own for the first time?

3___ I've been doing loads of training in preparation for the snowboarding season. Feeling pretty good and my legs are definitely getting stronger. Remember I had that summer job? Well, I saved up all summer and I'm going to Austria for a snowboard training camp in December. (Dead excited!) **4**___ Fancy coming for a visit and going to the mountains for the day? If only I knew someone who has a driving licence and their own car and could drive me there. Oh, that's right, I do … you! ☺

Revision is driving me crazy at the moment. I keep having these dreams where I get to the exam and realise that I missed all the lessons and don't know anything about the subject! **5**___ Really awful, but at least I'm relieved when I wake up! How are you getting on? You always seemed pretty calm about tests and exams. Do you feel like you're going to be ready in time? Maybe we could have a video call sometime and share some notes. **6**___ Good plan?

7___ Katy and I are off to the cinema on Saturday – going to see the new Wonder Woman film. Probably go for a burger afterwards. We both need a break from revision. Speaking of revision, I guess I'd better go and get on with some right now!!☹

Say hi to your sis, bro, mum and dad. **8**___ about coming to visit.

9___

Justin

1 Match phrases a–i with gaps 1–9 in Justin's email.

a ☐ It was great to hear
b ☐ Let me know
c ☐ Haven't seen you
d ☐ You like winter sports too, don't you?
e ☐ What else?
f ☐ What do you think?
g ☐ Argh!
h ☐ Cheers,
i ☐ Life's been busy here as usual.

2 Read the email again and complete the advice with *Do* or *Don't*.

1 *Don't* use a formal style.
2 _____ use full forms instead of contractions.
3 _____ use more informal quantifiers and intensifiers.
4 _____ include the subject and auxiliary verb if the meaning is obvious.
5 _____ use question tags and rhetorical question.
6 _____ use abbreviations, emoticons and interjections.

3 Find examples of the following punctuation marks in Justin's email.

1 comma after greeting
2 exclamation marks (including multiple exclamation marks)
3 comma after an introductory adverb
4 brackets and dashes
5 comma to separate three or more words
6 comma after sign-off

4 Punctuate this email correctly.

Hi Sid,

Great news Amazingly I passed all my exams even Maths I feel proud happy relieved and totally surprised

Take care

Nancy

5 WRITING TASK Write a reply to Justin's email from Exercise 1.

ACTIVE WRITING | An informal email

1 Plan your email.
- Think about your reaction to Justin's news.
- Make a note of some news of your own to tell Justin.
- Think about how to react to Justin's invitation and suggestions.

2 Write the email.
- Start with a friendly greeting.
- Use a chatty style, including informal quantifiers, intensifiers, question tags and rhetorical questions.
- Don't forget to use contractions, emojis and abbreviations.
- Finish with a friendly goodbye.

3 Check that …
- all the relevant information is there.
- there are no spelling, grammar or punctuation mistakes.

1 1A GRAMMAR AND VOCABULARY **Complete each short text or dialogue with the correct forms of the words in bold.**

MAKE / LOSE / STAY

> I can't believe we ¹*lost* touch after being such good friends at school. I'm so glad you ² _____ contact again. Let's make sure we ³ _____ in touch from now on.

SPREAD / MAINTAIN / ESTABLISH

> We can use social media to ⁴ _____ and ⁵ _____ contact with our online users, and to ⁶ _____ the message that we believe the voting age should be lowered to sixteen.

DELIVER / PASS ON

> **Amy** Will you ⁷ _____ a message to Bryony when you see her? Group 1 has cancelled and Group 2 is now coming at 9.15 a.m., but there are only seven of them, so … .
>
> **Brad** What? I'll never remember all that. Write it down and I'll ⁸ _____ it to her office later.

CARRY / CONVEY

> The artist has painted a bird ⁹ _____ a message to the king. I think the painter is trying to ¹⁰ _____ a message about power and importance here.

2 1B READING AND VOCABULARY **Replace the underlined parts with the correct forms of the phrasal verbs from the box.**

---

bring about   come across   figure out   make out
~~pick up~~   point out   spell it out   wipe out

---

1 This device will <u>receive</u> a signal from someone trapped under the snow after an avalanche. *pick up*

2 Contact with aliens could <u>cause</u> a big change in the way we see our place in the universe. _____

3 I'd like to <u>bring to your attention</u> a few important rules before the game begins. _____

4 It was raining so heavily that we could barely <u>see</u> the road ahead. _____

5 The arrival of the new shopping centre has <u>completely destroyed</u> local shops. _____

6 Let me <u>explain it clearly</u> for you: if you ever do that again, I will report you to the police. _____

7 We <u>found</u> the bottle containing the message while walking on the beach. _____

8 These days, it doesn't take a genius to <u>understand</u> that the Earth is round and not flat. _____

3 1B READING AND VOCABULARY **Complete the sentences with one word in each gap.**

1 I was so tired I simply couldn't take <u>*in*</u> what they were saying to me.

2 Do I really have to spell _____ the reasons you should quit smoking?

3 Please pay attention while we point _____ some of the safety features on this aircraft.

4 Sadly, the accident brought _____ a serious change in his personality.

5 She didn't speak English, but I managed to get _____ the fact I needed help.

4 1C VOCABULARY **Complete the song lyrics with one word in each gap.**

> Just wanted to make a favourable ¹*impression*.
> Only wanted to strike up a real ² _____ .
> Have a ³ _____ . Hit it ⁴ _____ .
> Come ⁵ _____ as cool.
> Make small ⁶ _____ , get along
> and spend some time with you.
>
> And now I'm standing on my own.
> Might as well have stayed at home.
>
> Must've tried too hard,
> 'cos you left me on my own.
> Paid you ⁷ _____ , yet here I am alone.
> Couldn't ⁸ _____ a bond, though I wanted to.
> You didn't ⁹ _____ to me
> although I took to you.
>
> And now I'm standing on my own.
> Might as well have stayed at home.

5 1E LISTENING AND VOCABULARY **Replace the underlined words with the adjectives from the box with a similar meaning.**

---

bewildered devastated ecstatic exasperated livid
tense ~~terrified~~

---

1 Tim didn't tell his friend how <u>frightened</u> he was by the final scene of the film they went to see. *terrified*

2 Leanne was <u>sad</u> when her best friend stopped speaking to her. _____

3 When Paul returned to find his new car scratched he was <u>angry</u>. _____

4 Charlotte was understandably <u>nervous</u> as she waited for the results of her blood test. _____

5 Leon was <u>thrilled</u> when he found out he'd got a place at Sheffield University. _____

6 Carla's dad was <u>annoyed</u> that once again she hadn't called to let her parents know she was safe. _____

7 Passengers were left <u>confused</u> after the departure gate was changed seven times. _____

6 ON A HIGH NOTE **Write a short description of a time when you received a surprising message.**

1 **For each learning objective, write 1–5 to assess your ability.**

1 = I don't feel confident. 5 = I feel confident.

	Learning objective	Course material	How confident I am (1–5)
1A	I can use the present and past tenses to talk about different actions.	Student's Book pp. 4–5	
1B	I can identify the author's opinion and talk about life on other planets.	Student's Book pp. 6–7	
1C	I can talk about making new friends.	Student's Book p. 8	
1D	I can use question tags and echo questions to keep a conversation going.	Student's Book p. 9	
1E	I can identify specific information in a radio interview and talk about emotional intelligence.	Student's Book p. 10	
1F	I can use fixed phrases to express emotions.	Student's Book p. 11	
1G	I can write an informal email.	Student's Book pp. 12–13	

2 **Which of the skills above would you like to improve in? How?**

Skill I want to improve in	How I can improve

3 **What can you remember from this unit?**

New words I learned and most want to remember	Expressions and phrases I liked	English I heard or read outside class

GRAMMAR AND VOCABULARY

1 Choose the correct words to complete the sentences.

1 Houston has finally managed to *establish* / *lose* contact with Apollo 13 again after nearly twenty-four hours of radio silence.

2 I've no idea where Sophie is now. We *stayed in* / *lost* touch after university.

3 Could you *spread* / *pass on* the message to Kim that I'll be ten minutes late?

4 Can I *figure* / *point* out that you are entitled to your own opinions, but not your own facts?

5 Over seventeen different species have been *wiped* / *spelled* out this year and it's only March.

/ 5

2 Complete the text with the words from the box. There are two extra words.

bewildered   bond   compliment   doubt   ecstatic   hit   ~~terrified~~   took

Yesterday I got Skip, my new dog, from the rescue shelter. Most of the animals there looked understandably **¹terrified** – all alone in their cages. But when I approached Skip, he stuck his nose through the bars and gently licked my hand. As you can probably imagine, I ²_____ to him immediately. The lady at the shelter warned me that it can take some time to create a real ³_____, but Skip and I went for a walk together and seemed to ⁴_____ it off straight away. When he realised he was coming home with me, he was ⁵_____, barking excitedly and jumping and turning. Without a ⁶_____, after twenty-four hours, I'm completely in love.

/ 5

3 Choose the correct forms to complete the sentences.

1 I ___ shopping when I heard the news.
   a have been   **b** was   **c** am shopping

2 The researchers ___ picked up a signal from space before that incredible day.
   a had been   **b** had never   **c** have never

3 I ___ that this is the best way to spread our message; we need to think of something different.
   a haven't agreed   **b** am not agreeing   **c** don't agree

4 Cinema tickets ___ more and more expensive these days.
   a got   **b** get   **c** are getting

5 When I got to the stadium, I ___ a huge queue.
   a joined   **b** was joining   **c** had joined

/ 5

4 Complete the sentences with question tags.

1 Let's go out for lunch, *shall we*?
2 Don't forget about Jill, _____?
3 I'm still your best friend, _____?
4 It wasn't the best party, _____?
5 You will be nice to her, _____?
6 It's your birthday today, _____?

/ 5

USE OF ENGLISH

5 Complete the sentences with the correct words formed from the words in bold.

1 Sorry, we're having technical problems and are *currently* working on a solution. **CURRENT**

2 She finds it difficult to strike up a _____ with somebody she doesn't know. **CONVERSE**

3 I don't think I made a _____ impression in the interview. **FAVOUR**

4 When Fiona learned that her little brother was healthy, it was a _____ off her mind. **WEIGH**

5 Penelope was _____ when her cat died. **DEVASTATE**

6 The smell in the room was almost _____ – I had to cover my nose with a tissue. **BEAR**

/ 5

6 Complete the conversation with one word in each gap.

Charlotte	I **¹made** contact with my second cousin Beth for the first time yesterday.
Phoebe	Oh, wow! That's cool. How did you find her?
Charlotte	Mum and I ²_____ chatting about family and I found her on social media. There were seventeen 'Beth Gerard's', but we figured ³_____ which one she was from her photo.
Phoebe	How did you get on with her?
Charlotte	We really ⁴_____ it off.
Phoebe	That's great! I mean, you never know how someone might react when you contact them online like that. It kind of puts you ⁵_____ the spot, doesn't it?
Phoebe	It does, yes. I know people who ⁶_____ stopped using social media completely because they're worried about privacy.

/ 5

/ 30

15

2A GRAMMAR AND VOCABULARY

Future forms for predictions

1 ⭐ Complete the sentences with the correct forms of *will* or *going to* and the verbs in brackets. Sometimes more than one answer is possible.

1 My grandfather is 89 years old, but he's in great shape, so I'm sure he *'s going to live/'ll live* (live) to be 100.

2 Many experts expect that technology _____ (improve) living conditions for people in the developing world, but there's no evidence of that.

3 Look at these statistics – they are very optimistic. Without a doubt, crime figures _____ (continue) to decrease in the near future.

4 Some people fear that robots _____ (take) control of society soon, but I think that's unlikely.

5 Our new facial recognition software is already very popular in Europe. We _____ (make) a fortune once we launch it in countries across the world.

2 ⭐ Match sentences 1–5 with explanations a–c.

1 ☐ We'll be sleeping under the stars at this time next week.

2 ☐ Sue and Fiona will have watched the entire first series by the end of today.

3 ☐ Please don't complain. I'll be revising while you're relaxing on the beach!

4 ☐ Unfortunately, we won't have arrived by the time the restaurant closes at 9 p.m.

5 ☐ By the time we reach the entrance, we'll have been waiting for three hours!

a an activity in progress at a specific time in the future

b an activity which will be completed by a specific time in the future

c an activity which continues up to a specific point in the future

3 ⭐ Choose the correct words to complete the sentences. In one sentence both answers are possible.

1 You've done so much revision you're *bound / unlikely* to pass your exams.

2 With such strong winds, the ski-lifts are *unlikely / sure* to be open.

3 Although we can't be certain, we think the pool is *sure / likely* to be busy today.

4 After her injury, it's *unlikely / likely* that Shana will reach the finals.

5 Without a map or GPS you are *bound / certain* to get lost if you don't know the area.

4 ⭐⭐ Complete the factfile with the forms from the box.

will be flying ~~will be leaving~~ will be spending
will be watching will have been training
will have been travelling will have covered
will have learned

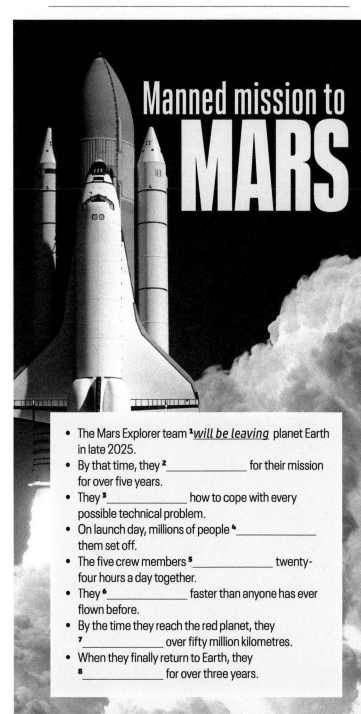

Manned mission to MARS

- The Mars Explorer team **1** *will be leaving* planet Earth in late 2025.
- By that time, they **2** _____ for their mission for over five years.
- They **3** _____ how to cope with every possible technical problem.
- On launch day, millions of people **4** _____ them set off.
- The five crew members **5** _____ twenty-four hours a day together.
- They **6** _____ faster than anyone has ever flown before.
- By the time they reach the red planet, they **7** _____ over fifty million kilometres.
- When they finally return to Earth, they **8** _____ for over three years.

5 ★★ Read the headlines and use the prompts to write sentences.

> President to visit UK on 23 October

1 By / 23rd October / special agents / finish / all their security checks

By 23 October, special agents will have finished all their security checks.

2 By / time the President arrives / people / wait / two years for an official visit

_____

3 On / 23 October / the President / address / MPs in the UK parliament

_____

> City centre closed to cars from 1 p.m. to 7 p.m. on Sunday for protest march

4 By / 4 p.m. / police / block / traffic into the city centre / for three hours

_____

5 By / 7 p.m. / all the protesters / finish / the march

_____

6 By / 7.05 p.m. / people / drive / through the city centre again

_____

6 ★★ Read the answers and write the questions.

1 *Will you be watching the match tomorrow?*
No, I won't be watching the match tomorrow.

2 _____
Yes, Laura will have finished school by 4 p.m.

3 _____
I'll have been training for nine years by the time I qualify as a surgeon.

4 _____
Yes, I'll have read both books by the weekend.

7 ★★★ USE OF ENGLISH Complete the second sentence using the word in bold so that it means the same as the first one. Use between two and five words, including the word in bold.

In the not-too-distant future …

1 driverless cars will almost certainly reduce the number of road accidents. **SURE**
driverless cars *are sure to reduce* the number of road accidents.

2 powerful computers will almost definitely become smaller, faster and cheaper. **CERTAIN**
powerful computers _____ smaller, faster and cheaper.

3 the human race probably won't go and live on another planet. **UNLIKELY**
the human race _____ on another planet.

4 smoking will almost certainly be banned altogether. **BOUND**
smoking _____ altogether.

8 ★★★ Complete the sentences with one word in each gap.

1 I hope that by the age of thirty, I'll *be* running my own successful tech business.
2 Is Svetlana likely _____ apologise for her behaviour?
3 By the time they get home, Lily and Dom will have _____ travelling for eighteen hours!
4 Do you think you'll _____ finished your project before next week's deadline?
5 I think it's likely that _____ the year 2050, doctors will have found a cure for cancer.
6 Three years _____ now, Harold will have gained his degree in astrophysics.

9 ★★★ Complete the text with the correct forms of the verbs in brackets.

By the time I get on the train at **London St Pancras** next Saturday, I [1]*'ll have been planning* (plan) this trip for two months! I [2]_____ (save up) enough money to pay for an Interrail pass which [3]_____ (allow) me to travel around Europe for one month. I've got a few days left before my trip, during which I [4]_____ (prepare) my bags and buying any last minute things I need for the journey. When I arrive at the platform on Saturday, my friend Jack [5]_____ (wait) for me. We [6]_____ (travel) everywhere by train and staying in different towns and cities on the way. By the end of the week, I hope we [7]_____ (reach) Madrid. I'm really excited about this trip. We've spent so much time preparing that I think our plan [8]_____ (bound/succeed). What could possibly go wrong?

10 ON A HIGH NOTE Make six statements about what you will be doing, will have done and will have been doing when/by the time you finish this English course.

1 ⭐ Match the compond nouns from the box with the definitions.

~~endangered species~~ exhaust fumes greenhouse effect ozone layer renewable energy toxic waste water scarcity wind turbine

1 Types of animals in danger of extinction. _endangered species_

2 Lack of water. _____

3 Power produced by wind, sun, etc. _____

4 A machine used to produce electric power. _____

5 Chemicals and other harmful waste products. _____

6 Poisonous gases produced by engines of non-electric vehicles. _____

7 Part of the stratosphere which limits the amount of ultraviolet radiation reaching the Earth. _____

8 Process by which gases trapped in the atmosphere cause the planet to heat up. _____

2 ⭐ Complete the crossword.

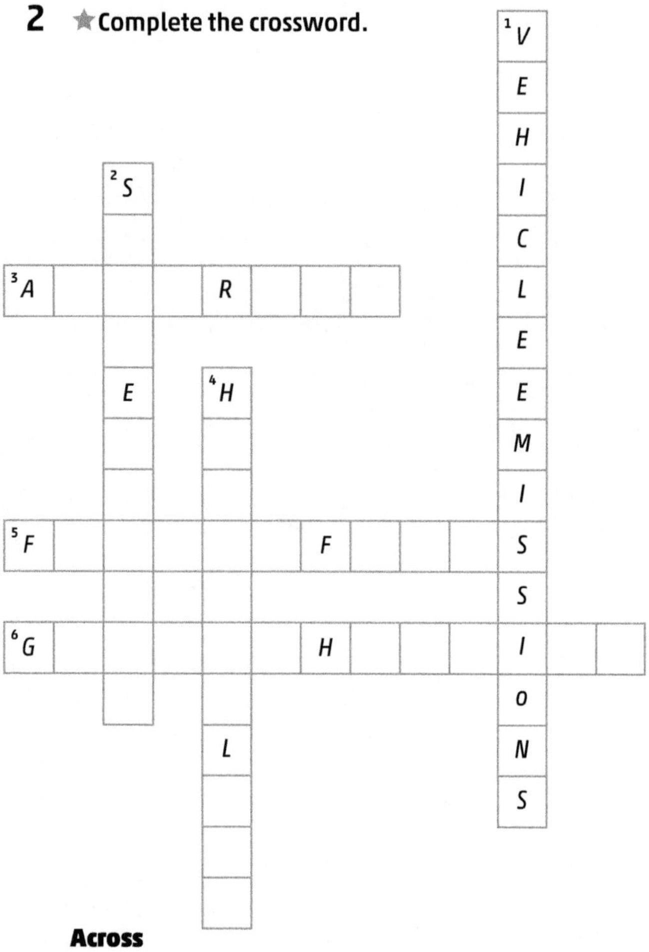

(crossword grid)
Vertical (1): V E H I C L E E E M I S S I S I O N S
2: S
3: A _ _ R _ _
E 4: H
5: F _ _ _ F _
6: G _ _ _ _ H _ _ _
L

Across

3 Rain that contains a lot of pollutants.

5 Examples of this are coal, oil and gas.

6 Gradual increase in the Earth's temperature.

Down

1 Synonym for 'exhaust fumes'.

2 Gradual destruction of the ground by weather or people.

4 Disappearance of areas that are home to plants and animals.

3 ⭐⭐ 🔊 9 Find the stressed word in these compound nouns. Listen and check.

1 (climate)change

2 industrial waste

3 wind turbine

4 endangered species

4 ⭐⭐ Complete the signs with one word in each gap.

> SAVE OUR TREES. STOP ¹*ACID* RAIN!

> Burning fossil fuels = a hole in the ozone ² _____ . Stop the cycle of destruction!

> MAKE PUBLIC TRANSPORT FREE TO REDUCE VEHICLE ³ _____ .

> CLOSE FACTORIES THAT PRODUCE ⁴ _____ WASTE NOW!

> The planet belongs to all living things: protect ⁵ _____ species and stop habitat ⁶ _____ .

> WATER ⁷ _____ WILL LEAD TO WAR! WE ARE THIRSTY FOR CHANGE!

5 ⭐⭐⭐ Complete the conversation with the compound nouns from Exercises 1 and 2.

Presenter On today's podcast – Peter Crumb, environmental activist. Peter, what's the biggest environmental issue the planet is facing?

Peter I think it has to be ¹_global heating_, by which I mean rising temperatures caused by the build-up of gases in the atmosphere, a process otherwise known as the ² _____ . We continue to burn ³ _____ despite knowing the harm they do to the environment and that they are certain to run out in the near future.

Presenter Yes, and we continue to drive cars that pollute the air with their ⁴ _____ .

Peter Indeed. You see, our refusal to properly adopt ⁵ _____ sources, such as solar power or wind farms with their majestic ⁶ _____ , is likely to mean things will get worse before they get better.

Presenter And do you think we are ever likely to change our behaviour?

Peter Well, I think public opinion is changing.

6 ON A HIGH NOTE Write a paragraph about threats to the environment in your region and what could be done locally to improve the situation.

2C LISTENING AND VOCABULARY

02

1 🔊 *10* **Listen to Part 1 of a lecture. What is the main topic? Choose the correct answer.**

a The impact of climate change on our clothing choices.

b Green is the new black: the rise of eco-fashion.

c How your clothes are ruining the natural environment.

2 🔊 *11* **Listen to Part 2 of the lecture and tick the things that are mentioned.**

1 ☑ water use
2 ☐ corruption
3 ☐ pesticides
4 ☐ chemical waste
5 ☐ child labour
6 ☐ consumerism
7 ☐ greenhouse gases
8 ☐ public opinion

3 🔊 *11* **Listen to Part 2 again and complete the sentences with no more than three words in each gap.**

1 It takes around *7600* litres of water to produce a pair of jeans.

2 _____ has caused severe damage to the environment in many countries.

3 What used to be the Aral Sea in Kazakhstan is now just _____.

4 Apart from the overuse of pesticides and water, clothes manufacturing also produces a lot of _____.

5 Because of 'fast fashion', the number of times people wear an item of clothing has gone down by _____ in the last fifteen years.

6 Multinational companies in the fashion industry are likely to continue prioritising _____ over ethical values.

Vocabulary extension

4 **Complete the text with the phrases from the box, which you heard in the recording in Exercises 1 and 2. Use the information in brackets to help you.**

common knowledge   in the name of   safe to say
share the blame   ~~well aware of~~   widely reported

Most people are **1** *well aware of* (know all about) the suffering that results from fur farming, yet all over the world animals are still mistreated and killed **2** _____ (for the sake of) fashion. Despite the fact that the issue has been **3** _____ (in the news a lot) and is now **4** _____ (known by everyone), fur is still seen by some people as a desirable luxury product. It is **5** _____ (certain) that if there was no demand for fur, then these farms would close. In reality, this means that consumers **6** _____ (are also responsible for the problem) with producers.

5 ON A HIGH NOTE **Would you stop purchasing clothing for environmental reasons? Write a short paragraph and explain your stance.**

Pronunciation

6 🔊 *12* **Read some words from the lecture in Exercises 1 and 2. How are the underlined vowel sounds pronounced? Listen and check.**

1 j<u>ea</u>ns, <u>ea</u>ch, f<u>ee</u>d, b<u>ei</u>ng
2 m<u>i</u>ddle, r<u>i</u>ver, s<u>i</u>mply, th<u>i</u>nk

ACTIVE PRONUNCIATION
/iː/ and /ɪ/ sounds

/iː/ and /ɪ/ are similar sounds in English. The spelling of words which include these vowel sounds is not always a clear guide to their pronunciation.

• /iː/ (long) typically appears in words which are spelled with ee (e.g. *seen*), ea (e.g. *please*), and ie (e.g. *piece*).

• /ɪ/ (short) typically appears in words which are spelled with i (e.g. *big, window, spirit*).

7 🔊 *13* **Write the words from the box in the correct column. Listen, check and repeat.**

~~extinct~~ freeze greenhouse habitat predict sea species   statistics

/iː/ feet	/ɪ/ fit
	extinct

8 🔊 *14* **Listen and notice how the vowel sound changes. Practise saying the pairs of words.**

1 st<u>ea</u>l st<u>i</u>ll
2 f<u>ie</u>ld f<u>i</u>lled
3 ch<u>ea</u>p ch<u>i</u>p
4 l<u>ea</u>k l<u>i</u>ck
5 sl<u>ee</u>p sl<u>i</u>p
6 wh<u>ee</u>l w<u>i</u>ll
7 f<u>ee</u>ling f<u>i</u>lling

9 🔊 *15* **Listen to these pairs of words. Tick the word you hear first.**

1 ☐ slip ☑ sleep
2 ☐ pill ☐ peel
3 ☐ bitten ☐ beaten
4 ☐ list ☐ least
5 ☐ fit ☐ feet
6 ☐ lid ☐ lead

10 🔊 *16* **Can you identify the /iː/ and /ɪ/ sounds in each sentence? Listen and check. Then practise saying the sentences.**

1 An increase in industrial waste will lead to habitat loss.

2 The key reason for this species' success is their big beaks.

3 Have you been drinking from reusable or single-use cups?

4 The disease spreads more quickly in humid conditions.

2D READING AND VOCABULARY

1 Match sentences 1–4 about four different animals with pictures A–D.

1 ☐ It is made angry by the colour red.
2 ☐ It buries its head in the sand when it is afraid.
3 ☐ It can only remember things for a few seconds.
4 ☐ It becomes two living creatures if cut in half.

2 Which of the sentences in Exercise 1 do you think is true? Read the article quickly and check your ideas.

3 Read the article again and match questions 1–10 with paragraphs A–E. Each paragraph may be chosen more than once.

Which paragraph …

1 ☐ contains good news for animals that might be hunted by a particular predator?
2 ☐ explains why a type of animal is not eaten as some people believe.
3 ☐ reveals that a particular animal's eyesight is more sensitive than is often believed.
4 ☐ suggests ancient origins for a particular myth.
5 ☐ mentions an important brain function that lasts much longer than commonly thought.
6 ☐ explains that a certain animal suffers from some vision deficiency but otherwise its eyesight is fine.
7 ☐ suggests that a particular truth will be a relief to a lot of people.
8 ☐ mentions a myth linked to the desire to avoid being seen by predators.
9 ☐ gives a specific example of an idiom in the context of the writer's family.
10 ☐ mentions a feeding behaviour that is often misinterpreted as an attack on a human.

Vocabulary extension

4 Match the highlighted words and phrases from the text with the definitions.

1 Not being able to fly. _flightless_
2 Hard pointed parts of an animal's head. _____
3 A way of navigating using sound. _____
4 An animal eaten by another animal. _____
5 Move quietly along the ground. _____
6 The ability to see well at night. _____

5 Complete the sentences with the correct forms of the words from Exercise 4.

1 My little brother screamed when he saw a spider _creeping_ out of the fruit bowl.
2 African buffalos are unusual because both males and females grow _____ on their heads.
3 As well as bats, marine animals such as dolphins and whales use _____ to help them navigate.
4 Penguins are _____ and have flippers.
5 Owls have extremely light-sensitive eyes and therefore excellent _____.
6 The leopard seal's most common _____ are squid and fish, but they eat penguins too.

ACTIVE VOCABULARY | Idioms with animals

In English, there are many common idioms that feature animals. In some cases, meaning can be guessed if you are aware of a particular animal's behaviour, e.g.:

the **lion's share** of something = the largest portion/amount of something (when lions eat their prey, they leave very little for other animals).

6 Complete the sentences including animal idioms with the words from the box. Use the information in brackets to help you.

bird   butterflies   dog   hawk   horses   ~~snail~~   wolf

1 The roads were so busy that the traffic was going **at a _snail_'s** pace (very slowly) – it took us two hours to get home!
2 Afraid that the children might hurt themselves while playing, the new kindergarten teacher watched **them like a _____** (watched them very carefully) during break time.
3 Just **hold your _____** (wait) before you go rushing off. Have you packed everything you need?
4 A little _____ **told me** (I don't want to say who it was) that you've bought us tickets for a concert for my birthday. Is it true?
5 I **had _____ in my stomach** (I was nervous) before my English exam.
6 Be careful – the new manager looks nice and friendly, but she's actually **a _____ in sheep's clothing** (more dangerous than she seems) and is very strict.
7 With far fewer jobs available than there are graduates, the post-graduate job market is **a dog eat _____ world** (it's very competitive).

7 ON A HIGH NOTE If you could have the powers of any animal, which would you choose and why? Write a paragraph giving your reasons.

A

UNIT VOCABULARY PRACTICE > page 25

ANIMAL MYTHS

A Criticising my brother's driving is like a red rag to a bull. He'll lose his temper and you'll end up walking instead of getting a lift! The idiom 'like a red rag to a bull' is a useful way of describing something that is guaranteed to make another person angry, but where does it come from? Well, it's common knowledge that the colour of blood makes bulls angry – that's why a matador's cape is red, right? Wrong: bulls are actually colour-blind and it is the movement of the cape, and not its colour, that makes them charge at you, horns first. This is one of many common myths about the walking, flying, swimming and crawling creatures with whom we share our beautiful planet.

B The idiom 'as blind as a bat' is often used to describe someone who can't find something that's right in front of them. However, even a thorough search is unlikely to reveal a truly blind bat because in fact, all species in the bat family have eyes and are capable of sight. About seventy percent of them use echolocation to navigate, but that doesn't mean they can't see. The remaining thirty percent, mainly the larger species, don't even use echolocation and have excellent night vision. Another bat myth is that they love human hair. While they are known to occasionally dive towards people at high speed, scientific evidence shows that they are actually hunting insects and are not irresistibly attracted to your beautiful long hair!

C The idiom 'to bury your head in the sand' means to ignore a problem in the hope that it will go away. The saying is based on the behaviour of ostriches, known for using their beaks to dig holes in which to hide their head from enemies. The only problem is that this is not actually normal ostrich behaviour. The myth that the world's largest flightless birds do this is probably based on the writings of Pliny the Elder. He was a famous Roman naturalist who suggested around two thousand years ago that ostriches 'imagine, when they have thrust their head and neck into a bush, that the whole of their body is concealed.' Considering ostriches are the fastest creatures on two legs and have a kick powerful enough to kill a lion, they are much more likely to run or fight than try to hide.

D Moving from underground to underwater, there are several common myths about marine creatures. Firstly, the idea that fish, and especially goldfish, have a memory of just a few seconds is something people seem to remember, but ought to forget. Experiments suggest a fish's memory is much better than that, and can be counted in months rather than seconds. Next, sharks and the disturbing idea that these incredible predators can detect a single drop of blood in the water from miles around. True, though these often solitary hunters have poor eyesight, they do have a highly developed sense of smell, with some species able to detect a single drop of blood in about fifty litres of water. However, rather disappointingly (unless you're a fish or another of the shark's favourite prey), their noses are not as sensitive as is generally believed when it comes to blood.

E Finally, let's head back to dry land where the insects and invertebrates (creatures without backbones) creep and crawl. Firstly, despite the rumours, earthworms do not actually become two separate worms if you split them in half. Only a limited number of earthworm species can survive such serious injury – only the front half of the worm (where the mouth is located) is able to feed and so survive. Moving from zero to eight legs, you'll no doubt be relieved and thankful that it's not true that over a lifetime people swallow a large number of spiders during their sleep. While sleeping, we make all kinds of noises and movements that warn spiders of danger and prevent them from becoming unwanted midnight snacks. So, armed with that knowledge, I wish you a peaceful night's sleep, and if you are curious to learn more, there are plenty more myths connected to animals that you can read about online.

B

C

D

2E SPEAKING

1 🔊 *17* Listen and repeat the phrases. How do you say them in your language?

SPEAKING | Problem-solving

EXPRESSING INDECISION

I'm **torn between** a new drinking fountain **and** a plastic recycling bin.

I'm **on the fence about** the advertising campaign.

I'm **having second thoughts.**

I **can't make up my mind.**

On the one hand, this is a fun idea, **but on the other hand,** not everybody can afford it.

I can't put my finger on it, but something's not right with the poster.

EXPRESSING AGREEMENT

You're **spot on!**

That's what I was going to say!

Absolutely!

EXPRESSING DISAGREEMENT

It **doesn't grab me.**

I **think we're on the wrong track.**

That's a good point, but I don't know if everybody will agree.

OK, but another option might be to reduce plastic use within the town.

Seriously?!

REACHING A DECISION

So, let's make a decision on this.

OK, so will we go with the first poster?

It looks as if we agree that the first poster is more suitable.

2 Choose the correct words to complete the sentences.

  1 It looks as *if* / *like* we agree that we need a recycling bin in each classroom.

  2 I'm *on* / *over* the fence about it to be honest.

  3 *Absolutely!* / *Seriously?!* That's exactly what I think too.

  4 OK, but another *option* / *decision* might be to wait a bit longer.

  5 So, let's *do* / *make* a decision on this, shall we?

  6 I'm having second *ideas* / *thoughts* about our decision.

DROWNING IN OLD CLOTHES?
BRING THEM TO CLOTHES SWAP DAY.

Swap old clothes for new
AT CLOTHES SWAP DAY

3 🔊 *18* Complete the conversation with the correct words from the Speaking box. Listen and check. Which poster do the friends decide to use?

Dan So we have to choose one of these posters to promote our environmental campaign – the school clothes swap day. What do you think? I'm **1**_torn_ between these two.

Sia That's what I was going to **2**_____! I can't make up my **3**_____ which one though. I mean – on the one **4**_____, the poster with the wave of clothes is visually striking, but on the other hand, the one with the two guys is quite funny.

Dan It is, but something about it doesn't **5**_____ me. I can't quite put my **6**_____ on it. Maybe it needs a better caption or something?

Sia That's a good **7**_____, but I'm not sure I can think of anything better.

Dan Maybe something like 'Clothes swap day – not just for girls!'

Sia Hmm. I think we're on the wrong **8**_____ with the gender thing. How about 'You never know what you'll find at clothes swap day'. Sort of like these two guys found each other among the clothes, if you know what I mean.

Dan I think you're **9**_____ on! I like it!

Sia OK, so will we **10**_____ with this one then?

Dan Definitely. I'll change the caption and print a few off.

4 ON A HIGH NOTE Write a short conversation between two friends who want to organise a fundraising event for their school. Use phrases from this lesson.

2F GRAMMAR

Future forms for plans and hopes

1 ⭐ Read the sentences. Then complete the rules with the structures and names of tenses in bold.

1 The shopping centre opens at 10 a.m. (**Present Simple**)
2 I'm **going to** give these old blankets to the charity shop.
3 I **will** take a packet of the paper straws, thanks.
4 As usual on the show, we'll be showing you how to reuse everyday items. (**Future Continuous**)
5 We're meeting early to go to the car boot sale. (**Present Continuous**)

Rules

a We use *Future Continuous* to talk about an action that is expected to happen in the normal course of events.
b We use _____ to talk about a timetabled or scheduled future event.
c We use _____ to talk about something which has already been decided.
d We use _____ to talk about a future arrangement with another person.
e We use _____ plus bare infinitive to talk about a future action decided at the moment of speaking.

2 ⭐ Choose the correct forms to complete the sentences about a monthly car boot sale.

1 The monthly sale *starts / is starting* at 10 a.m.
2 I *'m going to try / try* and sell all my old sports equipment.
3 As usual, they *'re / 'll be* selling tickets at the gate.
4 I *'m meeting / 'll meet* my cousin there at 9 a.m. to set up our stall.
5 It sounds fun – maybe we *'re going to / 'll* come along too.

3 ⭐⭐ Look at the poster and complete the sentences with the correct forms of the verbs in brackets. Sometimes more than one answer is possible.

ANNUAL
CHARITY DAY
Queen Anne's School
29 July, 9 a.m.

1 The annual charity day *begins* (begin) at 9 a.m.
2 29 July? I'm free, so I think I _____ (come).
3 It's been decided that we _____ (raise) money for the British Heart Foundation.
4 As in previous years, the head teacher _____ (announce) how much money we have raised at the end of the day.
5 On the 28, my classmates and I _____ (bake) cakes to sell.

4 ⭐⭐⭐ Put the words in order to make sentences. Then match the sentences with explanations a–d.

1 ☐ the winners / announce / they / to / are / about
They are about to announce the winners.
2 ☐ planning / we / go / on holiday / this summer / to / are
_____
3 ☐ are / you / apologise / at once / to / !
_____
4 ☐ begin / is / the concert / due / at 8 p.m. / to
_____
5 ☐ hoping / turtles and dolphins / to / we're / see
_____
6 ☐ of / my summer job / thinking / quitting / I'm
_____
7 ☐ the café / shut down / is / on Friday / to
_____

a for plans
b when something is happening very soon
c for timetabled events
d for formal or official arrangements, instructions or commands

5 ⭐⭐⭐ Rewrite the sentences using the words in bold.

1 I intend to sell this jacket online. **THINKING**
I'm thinking of selling this jacket online.
2 We will arrive at our destination very soon. **ABOUT**
_____
3 I've just decided to go home. **'LL**
_____
4 We intend to buy fewer clothes this year. **GOING**
_____
5 The timetable says the tram leaves at ten past. **DUE**
_____
6 The princess will open the new park. **TO**
_____

6 ON A HIGH NOTE Use each of the tenses and structures practised in Exercises 1 and 4 to write sentences about you and your plans for the next few weeks.

Begin with an appropriate formal greeting.

State your reasons for writing in the introduction.

In the main paragraphs, state the problem and offer some solutions.

In the final paragraph, ask the recipient of the email to take some action.

Mention that you expect a reply before you sign off.

Sign off with an appropriate farewell that matches the greeting you began with.

George Grouse
To: City Council
Subject: Air pollution

¹Dear Sir/Madam,

I am writing ²to express my concern about plans to construct a new concert hall on the site of the city park on Washington Road. While a concert hall would certainly be a desirable facility, the current plans present a number of major problems.

Like many city centre residents, my family and I live in an apartment and value the park for the access it provides to fresh air in a green environment. On any day, people of all ages can be found walking, jogging, cycling and rollerblading there. Outdoor exercise is vital for physical and mental well-being and I am ³worried that removal of the park would have a serious impact on residents' health. If the council is keen to promote fitness and well-being, plans for the concert hall must be reconsidered to allow space for this vital function to continue.

With its mature trees and good-sized lake, the park is home to many birds and wild animals. ⁴We are told that the city's expansion in recent years has already caused a great deal of habitat loss. I find it unacceptable that yet another part of the city's green space would be sacrificed under the current proposals. It is ⁵essential that preservation of the area for the benefit of the animal population is taken into consideration in any plans.

Given the drawbacks to locating the concert hall on the site of Washington Road Park, ⁶I urge you to seek an alternative location in an area which would benefit from development and not one which already has a clear and important purpose. I look forward to ⁷hearing from you.

⁸Yours faithfully,

George Grouse

1 Replace the underlined parts in the email with the words and phrases from the box.

concerned   ~~Dear Mrs Greco~~   I would ask you   It is said
vital   with regard to   your response   Yours sincerely

1 *Dear Mrs Greco*
2 _____
3 _____
4 _____
5 _____
6 _____
7 _____
8 _____

2 Find the word that is not possible in each sentence.

1 I am contacting you with regard to a(n) *complex / ideal / significant* problem.

2 This is a *fundamental / major / viable* problem for the town and its citizens.

3 What is needed is a *pressing / simple / workable* solution.

4 People need to *face / offer / address* this issue as a matter of urgency.

5 The most effective way to *tackle / deal with / implement* this problem is also the simplest.

6 We are ready to *face / provide / offer* a range of alternatives if necessary.

3 WRITING TASK Read the headline from a newspaper and write a formal email to your local council about the problem.

AIR POLLUTION FROM CARS IS A SIGNIFICANT PROBLEM IN OUR CITY AND NOT ENOUGH IS BEING DONE BY THE LOCAL GOVERNMENT TO TACKLE THE SITUATION.

ACTIVE WRITING | A formal email

1 Plan your email.
- Make a note of the problems air pollution can cause.
- Think about two or three possible solutions.

2 Write the email.
- Write an introduction, stating your reason for writing.
- Explain the problem and suggest solutions.
- Ask the council to take action and say that you expect a reply.
- Use an impersonal writing style including passives and hypothetical constructions.
- Avoid contractions and phrasal verbs.

3 Check that ...
- all the relevant information is there.
- there are no spelling, grammar or punctuation mistakes.

1 2A GRAMMAR AND VOCABULARY **Complete the blog post with one preposition in each gap.**

The #TRASHTAG Challenge

As a consequence **¹**_of_ the '#trashtag challenge' going viral on social media, thousands of people have begun clearing up rubbish from their neighbourhoods. The social media phenomenon has brought **²**_____ a change in people's attitudes to urban cleanliness and given rise **³**_____ hundreds of mini clean-up schemes across the country. Littering results **⁴**_____ a lack of responsibility and awareness, but the '#trashtag challenge' is helping to change that. Another big cause **⁵**_____ littering is the shortage of bins in public spaces, so we are asking the local council to find funding to increase both the number of bins and the frequency of rubbish collections. If you would like to help, click here to sign our petition. Your support could result **⁶**_____ concrete action and a cleaner environment for us all.

2 2B VOCABULARY **Complete the sentences with one word in each gap.**

1 A_cid_ rain is sometimes strong enough to damage the paint on your car.
2 Exhaust f_____ are extremely dangerous to human health.
3 Sometimes the only way to save an e_____ species is to move the last remaining animals to a zoo.
4 Known deposits of f_____ fuels may run out in the next 50 to 150 years.
5 Could technology provide a solution to global h_____?
6 The disastrous landslide was caused by soil e_____ after trees were cut down higher up the slopes.
7 Vehicle e_____ are only one of the many causes of climate change.

3 2C LISTENING AND VOCABULARY **Complete the weather report with the words and phrases from the box.**

cold   freak   gale-force   heat   ~~hot~~   humidity   pour scorching   soaked   sub-zero   torrential

And here's the world weather report. It's boiling **¹**_hot_ in Australia with the blistering **²**_____ reaching 45 degrees in many places this week.

Those **³**_____ temperatures continue southwards into Indonesia and Thailand, where it is particularly humid for the time of year – high **⁴**_____ in Vietnam too. You can expect to get **⁵**_____ in South East Asia next week, however, as the heatwave breaks and is replaced by **⁶**_____ rain and the risk of floods and even hurricanes in the coming weeks.

Crossing to Canada, it's a completely different story – heavy snow and **⁷**_____ temperatures making it a chilly minus 9 in Vancouver, and further north it's freezing **⁸**_____, reaching minus 28 in places.

4 2D READING AND VOCABULARY **Choose the correct words to complete the sentences.**

1 The *marine / poacher* caught a little *furry / slimy* hamster and gave it to his children as a lovely *chilly / cuddly* pet.
2 The pangolin is the only *reptile / mammal* wholly covered in *scales / claws*.
3 The dodo was a bird with a large *beak / scale*. Sadly, it's now *extinct / nocturnal*.
4 This species of bee is now *endangered / solitary* because of *lead poisoning / pesticides* used in agriculture.
5 The *skeleton / wing* of the sabre-toothed tiger shows that it was one of prehistory's largest *backbones / predators*.

5 2G WRITING AND VOCABULARY **Complete the email with the correct forms of the words from the box.**

contribute   ~~press~~   tackle   urgent   viable

Dear Sir/Madam,

I am writing with regard to the **¹**_pressing_ problem of single-use non-biodegradable plastics your restaurant uses.

The takeaway boxes that stay in your customers' hands for ten minutes could be in the ocean forever, so they **²**_____ to the problem of plastic waste. As the majority of your clients probably won't check if the box is recyclable before throwing it in the bin, I believe, it is your company's responsibility to **³**_____ this fundamental problem and make a significant change to your packaging system.

I would be grateful if you could offer a **⁴**_____ solution as it is a matter of **⁵**_____.

Yours faithfully,

Fran Bothered

6 ON A HIGH NOTE **What is the weather like in your country? Describe how it varies throughout the year.**

Returning to Europe and to Germany where **⁹**_____ weather means that **¹⁰**_____ winds have hit the city of Frankfurt and surrounding areas. The storms should finally die down tomorrow, but it's expected to **¹¹**_____ with rain for most of the next week.

That's the weather for now. We'll be back after the news.

02 Self-assessment

1 **For each learning objective, write 1–5 to assess your ability.**

1 = I don't feel confident. 5 = I feel confident.

	Learning objective	Course material	How confident I am (1–5)
2A	I can use a variety of forms to talk about future predictions.	Student's Book pp. 18–19	
2B	I can talk about threats to the environment.	Student's Book p. 20	
2C	I can understand signposting in a lecture and talk about climate change.	Student's Book p. 21	
2D	I can identify specific details in an article and talk about endangered species.	Student's Book pp. 22–23	
2E	I can use fixed phrases to express indecision, agreement, disagreement.	Student's Book p. 24	
2F	I can use a variety of forms to talk about plans and hopes.	Student's Book p. 25	
2G	I can write a formal email.	Student's Book pp. 26–27	

2 **Which of the skills above would you like to improve in? How?**

Skill I want to improve in	How I can improve

3 **What can you remember from this unit?**

New words I learned and most want to remember	Expressions and phrases I liked	English I heard or read outside class

GRAMMAR AND VOCABULARY

1 Complete the sentences with one word in each gap.

1 Lack of sleep can b<u>ring</u> a<u>bout</u> all sorts of mental and physical health problems.

2 Her refusal to pay the fine r_____ i_____ a short jail sentence.

3 Around the world, h_____ l_____ is having a serious impact on the survival of many species such as frogs.

4 Mountain gorillas are amongst the most e_____ s_____ with only a few hundred individuals left in the wild.

5 In Quibdó, Columbia there is no dry season and it p_____ with r_____ for 304 days a year on average.

6 Scientists agree that the burning of coal could l_____ t_____ global heating.

/ 5

2 Choose the correct words to complete the sentences.

1 The *blistering* / *heavy* snow means that it's difficult for birds to find food.

2 A grizzly bear could tear you apart with its powerful *claws* / *fins*.

3 These *extinct* / *nocturnal* creatures sleep by day and hunt by night.

4 This is one of the most complete fossilised dinosaur *skeletons* / *scales* ever found.

5 Two *primates* / *poachers* were arrested for hunting elephants for their ivory.

/ 5

3 Choose the correct forms to complete the sentences.

1 By the end of this term, we ___ English for five years and we still have two more years to do.
   a 'll have been studying
   b 'll be studying
   c 'll have studied

2 If you don't charge your phone now, it ___ completely by lunchtime.
   a will be dying
   b will been dying
   c will have died

3 You ___ sick if you eat any more cake.
   a will have been
   b are going to be
   c will be being

4 Long before her birthday, Jessica will already ___ how she wants to celebrate.
   a have been deciding
   b have decided
   c be deciding

5 In two weeks' time, I ___ on a beach in Fiji.
   a 'll be lying
   b 'll lie
   c 'll have been lying

/ 5

4 Use the prompts to write sentences.

1 Hmm ... I think / I / have / a California roll, / please
   Hmm ... I think I'll have a California roll, please.

2 We / plan / go home / as soon as this class finishes
   _____

3 you / meet / Lara tomorrow?
   _____

4 I / about / put / dinner on the table
   _____

5 At the moment / Rachel / think / help a charitable institution.
   _____

6 Samuel's train / leave / at 10 a.m.
   _____

/ 5

USE OF ENGLISH

5 Complete the conversation with one word in each gap.

Ian Soon we'll have [1]*been* queuing for this roller coaster for over an hour. My feet hurt.

Kelly We're nearly there, Ian. We're sure [2]_____ enjoy it after all this waiting!

Ian With our luck it will [3]_____ raining by the time we get on it.

Kelly Oh, [4]_____ you keep complaining all the time?

Ian Well, in fact, I am having [5]_____ thoughts about this. Last year my uncle got so scared on a roller coaster that he almost had heart attack.

Kelly Why are you always [6]_____ a pessimist?

/ 5

6 Choose the correct words a–c to complete the texts.

1
> Warning: heavy rain and ___ winds predicted for the next twenty-four hours.

   a scorching   b gale-force   c torrential

2
> Water ___ is a major problem on our island in the summer. Please do not wash your car.

   a heating   b loss   c scarcity

3
> Please do not approach bears. They may look ___, but they are dangerous wild animals!

   a solitary   b cuddly   c furry

4
> **Health Warning**: smoking ___ deadly diseases.

   a brings   b results   c causes

5
> Change of platform. The Liverpool train is now ___ to leave from Platform 17 at 06.59.

   a bound   b due   c planning

/ 5

/ 30

27

03 Influences

3A GRAMMAR AND VOCABULARY

Past and present habits

1 ⭐ Match sentences 1–7 with their meanings a–g.

1 ☐ Leo was forever bursting into tears as a child.
2 ☐ Sara is constantly showing off.
3 ☐ Nasreen will forget to take her contact lenses out.
4 ☐ My uncle would always take me swimming.
5 ☐ I used to love winding my brother up.
6 ☐ We watched that show every week.
7 ☐ He and I always mess about in Maths lessons.

a a repeated past action or state; it might still happen in the present
b a characteristic of a person which is typical of them
c a repeated action in the present
d an annoying repeated habit in the past
e a past state or action which no longer exists
f a habit or repeated action in the past, but not a state
g an annoying repeated habit in the present

2 ⭐ Complete the mini-conversations with the correct Present or Past Continuous forms of the words in brackets.

Jane Have you two fallen out again?
Billy To be honest, Ellen and I ¹*are always falling out* (always/fall out) and it really upsets me.

Emma Why did you and your fiancé split up?
Sue He ² _____ (constantly/give) compliments to my friend and then I saw them out together.

Callum Why don't you like the twins?
Mia They ³ _____ (forever/talk) behind people's backs.

Jasper Why did they stop playing rugby?
Jamie Because they ⁴ _____ (constantly/injure) themselves.

Fiona How do you put up with him?
Neil To tell you the truth, I ⁵ _____ (constantly/ask) myself the same question!

3 ⭐⭐ Complete the sentences with the correct forms of *used to* or *would* and the verbs in brackets. Sometimes more than one answer is possible.

1 When we were younger, my sister and I *used to share* (share) a bedroom.
2 How _____ (stay) in touch with your friends before you got your first phone?
3 My brother was the baby of the family and everybody _____ (make) a big fuss of him.
4 When I was a student, I _____ (run) a lot. I _____ (get up) really early and run ten kilometres before breakfast.
5 When I was young, I _____ (not think) I would ever become an adult.
6 Caroline's sister always _____ (be) the peacemaker in her family.
7 When Greta was younger, she _____ (suddenly/start) crying for no reason.

4 ⭐⭐ Match sentences 1–5 with responses a–e. Then complete the responses with *will/won't* or *would/wouldn't*.

1 ☐ 'Nobody wanted to play with him when he was little.'
2 ☐ 'My parents don't let me use their car.'
3 ☐ 'Amanda is thinking of leaving her husband.'
4 ☐ 'I never really believed anything he said.'
5 ☐ 'Dani's hearing is getting really bad.'

a 'Yes, well, he *won't* listen to a word she says.'
b 'Well, she _____ keep listening to heavy metal.'
c 'I'm not surprised. He _____ stop shouting at the other kids.'
d 'That's not surprising. He _____ tell the most ridiculous stories.'
e 'Well, you _____ go too fast whenever you drive.'

7 ⭐⭐⭐ Choose all the correct forms to complete the text. Sometimes more than one answer is correct.

> When I was at primary school, I didn't do well at school. My concentration span **¹___** very short, and I was constantly getting into trouble for not listening. I often **²___** bored in class. I **³___** out of the window all the time and daydream. I **⁴___** listen to what the teacher was saying and found it hard to focus. One time I **⁵___** asleep while we were writing a Maths test! It was so embarrassing.
>
> Now I've grown up and I am a father of twin boys. They are bright students with good grades, but it annoys me that they are always messing about instead of paying attention in class. Teachers often report that they **⁶___** late to almost every class and they **⁷___** to do their homework more often than not. I guess they remind me of myself! I hope things will get better as they grow older.

1 **a** would be **b** used to be **c** was
2 **a** would feel **b** felt **c** used to feel
3 **a** would stare **b** used to stare **c** was staring
4 **a** didn't **b** wouldn't **c** didn't use to
5 **a** fell **b** used to fall **c** would fall
6 **a** arrive **b** will arrive **c** are arriving
7 **a** will forget **b** would forget **c** forget

8 ⭐⭐⭐ USE OF ENGLISH Complete the second sentence using the word in bold so that it means the same as the first one. Use between two and five words, including the word in bold.

1 Lola starts crying if anyone criticises her. **WILL**
Lola *will burst into* tears if anyone criticises her.

2 Kenny didn't get angry when he was a child. **USE**
Kenny _____ his temper when he was a child.

3 Dad and I met on Tuesdays and Saturdays. **WOULD**
Dad and I _____ on Tuesdays and Saturdays.

4 Liam has a habit of blowing things out of proportion. **USUALLY**
Liam _____ things out of proportion.

5 I'm sorry to say that Fiona and I often teased a girl at school. **TO**
I'm sorry to say that Fiona and I often _____ fun of a girl at school.

6 Daria checks her phone every few minutes. It's so irritating. **FOREVER**
Daria _____ her phone. It's so irritating.

7 Did you have arguments with your brother when you were younger? **TO**
Did _____ out with your brother when you were younger?

9 ON A HIGH NOTE Write a paragraph comparing your English language skills as a beginner with your current abilities. Use structures from this lesson.

5 ⭐⭐ Complete the mini-conversations with one word or a contraction in each gap.

Max Did you **¹***use* to walk to school when you were little?

Scott No, my mum **²**_____ always give me a lift.

Doria My sisters **³**_____ use to argue, but these days they are **⁴**_____ falling out.

Helga It's the same for me. I **⁵**_____ always the peacemaker in our household.

Lia Why **⁶**_____ you always shouting at me?!

Jim Because you annoy me!

Lia You didn't **⁷**_____ to lose your temper so often.

Jim That's because you **⁸**_____ constantly winding me up!

Ahmed I'm exhausted.

Penny Well – you **⁹**_____ stay up late watching videos on YouTube. What do you expect?

6 ⭐⭐ Complete the sentences with the forms from the box. Then tick the sentences which express annoyance with somebody's behaviour.

> are forever going didn't use to get on ~~didn't use to like~~
> lived used to understand was constantly showing off
> will borrow would always whistle

1 ☐ When I was young, I *didn't use to like* fizzy drinks.

2 ☐ My aunt and uncle _____ on holiday. I don't know how they can afford it.

3 ☐ My elder sister _____ my clothes without asking me first.

4 ☐ I _____ with my nieces.

5 ☐ I _____ a lot of French when I was a child, but I've forgotten it now.

6 ☐ When we were in primary school, Mark _____ in front of the girls in class.

7 ☐ When I was a child, we _____ in London.

8 ☐ When we were hiking, Dylan _____ something to himself.

3B LISTENING AND VOCABULARY

1 🔊 **19** Listen to a radio programme about the influence of books. Match speakers 1–4 with types of books they chose a–d.

1 ☐ Oliver		**a**	self-help
2 ☐ Grace		**b**	historical non-fiction
3 ☐ Ellie		**c**	semi-autobiographical novel
4 ☐ Simon		**d**	young adult novel

2 🔊 **19** Listen again and choose the correct answers.

1 In the introduction, which of the following is presented as an opinion and not a fact?

   a Young people are particularly influenced by books.

   b Older people read less than younger people.

   c People read books for a wide variety of reasons.

2 Oliver didn't expect the book to be so

   a challenging. **b** easy. **c** interesting.

3 Why did Grace feel a personal connection to the book?

   a It features a character who is similar to her.

   b It deals with an issue which affects her.

   c It made her extremely emotional.

4 What does Ellie say about the book she read?

   a It wasn't fun to read.

   b It changed her life.

   c It taught her a valuable lesson.

5 When Simon got the book, he felt

   a surprised. **b** excited. **c** disappointed.

Vocabulary extension

3 Match the words from the box, which you heard in the recording in Exercise 1, with their definitions.

accessible bookworm ~~lasting~~ simplify worthwhile

1 Having an effect for a long time. *lasting*

2 Worth the time, money or effort spent. _____

3 Easy to understand and enjoy. _____

4 A person who loves to read and does it a lot. _____

5 Make something easier to understand. _____

4 🔊 **20** Complete the extracts from the recording with the words from Exercise 3. Listen and check.

1 I was worried it would be too difficult, but it was actually quite *accessible* and really fascinating.

2 In fact, it had such a _____ effect on me that I've decided to study History when I go to uni next year!

3 I'm a total _____ and the most influential thing I've read recently is a John Green novel called *Turtles All the Way Down*.

4 As usual he doesn't _____ things or soften them just because he's writing for young adults.

5 Some parts of it are extremely emotional and were difficult to read, but that's what makes it _____ in my opinion.

Pronunciation

5 🔊 **21** Listen to some pairs of sentences from the recording in Exercise 1, paying particular attention to how the underlined words differ from each other. What do you notice about their pronunciation?

1 **a** Some pick up a book in order to learn something new or find out information.

   b It contains some really inspirational ideas about how to make the most of your life.

2 **a** Oliver, let's start with you.

   b Can you believe that?

ACTIVE PRONUNCIATION
Weak vowel forms

If a word in a sentence does not carry the main message, English speakers usually make it sound 'weaker' by using the neutral vowel sound /ə/. This may take place with:

• determiners (e.g. *some, this*)

• conjunctions (e.g. *than, and*)

• pronouns (e.g. *he, them*)

• auxiliary verbs (e.g. *can, have*)

• prepositions (e.g. *at, of*)

However, when these words are emphasised, quoted or said at the end of the sentence, they can be pronounced with full vowels.

6 🔊 **22** Listen to these sentences. Which of the underlined words are strong forms?

1 At the time, I didn't know him at all.

2 Jack's charming and trustworthy, and he's very hard-working.

3 I have checked that we have all the documents.

4 She's thinking of taking some time off.

7 🔊 **22** Listen again and repeat the sentences in Exercise 6.

8 🔊 **23** Which words in these sentences have a weak form? Listen and check. Then practise saying the sentences.

1 He's always put him on a pedestal.

2 Some artists tend to be hypocritical.

3 Entertainment can be seen as a distraction.

4 Millennials and baby boomers could not be more different.

1 ⭐ Choose the correct words to complete the sentences.

1 Jenny is a very *capable* / *conceited* teacher and I'm sure you'll benefit from her lessons.

2 She's such a(n) *inspirational* / *tough* teacher that all her students want to be like her.

3 The doctor was always very *bigoted* / *charming* and knew what to say to help her patients relax.

4 It's fine to be *hypocritical* / *idealistic*, but sometimes you have to be practical too.

5 Truly *dedicated* / *pushy* musicians are constantly practising.

6 Why can't you act your age and stop being so *dedicated* / *immature*?

7 Jean proved she was *compassionate* / *charming* by volunteering to help out at an animal shelter.

8 He's a very *inspirational* / *decent* person and will always act in the proper way.

9 Delwyn would always get *defensive* / *trustworthy* if a teacher criticised his written work.

10 Was the politician being *sincere* / *modest* when he said the government would tackle climate change?

2 ⭐ Match the words from the box with their definitions.

bigoted ~~conceited~~ hypocritical modest passionate pushy tough trustworthy

1 Constantly telling people how great you are. *conceited*

2 Determined to get what you want. _____

3 Feeling very strongly about something. _____

4 Not talking in a proud way about your achievements. _____

5 Saying one thing, but doing something different. _____

6 Can always be trusted. _____

7 Able to deal with difficult situations. _____

8 Intolerant of other people's beliefs and practices. _____

3 ⭐⭐ Use the words from Exercise 2 to complete the descriptions.

1 Justin says he's worried about climate change, but he drives everywhere and goes on holiday by plane twice a year. He's *hypocritical*.

2 Candice won't take 'no' for an answer. She'll keep asking until she gets what she wants. She's _____.

3 Alberto is a highly skilled pianist, but he doesn't show off about it. He's _____.

4 Gosia hates anyone who is different from her. She's really _____.

5 Reena is in a lot of pain from her illness, but she doesn't complain or feel sorry for herself. She's _____.

6 Carolina believes she's a better person than all her friends. She's so _____.

7 If you want to be sure a secret is kept, tell Margo. She's _____.

8 Marcel's life is completely dedicated to tackling pollution. He's _____ about it.

4 ⭐⭐ Complete the sentences with the verbs from the box.

admire ~~find~~ follow look down on put set

1 I *find* Anne Hathaway inspirational because of her work as a UN goodwill ambassador.

2 How dare you _____ me – just because my parents aren't wealthy!

3 Will you please tidy your room and _____ a good example for your little brother?

4 Sharif's parents always _____ him on a pedestal – probably because he's an only child.

5 Gareth wants to _____ in his mother's footsteps and become a doctor.

6 I really _____ Greta Thunberg for her work in raising awareness of climate change.

5 ⭐⭐ Complete the online comment with one word in each gap.

WHAT'S BUGGING YOU TODAY?

Share it with the world at **haveyoursay.com**

Don't you just ¹loathe it when someone you ²a_____ proves to be a bad ³i_____ on others? It seems to happen all the time these days. Athletes who we ⁴i_____, singers whose music we find ⁵i_____, actors who we put on a ⁶p_____ because of their talents and abilities, activists that we admire as ⁷s_____ examples for hope and change. But instead of being figures that we can look up ⁸t_____, they turn out to be totally ⁹h_____! They say one thing and then do something completely different! It drives me crazy!

6 ON A HIGH NOTE Write a short news article about somebody famous who has been in the media recently. Use the words and phrases from this lesson.

3D READING AND VOCABULARY

1 Read the text quickly. Tick the section of a newspaper in which you would expect to find this article.

A ☐ **BUSINESS**   **B** ☐ SCIENCE

C ☐ LIFESTYLE   **D** ☐ **Books**

2 Read the text again and choose the correct answers.

1 How does the author feel about the fact that many people know very little about their ancestors' lives?

   a She suggests it is not important.

   b She finds it unfortunate.

   c She understands how it happens.

   d She thinks it is interesting.

2 What does the author say about modern genealogy?

   a It never has shocking results.

   b It is a new area of study.

   c It is a very profitable business.

   d It was invented by AJ Jacobs.

3 What does 'distress' mean in line 19?

   a confusion   **b** hatred

   c unhappiness   **d** jealousy

4 Why did AJ Jacobs feel the Global Family Reunion project was important?

   a He knew he could write an interesting book about it.

   b He thought it was extremely unusual.

   c He wanted to know more about his family.

   d He thought it carried a valuable message.

5 What does 'traced' mean in line 45?

   a contacted   **b** asked

   c remembered   **d** found

6 What does the author say is the most important lesson to come out of the Global Family Reunion?

   a a change in attitude to one's family

   b an increased sense of belonging

   c a more positive approach to others

   d the importance of family stories

Vocabulary extension

3 Match the highlighted words and phrases from the text with the definitions.

1 Related to someone who lived a long time ago.

   descended from

2 Relationships between two people, groups or countries. _____

3 A person's origins or background. _____

4 Members of your family not closely related to you. _____

5 Members of a family who lived a long time ago. _____

6 A different word for 'relatives'. _____

4 Complete the sentences with the correct forms of the words from Exercise 3.

1 I was born and brought up in the UK, but my family has its *roots* in Pakistan.

2 The only _____ I've ever met are my third cousins, who visited last year from the USA.

3 According to my great-grandmother, our family is _____ the Vikings!

4 Filipino families are known for having very close _____ between members.

5 Our family is particularly small and I have very few living _____.

6 My _____ first came to Europe during the 1700s.

ACTIVE VOCABULARY | Phrasal verbs with *back*

The particle used in a phrasal verb can sometimes help you understand its overall meaning. For example, the particle *back* often refers to the idea of returning to an earlier time.

- *think **back*** – remember an earlier time
- *put **back*** – return something to where it was earlier
- *give **back*** – return something you took earlier

---

5 Complete the sentences with the correct forms of the verbs from the box. Use a dictionary to help you if necessary.

come ~~get~~ give go put think

1 Lori returned the faulty items to the shop and *got* her money back.

2 I'd appreciate it if you could _____ the books back in the correct place when you've finished with them.

3 Please _____ back and visit us again soon!

4 We certainly won't be _____ back to that restaurant as the service was awful.

5 I often _____ back to my childhood in Africa and to what a beautiful place it was to grow up.

6 Could I borrow your scooter if I promise to _____ it back undamaged?

6 ON A HIGH NOTE Write a paragraph about an interesting member of your family.

THE GLOBAL FAMILY REUNION

How much do you know about your great-grandparents? Without them, and all your other ancestors, you wouldn't exist, yet sadly many of us find it difficult to remember their names, never mind the details of their lives. How quickly we are forgotten! Unless that is, someone in the family has an interest in genealogy and takes the time and trouble to research and produce a family tree.

• • •

The easy availability of home DNA testing kits allows anyone to find out about their roots. As a result, genealogy, or the study of families and their history, has become a big business. The users of such kits, however, often discover surprising facts. For example, they may find out that they are descended from ancestors of entirely different nationalities or races. Even more shockingly, especially for those involved, these tests have revealed that some parents are not in fact related to their children. This knowledge understandably causes great distress and throws families into conflict. Such cases are thankfully very rare. More importantly, looking back at our origins has the potential to reveal fascinating facts and teach us a great deal about our preconceptions and prejudices. This is one of the reasons why best-selling writer, AJ Jacobs, began an ambitious project to find and gather together as many of his distant relatives as possible. He called it the 'Global Family Reunion'.

Jacobs is no stranger to unusual projects. While researching his previous bestsellers, he attempted to read the entire Encyclopaedia Britannica from cover to cover, and in a different project, to follow every piece of health advice he could find. The idea for the Global Family Reunion event first came to him when he received an email from a stranger who said he was Jacobs' eighth cousin and had access to a database containing 80,000 people all of whom were related to Jacobs. This distant cousin had managed to get nearly 3000 relatives together for a 'reunion', and Jacobs thought that he could beat that record and at the same time write about his attempt. He felt that the world was in need of a story that emphasised the ties between people, and crossed the barriers of race and nationality. And so he set to work.

After using an online genealogy service to contact 100 of his distant relatives, Jacobs expanded his efforts and traced thousands more relations including a number of celebrities, who agreed to feature in his book holding signs saying, 'I am a cousin'. Among them were George Bush Senior, actors Daniel Radcliffe and Olivia Wilde and comedian Ricky Gervais. The project took a year, and as well as highs such as Sister Sledge agreeing to sing their hit 'We Are Family' at the event, there were also setbacks to cope with. Perhaps the worst of these was the news that a French family had managed to bring together 4500 relatives and break the world record that Jacobs was aiming for with his event. Disappointed, but not defeated, he carried on as he felt the message behind the project was more important than the record itself.

In the end the Global Family Reunion was a great success and Jacobs managed to unite 3700 members of his genetic family. Although it didn't break the record for the largest family reunion, it did set several other records and, perhaps more importantly, taught participants and readers of his book some very important lessons. First was the increased sense of belonging that comes from knowing just how many relatives you actually have. Next, the potential which that same knowledge has to cause a positive change of attitude towards strangers. Realising that everyone you meet could possibly be a genetic relative, makes it much easier to be more compassionate and forgiving to people you don't know. The event also helped emphasise how important and interesting it is to pass down family stories from one generation to the next. Perhaps the biggest thing to take away from Jacobs' project though is that if we are indeed all one big family, then racism, prejudice and hatred have no place in the world, and equality, tolerance and love are in fact what we owe each other.

3E GRAMMAR

Relative and participle clauses

1 ★ Choose the correct relative clauses to complete the sentences. Then choose *D* for a defining or *ND* for a non-defining relative clause.

1 Bluetooth, _b_, is actually a kind of wireless connection.   D / ND

2 The headset ___ is really uncomfortable to wear.   D / ND

3 Ergonomic keyboards, ___, make typing more comfortable.   D / ND

4 This record player, ___, was made in Italy.   D / ND

5 This is the Walkman ___.   D / ND

6 'BCC' is a function ___.   D / ND

a which often look rather strange

b ~~which sounds like a dental problem~~

c which can play records at three different speeds

d which allows you to copy someone into an email without the other recipients knowing

e which my mum used to play her cassettes on when she was a teenager

f which came with my phone

2 ★ Tick the sentences from Exercise 1 where you can replace *which* with *that*.

1 ☐ **2** ☑ **3** ☐ **4** ☐ **5** ☐ **6** ☐

3 ★★ Complete the text with *who*, *which*, *that*, *where* or *whose*. Find the sentence where you can omit the pronoun.

whatphone.com

★★★★☆

I-talk 7 review

The *I-talk 7*, ¹_which_ has been completely redesigned since the *I-talk 6*, is possibly the best new phone on the market. Produced in Korea, ²_____ I-talk has its headquarters, this is a bright new star in a competitive market. For those of you ³_____ budget won't stretch to more expensive brands, we really recommend the *I-talk 7*. Virtually all of the quality issues ⁴_____ affected the company's earlier models have been solved in the *I-talk 7*. Users ⁵_____ care about the quality of their photographs will be happy with the new dual lens camera. The only complaint ⁶_____ we can think of is that the range of colours is limited to blue, black and grey. If that's not a problem, this could be the phone for you.

4 ★★★ Rewrite each pair of sentences as one sentence using a relative clause.

1 I was talking about an app. It's really cool.
The app (which/that) I was talking about is really cool.

2 Tom lives round the corner. I play games with him.
_____

3 These headphones stopped working after two days. I paid a fortune for them.
_____

4 I bought my computer at a shop. It has closed down.
_____

5 I spoke to a technician. She was very helpful.
_____

5 ★★★ Rewrite the sentences using participle clauses.

1 What's the name of that website that sells retro-tech?
What's the name of that website selling retro-tech?

2 The flip phone, which was designed in the 90s, is rapidly becoming popular again.
_____

3 There are very few people who are still using analogue televisions.
_____

4 Users who are used to the old system may find the new one confusing.
_____

5 The classic computer, which was sold on eBay this morning, went for over £20,000.
_____

6 ★★★ Rewrite the sentences to make them more formal. Use the phrases from the box.

from which   in which   ~~to whom~~   with whom

1 My friend Tom, who I usually go to when I've got computer problems, is on holiday.
My friend Tom, to whom I usually go when I've got computer problems, is on holiday.

2 The website that I usually buy my games from has closed down.
_____

3 Sheffield, the town where I was born, is famous for producing great electronic music.
_____

4 The friend that I used to walk to school with now takes us in his car.
_____

7 ON A HIGH NOTE Write one sentence about each of the following topics using defining and non-defining relative clauses.

- an important personal possession
- a person you admire
- a place you enjoy going with friends
- your favourite social media platform
- a friend or relative's annoying habit

3F SPEAKING

1 🔊 24 Listen and repeat the phrases. How do you say them in your language?

SPEAKING | Generalising

TALKING ABOUT WHAT YOU THINK IS GENERALLY TRUE

On the whole, I don't like taking risks.

In general, I'm a very calm person.

In some/many/most cases, it's quicker to send an email than to talk on the phone.

Broadly speaking, Gen Z have an entrepreneurial spirit.

By and large, young people do more sport than older people.

More often than not, young people communicate using messaging apps.

Nine times out of ten, I agree with her, but this time I think she's wrong.

Ninety percent of the time, I include emojis in my texts.

To some/a great extent, electronic devices are a distraction in the classroom.

Older people **tend to think/say/believe** that teenagers spend too much time in front of a screen.

There's a tendency for elderly people **to** be suspicious of the Internet.

ACKNOWLEDGING THAT YOU ARE GENERALISING

This is a bit of a sweeping statement, but younger people often take offence very easily.

I may be overgeneralising, but I think young people are losing the art of conversation.

You might think this is an overgeneralisation, but old people can't handle technology.

2 Replace the underlined parts of the sentences with the correct phrases from the Speaking box. Use the words in bold.

1 <u>Broadly speaking,</u> Generation Z lead healthier lifestyles than Generation X did in the past. **LARGE**

   By and large

2 <u>Nine times out of ten,</u> a person's outlook on life becomes similar to that of their parents. **PERCENT**

   _____

3 <u>In most cases,</u> what seems shocking to one generation, appears normal to the next. **OFTEN**

   _____

4 <u>This is a bit of a sweeping statement,</u> but young people tend not to know much about their grandparents' pasts. **OVERGENERALISATION**

   _____

5 <u>In general,</u> our generation is no better or worse behaved than the previous one. **WHOLE**

   _____

3 Use the prompts to write sentences.

1 most cases / elderly people / not like / fast food

   In most cases, elderly people don't like fast food.

2 Children / tend / say / what they think

   _____

3 I / overgeneralising / but / I / believe / teenagers / be / very creative

   _____

4 some extent / older people / enjoy / spend / time at home

   _____

5 This / sweeping statement / women / be / usually / more emotional than men

   _____

6 Nine times / men / not talk / to their friends about / their feelings

   _____

4 Complete the conversation with the correct words from the Speaking box.

Teacher On the ¹*whole*, do you think life was better for your parents' generation, Will?

William No, I don't. ²_____ speaking, I think our lives are better. I mean – imagine having no phones or Internet!

Teacher Well, yes. What about you, Amanda?

Amanda There's a ³_____ for young people to think that life must have been worse without technology, but my dad is always saying how grateful he is to have seen what life was like back then. To some ⁴_____, I think people were more able to appreciate the simple pleasures in life.

Teacher That's interesting. And you Kurt?

Kurt Well, ⁵_____ and large, the world was a greener and less polluted place back then. However, I suppose in ⁶_____, I believe life is better these days.

5 ON A HIGH NOTE Write a short paragraph in which you make several generalisations about life in the past in your country.

3G **WRITING** | An opinion essay

Summarise the topic of the essay and state your position with regard to the topic.

Set out your arguments in two or three paragraphs, including the two topics given in the question.

Each paragraph should be about one main idea and should start with a topic sentence.

Include one idea of your own.

For each argument, give further details, reasons and examples.

Summarise the main points of the essay and restate your opinion on the topic.

[1]It is sometimes held that in our busy and technologically-advanced world, teenagers have little to learn from the elderly. However, [2]I firmly believe that there are many ways teens can benefit from the wisdom and experience of their grandparents.

Perhaps the most obvious topic which grandparents can tell us about is the past. This is particularly true of our individual family histories. [3]In my opinion, hearing our grandparents' stories of how historical events affected our own families helps us understand the past in new ways. The fascinating stories my grandmother tells about what happened to her and her brothers during WWII [4]are a great example of this.

Our lives may be different from those of our grandparents, but there are plenty of life lessons that we can learn from those who have lived much longer than us. Whether it is a clash between you and your parents or a row with a friend, [5]my personal conviction is that the best advice comes from those who have already dealt with such problems themselves.

Grandparents may not be able to teach us about modern technology, but there are plenty of valuable skills we can learn from them. Growing up, they may have learned how to sew or knit [6]for instance, or perhaps how to cook, bake, fix a bike or decorate a house. [7]Many people today feel that we teenagers lack such practical skills, so what could be better than to learn a new skill set from someone who loves you, has time for you and wants you to succeed?

In conclusion, [8]I would say that there are a great many things that teenagers can learn from their grandparents including family history, life lessons and practical skills.

---

1 Read the task below. Tick three topics which you could include as 'your own ideas' for the essay question.

Some people believe that grandparents have little to teach their teenage grandchildren in the modern world. Do you agree?

Write about ...
- family history.
- life lessons.
- your own ideas.

1 ☐ communication skills
2 ☐ caring for the elderly
3 ☐ non-digital games and activities
4 ☐ education for the over 70s
5 ☐ practical skills, e.g. baking or car mechanics

2 Now read the essay. Which topic from Exercise 1 did the author include as her own idea?

3 Read the underlined phrases in the essay. What are they used for? Choose *P* for personal opinions, *I* for impersonal views or *E* for supporting examples.

1 P / I / E   5 P / I / E
2 P / I / E   6 P / I / E
3 P / I / E   7 P / I / E
4 P / I / E   8 P / I / E

4   WRITING TASK Read the task below and write your opinion essay.

Some people say that parents put too much pressure on their children to succeed. Do you agree?
Write about ...
- the importance of success.
- the importance of finding your own way in life.
- your own ideas.

ACTIVE WRITING | An opinion essay

1 Plan your essay.
- Do you agree or disagree with the statement?
- Make some notes which support your opinion.
- Make a note of at least one idea of your own which supports your view.

2 Write your essay.
- Use a formal/semi-formal writing style.
- Begin each new paragraph with a topic sentence.
- Give your personal opinion, as well as phrases for more impersonal views.
- Back up your opinion with reasons and examples.

3 Check that ...
- all the relevant information is there.
- there are no spelling, grammar or punctuation mistakes.

1 **3A GRAMMAR AND VOCABULARY** Match phrases 1–8 with situations a–h.

1. ☐ be the peacemaker
2. ☐ empathise with somebody
3. ☐ give somebody a compliment
4. ☐ make fun of somebody/something
5. ☐ make up with somebody
6. ☐ show off
7. ☐ talk behind somebody's back
8. ☐ tell somebody off

a. Poor you! I know exactly how you feel.
b. Have you heard the gossip about Karen?
c. You look very intelligent in those glasses.
d. Of course I got top marks in all my exams as usual.
e. OK! Calm down you two – there's no need to shout at each other.
f. Ha ha! You dropped your ice cream!
g. Let's forget about it, OK? I love you and I'm sorry.
h. Why is your room such a mess? I've told you before to keep it tidy!

2 **3A GRAMMAR AND VOCABULARY** Complete the email with one preposition in each gap.

> Dear Agony Aunt,
>
> I badly need your advice. I can't put **¹**_up_ with my younger sister's childish behaviour anymore. She keeps on blowing things **²**_____ of proportion and having a go **³**_____ me just because I want to hang out with my friends without her. Sometimes, I think she tries to wind me **⁴**_____ on purpose just before I go out. She either messes **⁵**_____ or loses her temper over unimportant things. Then, she often bursts **⁶**_____ tears and I don't know how to help her. Telling the truth, I don't enjoy it when we fall **⁷**_____. Please, help me Agony Aunt.
>
> Regards,
>
> Jane

3 **3B LISTENING AND VOCABULARY** Complete the questions sent to a problem page with one word in each gap.

4 **3C VOCABULARY** Choose the correct words to complete the sentences.

1. You're so *hypocritical / idealistic* – you say one thing and then do exactly the opposite.
2. Greg may look *tough / defensive*, but he's actually as soft as a kitten.
3. He's too *modest / dedicated* to tell you about his academic and career success.
4. My uncle is a very *inspirational / capable* plumber – he made a fantastic job of our bathroom.
5. She is definitely not *trustworthy / passionate* enough to be given a key to our home.
6. Rudi is a *pushy / compassionate* person who always tries to understand others' feelings.
7. I admit that I'm *immature / decent* sometimes, but we all need to have fun now and again.
8. I'm sorry, but I don't think you mean what you say. I just don't believe that you're *charming / sincere*.

5 **3D READING AND VOCABULARY** Complete the lyrics for a rap song with the words and phrases from the box.

beg day home malnourished meet skinny ~~to-mouth~~ together

BEATS FROM THE STREETS

On the streets. On the streets.
These are the real beats from the streets.

It's not posh down south when you're living hand - **¹**_to-mouth_.
Hunger never goes away when you're living **²**_____ -to-day.
You get your breakfast from the trash, then **³**_____ for some cash.
Always **⁴**_____ and thin when your meals come from the bin.

On the streets. On the streets.
These are the real beats from the streets.

Never make ends **⁵**_____ when you're living on the streets.
⁶_____ and cold; only young, but feeling old.
Some gather **⁷**_____ to shelter from the weather.
Others stay alone, but no one ever feels at **⁸**_____.

On the streets. On the streets.
These are the real beats from the streets.

6 **ON A HIGH NOTE** Write a brief description of what makes a good friend. Mention the kind of behaviour and character traits you would not want in a friend.

SEND YOUR PERSONAL PROBLEMS TO OUR WEBPAGE AND GET PRACTICAL ADVICE FROM OTHER USERS.

- How can we prepare our dog for the arrival of a **¹**n_ew-bor_n baby into the family?
- I've **²**f_____d four out of my six exams and my parents are furious. What should I do?
- I'm thinking about **³**s_____g up with my fiancé. Is it OK to do it by text message?
- I've had a **⁴**m_____g with my best friend about money. Now she won't speak to me. What can I do?
- How can I avoid a **⁵**c_____h between me and my parents over what time I should come home at the weekends?
- My parents are **⁶**r_____g to the USA, but I was hoping to go to university here. Should I go with them?

03 | Self-assessment

1 For each learning objective, write 1–5 to assess your ability.

1 = I don't feel confident. 5 = I feel confident.

	Learning objective	Course material	How confident I am (1–5)
3A	I can use a variety of forms to talk about present and past habits.	Student's Book pp. 34–35	
3B	I can distinguish between opinion and facts in a radio programme and talk about life events.	Student's Book p. 36	
3C	I can talk about personal qualities and behaviour.	Student's Book p. 37	
3D	I can identify attitudes and feelings of characters in a text and talk about different cultural backgrounds.	Student's Book pp. 38–39	
3E	I can use defining and non-defining relative clauses to give additional information.	Student's Book p. 40	
3F	I can use generalisations to talk about something that is usually true.	Student's Book p. 41	
3G	I can write an opinion essay.	Student's Book pp. 42–43	

2 Which of the skills above would you like to improve in? How?

Skill I want to improve in	How I can improve

3 What can you remember from this unit?

New words I learned and most want to remember	Expressions and phrases I liked	English I heard or read outside class

GRAMMAR AND VOCABULARY

1 Complete the text with one preposition in each gap.

EASYTV.CO Jenny123

My favourite character on TV is Meredith from *Good times, Bad times.* I'd love to have a friend like her. She would never talk **1** *behind* someone's back and isn't the type to let anyone **2**_____, or show **3**_____ about her skills and achievements. She always empathises **4**_____ the other characters, even if they sometimes make fun **5**_____ her. I think Meredith is a really good role model that everybody should look **6**_____ to.

/ 5

2 Choose the correct words to complete the sentences.

1 Harry can't stand being wrong and gets very *conceited / defensive* if you say anything critical of him.

2 Jeremy *handled / flunked* his French exam three times in a row.

3 It was very *decent / hypocritical* of you to help me with my homework when you were so busy.

4 I said I was just looking, but the sales assistant kept trying to sell me things in a very *dedicated / pushy* way.

5 Cerys had a big *clash / misunderstanding* with her sister and now they're not speaking to each other.

/ 5

3 Complete the sentences with the forms from the box.

didn't use to like it   ~~is forever asking~~   used to order
will leave   will play the drums   would always remember

1 Our teacher *is forever asking* us difficult questions about English grammar!

2 Wendy isn't trustworthy – she _____ the doors unlocked and forget to feed the dog.

3 Before we started working on our fitness, we _____ pizza every night.

4 The neighbours _____ when we played our music loud.

5 I used to rely on my sister because she _____ everyone's birthdays.

6 The most annoying thing my sister does is that she _____ on Sunday mornings.

/ 5

4 Complete the sentences with *where*, *which*, *whom*, or *0* (no pronoun). Add commas where necessary.

1 Who was that woman *0* taking photographs at the party?

2 I waited in a long queue _____ was boring.

3 Passengers _____ sitting in window seats have the best views.

4 The receptionist with _____ I spoke was very helpful.

5 Warsaw _____ I grew up is the largest city in Poland.

6 The boy to _____ I was talking yesterday was my cousin.

/ 5

USE OF ENGLISH

5 Choose the correct words a–d to complete the text.

I just got your text about Sparky. If I were you, I wouldn't make **1**___ of him when he behaves badly. My previous dog **2**___ forever messing about. He **3**___ wind us up when digging in our garden; he was so dedicated to this activity that my mum would constantly lose her **4**___. Eventually, we sought help of a dog trainer. If you'd like to **5**___ in our footsteps, I can give you her number.

1	**a** fun	**b** up	**c** a fuss	**d** ends
2	**a** will be	**b** was	**c** would	**d** were
3	**a** would	**b** used	**c** was	**d** is
4	**a** anger	**b** temper	**c** mess	**d** behaviour
5	**a** go	**b** look	**c** follow	**d** find

/ 5

6 Complete the second sentence using the word in bold so that it has a similar meaning to the first one. Use between two and five words, including the word in bold.

1 I admired my older brother when we were kids. **LOOK**

I used *to look up to* my older brother when we were kids.

2 The hairdresser Agata usually goes to is on holiday this week. **WHOM**

The hairdresser _____ is on holiday this week.

3 My dog will usually bark at strangers. **TENDS**

My dog _____ at strangers.

4 Laura bites her nails all the time. **CONSTANTLY**

Laura _____ her nails.

5 Hypocritical people are not trustworthy. **TRUST**

I don't _____ are hypocritical.

6 I can't tolerate Mark's rude behaviour. **PUT**

I can't _____ Mark's rude behaviour.

/ 5

/ 30

04 Inside story

4A GRAMMAR AND VOCABULARY

Narrative tenses; Past Perfect Simple and Continuous

1 ★★ Put the sentences in order to make a story. Then match the sentences with their meanings a–f.

- ☐ I stopped my car, got out and stood in the road to see what it was.
- ☑ At midnight last night, I was driving back to my home in the country.
- ☐ I felt tired because I had been driving all day.
- ☐ By the time I got to the field, the object had disappeared.
- ☐ Suddenly, I saw an object in the sky.
- ☐ While I was watching the object, it fell into a field.

Past Simple
a ☐ an action that started and finished in the past
b ☐ actions which follow each other in a story

Past Continuous
c ☐ an action in progress at a specific point in the past
d ☐ an interrupted past action

Past Perfect Simple
e ☐ an action which took place before another past action

Past Perfect Continuous
f ☐ a situation or an action which continued up to a certain time in the past

2 ★★ Read the situations and use the prompts to write sentences in the Past Perfect Continuous.

1 Anne got into trouble at school for using her phone.
  She / text / during lessons
  She'd been texting during lessons.

2 Gavin had ink all round his mouth.
  He / chew / his pen / during the exam
  _____

3 The central square was underwater.
  It / rain / for five days
  _____

4 The gang was convicted of fraud.
  They / print / fake money
  _____

5 The president was assassinated while giving a speech.
  He / speak / at a political protest meeting
  _____

3 ★★ Complete the text with the forms from the box.

had been investigating   ~~had been working~~   had fallen
had just finished   had never seen
had never witnessed   had they seen

Professor Lindeman was exhausted. He [1]*had been working* late all week long on his paper regarding the possibilities of alien life existing in our universe. He [2]_____ for the night when he noticed a strange light outside the window. He [3]_____ anything like it. For many years, he [4]_____ UFO sightings and other bizarre events, but he [5]_____ one himself. Was this it? He rose and moved towards the window. [6]_____ his research and come to abduct him? As he reached the window, he felt something touch his shoulder. He jumped and suddenly he was back in his chair. His wife was shaking his shoulder. He [7]_____ asleep at his desk again.

4 ★★ Complete the sentences with the correct Past Perfect Simple or Past Perfect Continuous forms of the verbs in bold.

1 **PLAY**
  a Clara's music player *had been playing* for nineteen hours when the battery ran out.
  b Clara's music player _____ nearly two hundred songs when the battery ran out.

2 **ELIMINATE**
  a Inspector Fielding _____ all the other suspects when he arrested Stokes.
  b Inspector Fielding _____ suspects at an impressive rate.

3 **EXPOSE**
  a The journalist _____ four corrupt MPs in the previous three months.
  b The journalist _____ corrupt MPs for his entire twenty-year career.

4 **EAT**
  a The prince _____ breakfast when he collapsed.
  b The prince _____ something poisonous during breakfast.

5 **DROP**
  a Viola _____ several hints regarding what she wanted for her birthday.
  b Viola _____ hints all week regarding what she wanted for her birthday.

5 ⭐⭐ Tick the correct sentences. Then rewrite the remaining sentences to make them correct.

1 ☑ Until that night, Mark had never believed in UFOs.
_____

2 ☐ By the time we opened the door, the noises already stopped.
_____

3 ☐ The other day, I was talking to a man who said he had seen Elvis in a café in Prague.
_____

4 ☐ Suddenly, I was hearing a noise, so I was going upstairs and opening the door to the attic.
_____

5 ☐ The hikers had been walking in the mountains for six hours when they saw something strange.
_____

6 ☐ While he was performing, the magician had accidentally revealed the secret behind his famous trick.
_____

7 ☐ While I rowed a boat across Loch Ness, a large creature suddenly appeared in the water next to me!
_____

6 ⭐⭐ Complete the sentences with the correct forms of the verbs in brackets.

1 When Kiara arrived at the party, the boys _had already eaten_ (already/eat) the food.

2 There was a strange smell because someone _____ (cook) fish.

3 Loud music _____ (play) and the guests were dancing or chatting to each other.

4 Ryan _____ (wait) all week for the chance to ask Charlotte to dance.

5 While they _____ (dance), there was a power cut and the music stopped.

6 They lit some candles and then everyone _____ (sit) in a circle and told scary stories.

7 ⭐⭐ Complete the story with the correct forms of the verbs from the box.

~~come~~ disappear do kidnap leave organise play switch wait work

The mystery of Lionel the caretaker

I was reading a newspaper the other day when I **¹**_came_ across a fascinating story. It was about a school caretaker who **²**_____ in mysterious circumstances. Lionel Brigg **³**_____ at the school for exactly twenty-five years on the day he vanished. He was a friendly, polite man who was popular with everyone and who always **⁴**_____ his job well. The staff and students **⁵**_____ a surprise party to celebrate Lionel's twenty-five years at the school. Everyone **⁶**_____ for him in the assembly hall when the head teacher stood up, **⁷**_____ on the microphone and announced that Lionel couldn't be found anywhere. The party was cancelled. While everyone **⁸**_____ the school, the rumours began. Some said he had been killed. Others claimed he **⁹**_____ the lottery for years and he'd finally won a fortune and gone to the Caribbean. Someone even said aliens **¹⁰**_____ him in a spaceship. Whatever the truth was, Lionel was never seen again.

8 ⭐⭐⭐ Use the prompts to write questions about the story in Exercise 7. Use the Past Perfect Simple or Past Perfect Continuous.

1 How long / Lionel / work / at the school / when / disappear?
How long had Lionel been working at the school when he disappeared?

2 How / the staff and students / plan / to celebrate?
_____

3 What / happen / Lionel?
_____

4 play / the lottery / for years?
_____

5 aliens / take him away / spaceship?
_____

9 ON A HIGH NOTE Write a paragraph to complete the story in Exercise 7 explaining what happened to Lionel. Use at least two examples of the Past Perfect Simple and Past Perfect Continuous.

4B VOCABULARY | News reporting

1 ⭐ Match the two parts of the sentences.

1 ☐ I never click on clickbait
2 ☐ The band's amazing video had gone
3 ☐ Their app is great, but it will never generate
4 ☐ Scientists have suggested that humans have shorter
5 ☐ A new experiment could finally shed
6 ☐ A Singaporean couple have hit
7 ☐ A judge has ruled it is not in the
8 ☐ As a serious newspaper we always attempt to present
9 ☐ I rarely trust a sensational report unless I can verify its
10 ☐ The murdered journalist had tried to expose

a attention spans than goldfish.
b public interest to reveal the details of the recent murders.
c headlines, though sometimes I'm tempted.
d enough revenue to keep their business alive.
e both sides of a story and give the full picture.
f corruption in the national government.
g the headlines after giving birth to quintuplets.
h viral before the song had even become a hit.
i sources multiple times on the Internet.
j light on the mysteries of dark matter.

2 ⭐ Complete the crossword. What's the mystery word?

Crossword:
1 (across) E X C L U S I V E
2 H _ _ _ _ B _ _
3 B _ _ _ _ _ _
4 H _ _ _ W _ _ _ _ _
5 H _ _ – H _ _ _
6 Q _ _ _ _
7 N _ _ _ _ _ _
8 T _ _ _ _ _ _

1 A story published only in one paper/magazine.
2 Extremely sad.
3 Considering all sides equally.
4 Causing feelings of happiness.
5 Including strong criticism.
6 Unusual in an interesting way.
7 Important enough to be reported in the media.
8 Relating to events happening now.

The mystery word is _____.

3 ⭐⭐ Choose the correct adjectives to complete the extract from a radio show.

AND IN TODAY'S PAPERS ...

The Courier leads with a [1]*balanced / hard-hitting* article accusing the prime minister of lying to parliament and the country. Supposedly [2]*off the record / quirky* comments from the deputy have made things very difficult for the PM this week and clearly *The Courier* doesn't want to let the story go. *The Gazette* has a [3]*heartwarming / heartbreaking* report on the thousands of victims of Hurricane Ivona and *The Record* leads with the same. *The Record* also has [4]*a topical / an exclusive* interview with United manager, Cyriac Jones, about his decision to leave the club after twenty-two years. And in *The Star* it's the usual [5]*sensational / viral* celebrity nonsense. Jenny, back to you ...

4 ⭐⭐ Complete the text with the words from the box.

awareness   balanced   corruption   light   newsworthy   ~~public~~   revenue   sensational   sides   verify

THE DAILY TARGET: OUR CORE VALUES

We believe it is the media's role to act in the [1]*public* interest and to report a range of [2]_____ stories and relevant opinions which inform readers and allow them to make up their own minds about current events. *The Daily Target* will never produce [3]_____, one-sided stories, but instead will seek to raise [4]_____ of important issues and only report information from sources we have been able to [5]_____. We believe in [6]_____ news articles that present all [7]_____ of a story. In our political reporting, we aim to shed [8]_____ on the way in which our country is run and to expose [9]_____ wherever we find it. We generate [10]_____ through advertising, but also through the kind contributions of our readers. Click here to find out more.

5 ON A HIGH NOTE Write a paragraph saying whether you agree or disagree with the following statement, and why.

Most young people are not interested in world news.

Negative inversion

1 ⭐ **Choose the correct forms to complete the sentences.**

1 At no time *is / it is* the use of such language acceptable.
2 Not only *did I feel / felt I* relaxed, but also happy and safe.
3 Under no circumstances *I will ever / will I ever* do that again.
4 Seldom *I had seen / had I seen* such a lucky escape.
5 Little *did they know / they did know* that I had more money in my back pocket.
6 Scarcely *the tickets had gone / had the tickets gone* on sale when they were sold out.
7 Hardly *we had begun / had we begun* when things started to go wrong.
8 No sooner *had they introduced / they introduced* us than we began to discover similarities between us.

2 ⭐⭐ **USE OF ENGLISH Choose the correct words a–c to complete the text.**

1 a he arrived   b did he arrive   c had he arrived
2 a would he   b he would   c were he
3 a Little they did know
   b Little did they know
   c Little they were known
4 a they'd begun   b had they begun   c they began
5 a Not only my father is
   b My father is not only
   c Not only is my father

While travelling in Thailand in 2001, my dad and his friends had a very lucky escape. He was at a railway station in the south of the country hoping to catch a train to the capital, Bangkok. He joined the queue for tickets, but no sooner ¹___ at the ticket window than he was told that the train was full. According to the clerk, under no circumstances ²___

3 ⭐⭐ **Rewrite the sentences to make them correct.**

1 No sooner Nick arrives at work than people start knocking on his office door.
No sooner does Nick arrive at work than people start knocking on his office door.
2 At no circumstances are students allowed to take exam papers out of the room.
_____
3 In no way this article represents my views.
_____
4 Scarcely the film had started when members of the audience began to walk out of the cinema.
_____
5 Seldom had Ahmed left the car showroom when his new car began to make a strange noise.
_____
6 Not only were you late, but were you also inappropriately dressed.
_____

4 ⭐⭐⭐ **Complete the sentences with the words in brackets and an appropriate auxiliary verb.**

1 *Barely had we arrived* (we/arrived/barely) when dinner was served.
2 _____ (left/no/they/sooner) the hostel than it started to rain.
3 _____ (only/it/not) the worst holiday we'd ever had, but also the most expensive!
4 _____ (in/way/saying/I/no) it is your fault, but we do need to find a solution.
5 _____ (rarely/felt/I) so unwelcome at someone's house.
6 _____ (imagine/Jordan/little) that Karen was actually working for the police.
7 _____ (we/seldom/see) such an emotional reaction from a politician.
8 _____ (been/there/never) such a need for a superhero-like figure to save the day.

5 ON A HIGH NOTE **Write a short news report about a lucky escape. Use at least three negative inversions.**

and his travelling companions be able to travel to Bangkok that day as planned, as the next available seats were not until the following day. ³___ how lucky they were.

Disappointed, the group left the station, went for some food and then later found a cheap hotel for the night. Once in their hotel room, they switched on the TV news, and hardly ⁴___ to watch when they realised what a lucky escape they had had. That afternoon, there had been a bomb in the station at exactly the time they would have been waiting for the afternoon train. Several people were killed and dozens injured. ⁵___ lucky to be alive, but, as I wouldn't be here without him, so am I.

1
Read two short web posts about the popularity of radio. Match photos A–D with the texts in which they are mentioned.

'Against' post: _A_, ___
'For' post: ___ ___

2
Read the web posts quickly and answer the questions.

1 What, according to Olivia, is the main reason why young people seldom listen to the radio?

_____

2 What three advantages to listening to the radio does Xander mention?

_____
_____
_____

3
Read the web posts again. Match sentences A–H with gaps 1–6 in the texts. There are two extra sentences.

A If you do this, you never have to listen to music you don't like.

B After being plunged into silence, I realised that as usual, I'd been half-listening to the radio for the last eight hours.

C According to research, eighty-nine percent of the UK population over the age of fifteen listened to the radio every week in 2018.

D That of course requires a reliable Internet connection and decent battery life.

E They reveal that we are abandoning radio in huge numbers.

F This is especially true when we are busy studying, exercising, cooking or whatever else we do with music in the background.

G Unfortunately, such services are still too expensive for many young people to afford.

H When I asked my friends about their listening habits the following weekend, they all confirmed the same thing.

Vocabulary extension

4
Complete the sentences with the highlighted words from the text. Use the information in brackets to help you.

1 A(n) _overenthusiastic_ (too excited) DJ described the young band as 'the next Beatles'.

2 Cleaning is so _____ (boring) that without the radio to listen to, I'd never get round to it.

3 My parents listen to _____ (old-fashioned) rock and roll from the 60s.

4 While streaming services bring _____ (excellent) choice to customers, they do not always benefit artists.

5 In the video, I'd also like to include some _____ (played while some other activity is going on) music.

5
Complete the text with the words from Exercise 4.

My dad is in his late forties and still into the [1]_old-school_ dance music he listened to when he was a teenager. Although cassette players are basically obsolete these days, he's still got one and he uses it to play old tapes from the clubs he went to in the 90s. He gets a bit [2]_____ to be honest – dancing around the living room and going on about how [3]_____ the 90s were. Although it's a bit annoying, it's also kind of funny and some of the music is actually pretty good. Sometimes, when we have a party, we play his songs as [4]_____ music and most people say they like them. But there are some songs that are so repetitive and badly produced that I find them completely [5]_____!

ACTIVE VOCABULARY
Adverb–adjective collocations

Many common collocations are formed using an adverb followed by an adjective (e.g. _quietly confident_, _deeply moving_).

6
Complete the collocations with the correct adverbs from the box. Use a collocations dictionary to help you if necessary.

actively   bitterly   ~~deeply~~   highly   perfectly   readily

1 The results of the last election have left the country _deeply_ divided.

2 I was _____ disappointed not to get an offer to study at Edinburgh University.

3 Printed information is _____ available for anybody who doesn't have access to the website.

4 It's _____ normal to feel nervous before a public performance.

5 This weekly radio show is _____ recommended for fans of movie soundtracks.

6 I'm _____ involved in the student council at our school.

7
ON A HIGH NOTE Write a short paragraph describing your listening habits.

AT **FORANDAGAINST.NET**
EVERY STORY HAS TWO SIDES

Against: by Olivia, 19 yrs

• • •

The last time I visited my grandfather, he was singing along to the old-school radio he still has in the corner of his kitchen. It struck me that I hadn't intentionally sat down and listened to the radio for as long as I could remember. **1**___ None of us ever listens to the radio, unless we happen to hear it at our grandparents' or when passing a building site!

As a source of music and information, it seems that radio is out of date in the eyes (or more appropriately, the ears) of the digital generation. Statistics support this anecdotal evidence. **2**___ Major radio stations in the UK seem to be satisfied with keeping their older audience happy. Conversely, streaming services such as Spotify and Tidal now account for over fifty percent of millennials' daily listening. It should come as no surprise that those aged fifteen to nineteen do nearly half their listening on smartphones. Never has it been easier to choose your own music, or to take it with you wherever you go. In fact, I have to wonder why anyone would want to listen to someone else's selection when it's so easy to create your own playlists. **3**___ Plus, if you pay for your streaming service, you also eliminate the annoying adverts that invade your headspace constantly on many commercial stations.

If I'm relaxing, I usually choose to watch rather than listen. This means I go to YouTube or similar, and never the radio. If I'm working, the last thing I want is an overenthusiastic DJ talking nonsense, followed by a song I don't like, and then another three minutes of mind-numbing adverts. No, I'm afraid I can only conclude that radio is practically dead and gone. The fact that anyone under the age of forty would tune in at all is a total enigma to me.

For: by Xander, 17 yrs

• • •

Just a few minutes ago, the digital receiver in the living room switched itself off automatically. **4**___ This happens a lot in our house. My dad switches the news on first thing in the morning and the station ends up playing all day long. To be honest, I enjoy the background noise and music: home wouldn't be home without it.

Radio has been around forever and despite recent claims in printed media that it is dying, there is evidence to suggest it is very much alive. **5**___ The medium is also moving with the times and over half of all UK listeners now tune in digitally, whether at home, in the car or on the move. You can even 'watch' your favourite radio shows via live feeds online.

Sure, there are streaming services and with them access to more music than you could possibly listen to in a lifetime. While I don't claim to speak for all young people, I'm quietly confident that most of us don't want to have to choose our own music all the time. **6**___ In fact, radio is a tremendous way to discover new songs, artists and even styles of music that you might never think to search for yourself. Let's not forget that radio is also much more than just music. There's news, sports, discussion, interviews, factual shows and a whole lot more besides. Radio is here to stay so turn on, tune in, and listen up!

1 🔊 **25** Listen to a radio phone-in programme about people who experienced fifteen minutes of fame. Tick the subjects which are mentioned.

1 ☑ a piece of research   4 ☐ a photograph
2 ☐ a fashion show   5 ☐ a book
3 ☐ a race   6 ☐ a fire

2 🔊 **25** Listen again. What does each person say about their fifteen minutes of fame? Match speakers 1–4 with sentences a–g. There are three extra sentences.

1 ☐ Kathy   3 ☐ Sarah
2 ☐ Gary   4 ☐ Naveen

a He/She was treated like a hero.
b His/Her school life became easier as a result.
c He/She got a technology-related job because of what happened.
d He/She earned a large amount of money afterwards.
e He/She finds it difficult to listen to a recording of the event.
f His/Her whole family had fifteen minutes of fame.
g He/She thinks that new technology makes it easier to do what she did.

Vocabulary extension

3 Match the words and phrases from the box, which you heard in the recording in Exercise 1, with the definitions.

an honour   in the spotlight   ~~infamous~~   prestigious
stardom   world-renowned

1 Well-known for a negative reason. _infamous_
2 A rare opportunity that makes you feel proud.
_____
3 A university or institution which is very much respected. _____
4 Something known globally. _____
5 A synonym of the word 'fame'. _____
6 Having the attention of the media. _____

4 Complete the sentences with the words and phrases from Exercise 3.

1 Many people dream of being famous, but the realities of _stardom_ are not always positive.
2 Cyclist, Norman Cooper, is _____ this week after setting a new world record in Paris.
3 The prime minister attended one of the most _____ schools in the UK.
4 _____ murderer, Bruce Wilson, was finally caught by Spanish police last week.
5 Quality Swiss watches are _____ and can cost tens of thousands of euros.
6 An invitation to meet the princess is considered _____ and is rarely refused.

5 ON A HIGH NOTE Write a short paragraph about a time when you or someone you know experienced fifteen minutes of fame.

Pronunciation

6 🔊 **26** Read some sentences from the radio phone-in programme in Exercise 1. Find the stressed syllables in the underlined words. What happens to the unstressed syllables? Listen and check.

1 I'd spent a long time researching journalism, privacy, and the law in connection with the (infamous) accident that killed Princess Diana.
2 There was a small cash prize and my work was printed in a prestigious academic journal.
3 It was a real honour, and the photo appeared in several national magazines and newspapers.
4 Not only were we on the local TV news, but we also got our picture in the newspaper.

ACTIVE PRONUNCIATION
/ə/ sound in adjectives

The sound /ə/ is the most common vowel sound in English. It is found in unstressed syllables and it can be spelt with any vowel letter. It appears in many words, including the suffixes which we use to create adjectives:

• -ous /əs/ (e.g. danger**ous**)
• -al /əl/ (e.g. intention**al**)
• -able/ible /əbl/ (e.g. comfort**able**)
• -ful /fəl/ (e.g. pain**ful**)
• -less /ləs/ (e.g. rest**less**)

7 🔊 **27** Listen and find the unstressed syllable with the sound /ə/ in each adjective. Then practise saying the words.

1 e(dible)
2 beautiful
3 global
4 useless
5 famous

8 🔊 **28** Find the unstressed syllable with the sound /ə/ in the underlined words. Listen and check.

1 The governor's excuses are (laughable).
2 Journalists must be careful to get their facts right.
3 Colin wandered aimlessly around the village.
4 The man was furious when his name was revealed in the newspaper.
5 The subject of the documentary is really topical.

9 Practise saying the sentences from Exercise 8.

1 🔊 *29* Listen and repeat the phrases. How do you say them in your language?

SPEAKING | Telling an anecdote

SAYING THAT AN ANECDOTE IS ABOUT TO START

You'll never believe what happened to me the other day.

That reminds me of the pop star I met in my local supermarket.

That reminds me of a time when I met a pop star in my local supermarket.

Have I ever told you about the time we were invited to Buckingham Palace?

A friend of a friend told me this story.

GIVING BACKGROUND INFORMATION (PEOPLE, TIME, PLACE)

I was travelling down to London from Oxford on the train.

Well, I'm not sure if you know my colleague, Joe, **but** he's actually related to the Queen!

There was this guy who had been working there who was related to Andy Murray.

INTRODUCING A TURNING POINT IN THE SEQUENCE OF EVENTS

Anyway, to cut a long story short, I decided to go round and see him.

Suddenly, I heard a loud noise.

No sooner had I got on the train **than** I noticed it was going in the wrong direction.

Hardly had we got off the train **when** I realised I'd left my bag under my seat.

It turned out that the train was the express service to Edinburgh.

Before we knew what was happening, the train pulled out of the station.

Guess what?

SHOWING THE SPEAKER'S ATTITUDE (THIS CAN HAPPEN AT ANY POINT, AND MORE THAN ONCE)

Obviously, I was a bit taken aback.

I couldn't believe what was happening.

Obviously, he was trying to travel without a ticket.

Presumably, he had left his wallet in the taxi.

Unbelievably, he had spent the whole journey in the toilet.

Apparently, another passenger had bought a ticket for him.

And then, to top it all, I realised I had lost my wallet!

I mean – I've done it, haven't you?

No word of a lie!

Would you believe it?

ROUNDING OFF THE ANECDOTE

It was probably the most embarrassing moment of my life!

I'll never forget the day I went to work in my pyjamas!

I'll never do that **again.**

---

2 Put the words in order to make sentences from anecdotes.

1 what / to us / couldn't / I / believe / was happening
I couldn't believe what was happening to us.

2 I / have / I / told you / about the time / a fairy / saw / ever / ?
_____

3 to cut / anyway / it was / short / a total disaster / a long story
_____

4 knew / was running / before / towards us / the bull / was happening / we / what / !
_____

5 was / obviously / aback / a bit / taken / by the whole thing / I
_____

6 never / to me / the other day / what / happened / you'll / believe
_____

3 Replace the underlined parts with the comment adverbs from the box.

apparently ~~obviously~~ personally presumably surely theoretically

1 It was clear that under no circumstances could I let that happen. *Obviously,*

2 In theory, there is no way the branch could snap. _____

3 I can only assume she forgot to check the locks before leaving for the night. _____

4 It seems that luck was on his side that afternoon. _____

5 I'm certain that someone would have noticed the missing lifeboat. _____

6 If you ask me, I think they were foolish to even consider such a move. _____

4 🔊 *30* Put the sentences in order to make an anecdote. Listen and check.

That reminds me of a scary story I heard not long ago …

a ☐ Would you believe it? It was probably the scariest moment of her life.

b ☐ Obviously, she was terrified, but then she felt her dog lick her hand in the darkness.

c ☐ But then the next morning she woke up to find the dog was missing.

d ☐ She was just falling asleep when suddenly, she heard strange noises and movement from under the bed.

e ☐ And there was a note next to her pillow that said 'people can lick hands too'.

f ☐ Apparently, that calmed her down and she went back to sleep.

g ☑ There was this girl in bed at home, alone except for her faithful dog.

5 ON A HIGH NOTE Write a funny or scary anecdote.

Give your story a catchy/interesting title.

Make sure your story has a clear structure – a beginning, middle and end.

Consider starting the story in the middle of the action for dramatic effect.

Use time linkers to show when things happened.

Use negative inversion to add emphasis.

Use direct speech to make your story more interesting.

MISSING IN THE HILLS

Paco had vanished into thin air. He and ¹Jamie had taken their familiar Saturday morning train ride from the city to the country, then hiked up into the stunning Derbyshire hills. When they reached a fork in the path, Jamie stopped to consult the map. ²It was raining and, though visibility was poor, Jamie was sure that Paco had been just behind him. Glancing round now though, he found himself utterly alone.

An hour later and ³Jamie was still searching when suddenly, he spotted a movement to his left. His heart started pounding. 'Paco!' he yelled, 'Is that you?' Again, there was movement followed by the sudden shock of a deer crashing out of the trees and racing down the steep hill. Jamie's wide eyes followed until they settled on the blue-grey peaks that filled the horizon. How would he ever find his friend out here?

⁴Jamie had been searching unsuccessfully for several hours. Not only was he desperately worried about Paco, but he was also shivering with cold. He came across a deserted looking hill-top pub, and hoping for a warm drink, he went inside. To his surprise, ⁵he found a group of young people chatting and unpacking their drones. 'We're the Derbyshire Drone Society' said a young woman brightly, 'I'm Chloe. Is everything alright?' Jamie asked for help and within minutes, six drones with cameras had joined the search.

'I think I see him!' yelled one of the pilots suddenly. 'Hold tight!' warned Chloe as, guided by one of the drones, she and Jamie sped off to the rescue on her off-road motorbike. When they reached the spot, Jamie called out, and all of a sudden there was Paco, muddy and exhausted but alive. He leapt into Jamie's arms; relieved Jamie was finally reunited with his faithful dog.

1 Read the story and choose the statement that is true.
The twist in the story is that …
  a it was all just one of the main character's dreams.
  b one of the main characters is not actually human.
  c the story actually takes place far into the future.

2 Match underlined parts 1–5 from the story with their functions a–e. Then write what tense the underlined parts are in.
  a ☐ a single completed action in the past _Past Simple_
  b ☐ an action completed before a time in the past
  _____
  c ☐ an event in progress interrupted by a single action
  _____ _____
  d ☐ an ongoing action forming the background to a story _____
  e ☐ a situation or action in progress up to a time in the past _____

3 Find adverbs and adverbial phrases in the story and write them in the correct column.

Manner	Place	Time
suddenly		

4 Rewrite the sentences with the words in brackets in the correct place. There may be more than one correct answer.
  1 The object in the sky disappeared. (into thin air, suddenly, quickly)
  _____
  2 Louise tried to find an apartment. (in the area, for months, unsuccessfully)
  _____

5 WRITING TASK **Write your story.**

ACTIVE WRITING | A story

1 **Plan your story.**
  • Think of a catchy/interesting title for your story.
  • Think about where and when your story takes place, and who the main characters are.
  • Think of a beginning, middle and end.
  • Decide if your story will have a twist.

2 **Write your story.**
  • Use a variety of past tenses and time linkers, interesting verbs and adverbs.
  • Include some direct speech for interest and negative inversion for emphasis.

3 **Check that …**
  • you have correctly placed the adverbs you used.
  • there are no spelling, grammar or punctuation mistakes.

1 4A GRAMMAR AND VOCABULARY **Choose the correct words to complete the sentences.**

1 The king was *assassinated / abducted* using poisoned food.

2 Police have so far failed to *eliminate / capture* the escaped prisoners.

3 Attempting to pay for something with fake bank notes is *fraud / hoax*.

4 The woman has always *maintained / revealed* her innocence despite being found guilty in court.

5 Investigators found several important *hints / clues* at the crime scene.

6 I always thought there was something slightly *topical / weird* about the two of them.

7 This is one of the most *bizarre / puzzle* stories we've ever reported.

8 The accused *claimed / exposed* that he was abroad at the time the crime was committed.

2 4B VOCABULARY **Complete the texts with the words from the box.**

clickbait   expose   interest   ~~raise~~   revenue   shed
spans   viral

WANTED: Investigative journalist to join our team and help **1** *raise* awareness of important local issues, **2**_____ light on the facts behind the headlines and **3**_____ corruption in local business and politics. If you dream of reporting in the public **4**_____, visit our website for more details.

Got what it takes to write successful 5_____ **headlines?** Know what's required to appeal to short attention **6**_____ and make a story go **7**_____? If so, you could be the one to help us generate **8**_____ while advancing your own career.
Contact Clickplus Marketing for more details.

3 4B VOCABULARY **Complete the sentences with one word in each gap.**

1 I prefer a newspaper with b*alanced* reporting rather than something that's always one-sided.

2 I like to read the main news, but I also like quirky, h_____ articles that make me smile.

3 Only in today's *Guardian* – a hard-hitting e_____ story for those interested in European politics.

4 *Save-A-Stray Magazine* is full of h_____ stories about stray animals living on the streets around the world.

5 My mother loves reading magazines with s_____ gossip about celebrities' marriages and divorces.

6 Comments made off the r_____ should not be reported publically even if they're newsworthy.

4 4D READING AND VOCABULARY **Match the two parts of the sentences.**

1 ☐ When Bob was offered a job abroad, he immediately seized

2 ☐ When I saw some hooligans smashing the windows, I immediately reported

3 ☐ The minister promised to release

4 ☐ Jane felt overworked and has put in

5 ☐ Sue laughed off

a a statement to the press in the afternoon.

b a request for a month's holiday.

c the accusation that she spread the gossip.

d the incident to the police.

e the opportunity.

5 4E LISTENING AND VOCABULARY **Rewrite the sentences with the words in brackets in the correct place.**

1 I love this because it my father's exactly as I remember him. (captures, likeness, shot)

I love this shot because it captures my father's likeness exactly as I remember him.

2 This photo is beautifully and for me it the bitter cold of winter. (composed, evokes, landscape)

_____

3 This one is really badly meaning half my face is missing, plus with everyone like that it looks fake. (cropped, posing)

_____

4 This one was taken just before our relationship ended, so the is particularly as far as I'm concerned. (poignant, subject matter)

_____

6 4G WRITING AND VOCABULARY **Choose the correct words to complete the sentences.**

1 The speaker kept on *mumbling / yelling* quietly under his breath, but I could understand what it was he was saying.

2 She *shrieked / snapped* in pain when the car ran over her foot.

3 Tom *wandered / tiptoed* past his father's office desperate not to be heard.

4 At last she *spotted / gazed* a figure on the horizon and began running towards it.

5 He had only *glanced / peered* at the photograph so couldn't remember any details about it.

6 Jenny stop it! It's rude to *peer / stare* at people.

7 He *muttered / bellowed* something about teenagers, but I couldn't hear exactly what he said.

7 ON A HIGH NOTE **Write a short paragraph describing a photograph that is special to you in some way. What happened before and after the photograph was taken?**

1 For each learning objective, write 1–5 to assess your ability.

1 = I don't feel confident. 5 = I feel confident.

	Learning objective	Course material	How confident I am (1–5)
4A	I can use narrative tenses to talk about past events.	Student's Book pp. 48–49	
4B	I can talk about the news.	Student's Book p. 50	
4C	I can use negative inversion to add emphasis.	Student's Book p. 51	
4D	I can recognise bias in news reports and talk about protests.	Student's Book pp. 52–53	
4E	I can identify specific details in a radio programme and talk about photos.	Student's Book p. 54	
4F	I can tell an anecdote.	Student's Book p. 55	
4G	I can write a story.	Student's Book pp. 56–57	

2 Which of the skills above would you like to improve in? How?

Skill I want to improve in	How I can improve

3 What can you remember from this unit?

New words I learned and most want to remember	Expressions and phrases I liked	English I heard or read outside class

GRAMMAR AND VOCABULARY

1 Choose the correct words to complete the sentences.

1 As many people had suggested, the UFO sighting turned out to be a *puzzle / hoax*.
2 He was a total *enigma / fraud* and police weren't able to find a single record of his existence.
3 A local businessman was *abducted / revealed* in the city centre on Saturday by two men in a van.
4 This documentary finally sheds *interest / light* on the mystery of the disappearance of flight 102.
5 The president *hit / exposed* the headlines again by choosing to play golf rather than work.

/ 5

2 Complete the sentences with the words from the box. There are two extra words.

corruption   muttering   neighbourhood   peering
quirky   ~~sensational~~   statement   suspicion

1 This so called 'news' paper contains nothing but *sensational* celebrity gossip.
2 Having lost all his money, he could be heard _____ to himself about how unfair life was.
3 The men were arrested on _____ of murder.
4 There has been a series of robberies in the _____, so residents are being warned to lock their doors.
5 This English stand-up comedian has a particularly _____ sense of humour.
6 He's the famous journalist exposing _____ in public life.

/ 5

3 Complete the conversation with the correct forms of the verbs in brackets.

Pat So how was the film?

Jez Well, the whole evening was a disaster. By the time the bus arrived, I **1** *'d been waiting* (wait) in the rain for twenty minutes, and when I finally met up with Gavin and got to the cinema, the film **2** _____ (already/start).

Pat Oh no! Was it a good film at least?

Jez Well, I don't know. We had been watching for about fifteen minutes when the screen **3** _____ (go) blank.

Pat What?

Jez Apparently they **4** _____ (not check) the projector properly, and it broke down. While we **5** _____ (wait) for them to fix the projector, they offered us tickets to the other film that was showing, but Gavin had already seen it.

Pat Oh, dear. So what **6** _____ (you/do)?

Jez Well, we got our money back and then caught the bus home. A total waste of an evening!

/ 5

4 Put the words in brackets in order to complete the sentences.

1 (had / scarcely / arrived / we) *Scarcely had we arrived* at the beach when it began to rain.
2 (time / at / no / did / believe / I) _____ he would actually turn up on our doorstep.
3 (way / no / is / she / in / saying) _____ she won't take part in the debate.
4 (think / little / they / did) _____ someone was recording every word they said.
5 (do / see / seldom / you) _____ such beautiful animals up close.
6 (so many / never / people / have) _____ turned up at elections.

/ 5

USE OF ENGLISH

5 Complete the text with the correct words formed from the words in bold.

This website aims to raise **1** *awareness* (**AWARE**) of issues that affect young people who have left school and are in full or part-time employment. Each week it presents **2** _____ (**TOPIC**) discussions and up-to-the-minute news aimed at younger **3** _____ (**WORK**) and those taking part in vocational training and apprenticeships. The stories it includes are always **4** _____ (**NEWS**) and the articles contain a great deal of **5** _____ (**INFORM**) that is likely to attract the **6** _____ (**ATTEND**) of anyone with a job aged between sixteen and twenty-five.
I recommend it highly.

/ 5

6 Complete the second sentence using the word in bold so that it means the same as the first one. Use between two and five words, including the word in bold.

1 The plane had just taken off when the emergency lights came on. **HARDLY**
   Hardly had the plane taken off when the emergency lights came on.
2 I arrived at the shop but it was already closed. **HAD**
   By the time we arrived at the shop, _____ closed.
3 I queued for an hour before I got to the front. **BEEN**
   I _____ for an hour when I got to the front.
4 Millions of people watched the video during the first twenty-four hours it was online. **VIRAL**
   The video _____ within twenty-four hours.
5 We didn't expect to have to pay for dinner. **CIRCUMSTANCES**
   _____ we expect to have to pay for dinner.
6 Where did he work before he went to prison? **LIVING**
   What did he _____ before he went to prison?

/ 5

/ 30

51

5A **GRAMMAR AND VOCABULARY**

Gerunds and infinitives

1 ⭐ **Match the two parts of the sentences.**

1 ☐ I know I should resist, but I can't help
2 ☐ Many people fail
3 ☐ Experts encourage
4 ☐ Let the delicious flavours
5 ☐ The curry is so spicy I have difficulty
6 ☐ Do you happen
7 ☐ Jack's parents tried to force
8 ☐ The smell was so terrible Mum made

a tempt your taste buds.
b to know where I can get my hearing tested?
c him to eat broccoli when he was a child.
d scratching when I've got an insect bite.
e to understand the strong link between smell and taste.
f me open all the windows.
g tasting anything except the chilli.
h us to take regular breaks from staring at our computer screens.

2 ⭐ **Choose the correct forms to complete the sentences.**

1 I tend *to remember* / *remembering* I'm not wearing my reading glasses when my eyes begin to ache.
2 Is it usual for under-eighteens *to pay* / *paying* for eye tests?
3 I'm short-sighted, so I wear glasses *helping* / *to help* me see objects in the distance.
4 You're the second person *to ask* / *asking* me if my hearing is OK today.
5 You risk *to damage* / *damaging* your eyesight if you stare at the Sun.
6 My dog is brilliant at *detect* / *detecting* smells.
7 *To tell* / *Telling* these smells apart can be very difficult for some people.
8 While *working* / *to work* as a chef, I developed a keen sense of smell.
9 To avoid *to damage* / *damaging* your glasses, always keep them in the case provided.
10 We encourage you *having* / *to have* your glasses cleaned and checked regularly at one of our stores.

3 ⭐⭐ **Complete the text with the correct forms of the verbs in brackets.**

I held a snake for the first time at a small zoo in the south of England. I was surprised ¹*to find* (find) that it was dry and not wet. While ²_____ (hold) the snake, I felt it begin ³_____ (wrap) itself round my arm, but I didn't feel threatened. I don't think it intended ⁴_____ (do) me any harm. In fact, it seemed ⁵_____ (want) to show me affection. Nothing about the snake was what I'd expected. I felt lucky that it had let me ⁶_____ (touch) it.

4 ⭐⭐ **Complete the texts with the correct forms of the verbs in bold and an object where necessary.**

READ

Gavin tries ¹*to read* for at least an hour every day. He enjoys ²_____ while he's travelling to school. His mum won't let ³_____ at the dinner table though.

DO

Anastasia's parents make ⁴_____ her homework as soon as she gets in from school. They encourage ⁵_____ it before anything else. The only way she can avoid ⁶_____ it is if she has after-school activities.

WATCH

Ola can't stand ⁷_____ violent films or TV series. She refuses ⁸_____ anything where violence is shown as entertainment. ⁹_____ comedies on the other hand, she finds a gre=at pleasure.

5 ★★ Complete the text with the correct forms of the verbs from the box.

approach   attack   be   ~~have~~   hunt   know   smell
steal   take

BEWARE
THE BEARS!

Imagine ¹*having* a sense of smell 700 times more powerful than a human. Grizzly Bears' noses are so good that they are able ²_____ a potential meal from up to eighteen miles away. This is why it is so important ³_____ careful when you are camping in Grizzly country. The bears will be the first ⁴_____ if you leave food out, and you won't be able to prevent them from ⁵_____ your campsite if they are hungry. ⁶_____ your food is much easier than spending time ⁷_____ and while bears are not likely ⁸_____ humans, can you really afford ⁹_____ the risk?

6 ★★ Read the sentences. What function do they have? Write *N*, *B* or *P*.

N = This is normal.

B = This is slowly becoming normal.

P = This was true in the past, but is no longer true now.

1 I'm getting used to wearing a hearing aid. *B*
2 Kenny used to have a sensitive palate. ___
3 Brianne is used to people asking her for advice. ___
4 We're already used to the Irish accent. ___
5 They're getting used to being vegetarians now. ___
6 Visitors used to be able to make out the sea from here. ___

7 ★★★ Complete the sentences with the correct forms of (*be/get*) *used to* and the verbs in brackets.

1 Although it's still a bit strange, Chris *is getting used to living* (live) in the student halls instead of at home with his parents.
2 I couldn't concentrate on audio books at first, but now I _____ (listen) to them and prefer them to reading a normal book.
3 When my sister was a child, she _____ (suck) her thumb all the time.
4 Joel _____ (not do) any exercise at all, but now he runs marathons regularly.
5 Bonnie _____ (get up) early after growing up on a farm.
6 I _____ (be) vegetarian eventually although it took a long time for me to stop missing chicken.

8 ★★★ Rewrite the sentences using the correct forms of *used to*, *be used to* or *get used to*.

1 It's normal for me to find cat hairs on my clothes.
I'm used to finding cat hairs on my clothes.
2 Life on the island is slowly becoming normal for the family.
_____
3 Fiona didn't like the smell of fish in the past.
_____
4 Waking up early was slowly becoming normal for Gina.
_____
5 Tim played guitar in a jazz band in the past.
_____
6 It was normal for Greta to speak to large groups of people.
_____

9 ★★★ USE OF ENGLISH Complete the second sentence using the word in bold so that it means the same as the first one. Use between two and five words, including the word in bold.

1 Using this switch, you can turn off all the lights in the house. **ENABLES**
This switch *enables you to switch* off all the lights in the house.
2 It's my job to test people for colour-blindness. **RESPONSIBLE**
I _____ people for colour-blindness.
3 Would you like to try the smelly blue cheese? **FANCY**
Do you _____ the smelly blue cheese?
4 We told him that listening to his headphones at such a high volume was a bad idea. **ENCOURAGED**
We _____ to his headphones at such a high volume.
5 Perfume makers are forbidden from smoking. **ALLOWED**
Perfume makers _____ smoke.
6 Our chemistry teacher forced us to smell the horrible brown liquid. **MADE**
Our chemistry teacher _____ the horrible brown liquid.

10 ON A HIGH NOTE Write a short paragraph about a situation in your life when you had to change your habits or routine, or adapt to new circumstances. Describe the situation and your emotions, and how you coped with the change.

5B VOCABULARY | The senses

1 ★ Do the words describe pleasant ☺ or unpleasant ☹ smells? Choose the correct emojis.

1 aroma ☺/☹ 5 smelly ☺/☹
2 mouth-watering ☺/☹ 6 stench ☺/☹
3 overpowering ☺/☹ 7 stink ☺/☹
4 scent ☺/☹ 8 subtle ☺/☹

2 ★ Choose the correct words to complete the description.

With twenty minutes to kill, I chose a pleasant-looking café near the river. The [1]*stink / aroma* of fresh coffee hit me as soon as I opened the door. I ordered a cup and sat down by the window. The seat was comfortable and whatever they were preparing in the kitchen smelled [2]*mouth-watering / overpowering*. 'Croissants' apparently, 'and fresh ones, not frozen' said the owner with considerable pride. I ordered two with honey and butter. The honey was delicious; 'local', apparently, and very [3]*smooth / spiky* with a [4]*subtle / smelly* hint of lavender. The delicate [5]*stench / scent* of the flower garden at the rear of the café came in through the window and added to the pleasant sense of relaxation.

3 ★ Match the words from the box with the descriptions.

chirp crunch hum pop rustle screech ~~sizzle~~
thud

1 Steaks under the grill. *sizzle*
2 A room full of switched on computers. _____
3 Biting into a slice of well-toasted bread. _____
4 A cork being pulled out of a bottle. _____
5 A heavy book dropped on a wooden floor. _____
6 A car's tyres as the driver takes a corner too fast.
_____
7 Hungry baby birds. _____
8 A bag of sweets in the cinema. _____

4 ★★ Complete the sentences with one adjective in each gap.

1 The jar's paper label came off in the dishwasher, but the *sticky* glue remained on the glass.
2 The children decided the hedgehog was simply too s_____ to pick up and left it alone.
3 The c_____ cloth hurt the little girl's face as her mother wiped her clean.
4 The si_____ material of Bethany's new dress felt wonderful against her legs.
5 The f_____ young chick weighed almost nothing in her hand.
6 Enid didn't believe that the miracle cream would make her skin look young and s_____.
7 After ten days in the fruit bowl, the kiwis were unpleasantly sq_____.
8 Vernon's wool jumper was p_____ against his skin, and was making him uncomfortable.

5 ★★ 🔊 *31* Choose the correct words to complete the mini-conversations. Listen and check.

Overheard at the campsite.

Kurt   What's that awful [1]___?
Uma   I don't know, but it really [2]___.
Kurt   We can't camp here. We'll have to move the tent.
Uma   But it's already dark, Kurt!

Lenny   Lenny! Wake up! Can you hear the [3]___ of the bacon I'm frying for our breakfast?
Norm   Yes, I can. Plus the whole campsite can probably smell that [4]___ smell.
Lenny   Am I a good friend, or what?
Norm   The best, Lenny. I'll make the coffee.

Marcus Argh! Argh!
Sophie What! What is it?
Marcus I can feel something [5]___ in the bottom of my sleeping bag!
Sophie Eeew! What is it?
Marcus I don't know ... wait ... argh! Sorry, but it felt kind of [6]___ like a grape then it [7]___ when I squashed it, and now I've got something [8]___ on my fingers.
Sophie Eeew! I'm never going camping ever again.

1 a aroma   b scent   c stench
2 a stinks   b chirps   c thuds
3 a sizzle   b crunch   c hum
4 a overpowering b fluffy   c mouth-watering
5 a squishy   b smelly   c silky
6 a prickly   b smooth   c spiky
7 a screeched   b popped   c hummed
8 a sticky   b rustling c crunching

6 ON A HIGH NOTE Imagine you are sitting in a busy park on a sunny day. Write a paragraph describing what you can smell, hear and feel.

Verbs with gerunds and infinitives

1 ⭐ Complete the sentences with the structures from the box.

---

deserved discussing   heard the bottle smash
needs paying   ~~regretted drinking~~   remember dreaming
see Ben fall   stop looking
watched Igor and Natalia dancing

---

1 Carl _regretted drinking_ a second can of energy drink.
2 Did you _____ off his bike yesterday?
3 The water bill _____ this week.
4 I _____ I could fly last night.
5 Carolina _____ as it hit the floor.
6 Svetlana _____ together.
7 Graham thought the idea _____.
8 Please _____ at your phone.

2 ⭐ Match each pair of sentences with their meanings a–b.

1 ☐ Why don't you try using a different app to see if it's any better?
2 ☐ Emma tried to sing the highest note, but she couldn't quite manage it.
  a Make an effort to do something difficult.
  b Do something as an experiment to see what happens.

3 ☐ Alice remembered to add salt to the soup she was making.
4 ☐ Harry remembered meeting Gina for the first time.
  a Remember something, then do it.
  b Remember that you did something earlier.

5 ☐ Felix went on to become a vet after graduating from university.
6 ☐ Donald went on dancing even after the music had stopped.
  a Do something after completing something else.
  b Continue an activity without stopping.

7 ☐ I'm sorry, I've forgotten borrowing your dictionary.
8 ☐ I forgot to tell you that I'm allergic to nuts.
  a Forget that you need to do something.
  b Forget about something that happened earlier.

9 ☐ I mean to tell her exactly what I think of her.
10 ☐ My summer job will mean getting up early every morning.
  a Say that one thing will result in another.
  b Say that you intend to do something.

11 I regret selling my mountain bike.
12 I regret to say we are unable to offer you a place on the course.
  a Feel sorry about something you did or didn't do.
  b A formal way to say you are sorry about a situation.

3 ⭐⭐ Complete the sentences with the correct gerund or infinitive forms of the verbs in brackets.

1 Always remember _to wash_ (wash) your hands before you start cooking.
2 Getting the grades I need for university means _____ (study) hard for the next six months.
3 Once your child can walk, he or she needs _____ (watch) all the time.
4 Can we stop at the service station _____ (use) the bathroom?
5 I really regret _____ (go) out last night as I'm exhausted this morning.

4 ⭐⭐ Choose the correct forms to complete the sentences. Then write **C** for a complete action or **I** for an incomplete action.

1 We listened to Whitney *sing / singing* the national anthem from beginning to end. _C_
2 Jay stood in the garden and felt the rain *fall / falling* on her face. ___
3 Did you see the racing cars *touch / touching* just then on the corner? ___
4 He heard the baby next door *cry / crying* every night through the thin walls. ___

5 ⭐⭐⭐ Complete the text with the correct forms of the verbs from the box.

---

go on/develop   need/clean   remember/smell
~~smell/toast/burn~~   stop/breathe in   try/pay   try/repeat
would like/improve

HOW TO IMPROVE YOUR SENSE OF SMELL

How well-developed is your sense of smell? Can you ¹_smell toast burning_ in the neighbours' kitchen, or tell when the bathroom ²_____ before anyone else? If you ³_____ your sense of smell, read on!

Step 1

⁴_____ more attention to familiar smells. For example, before you drink your coffee, ⁵_____ the delicious aroma. If you ⁶_____ your food and drink regularly, your sense of smell will start to improve.

Step 2

⁷_____ your sense of smell by training your nose. Choose a few familiar, pleasant scents and take a minute to really smell them. ⁸_____ this several times a day and your nose will become more sensitive.

6 ON A HIGH NOTE Write a short paragraph about something that you believe deserves doing. Have you ever tried doing it? If so, did you like doing it? Explain why.

5D READING AND VOCABULARY

1 Look at the photos. Which of the five senses are you going to read about?

_____

2 Read the article quickly. What do you think would be the best title?

a Genetic eye conditions

b Colour vision

c Art and the eyes

3 Read the article again and answer the questions.

1 Which eye colour is least common among the world's population? _green_

2 What is unusual about the eyes of someone with heterochromia? _____

3 What do some heterochromia sufferers do to hide their condition? _____

4 What causes the condition known as tetrachromia? _____

5 What is unique about the artist Concetta Antico? _____

6 What drawback of tetrachromacy is described? _____

7 What simple description of synaesthesia is given in the text? _____

8 What skill is synaesthesia often associated with? _____

9 In what way does Nick Ryan say he benefits from his synaesthesia? _____

10 Where was Nick Ryan's artwork shown to the public? _____

4 Decide if statements 1–6 are true or false.

1 ☐ The most common eye colour is brown.

2 ☐ There are thought to be more people with heterochromia than with green eyes.

3 ☐ Heterochromia has a negative effect on eyesight.

4 ☐ The colour vision of a tetrachromat is about 100 times more complex than that of a non-tetrachromat.

5 ☐ Synaesthesia always affects the way a person sees.

6 ☐ Nick Ryan worked with musician Imogen Heap to produce his audio-visual experience.

Vocabulary extension

5 Match the highlighted words from the text with the definitions.

1 Light form of a colour. _pale_

2 Coloured part of the eye. _____

3 Impossible to see. _____

4 Tell the difference between. _____

5 Very bright. _____

6 See (also hear) or notice. _____

7 Using both sight and sound. _____

8 A particular type of a colour, e.g. olive green. _____

6 Complete the sentences with the words from Exercise 5.

1 I never buy _audio-visual_ equipment online unless I've already tested it in a shop.

2 That yellow is too bright for this room – I would prefer _____ yellow.

3 The artist is famous for her use of bright colour – here she uses particularly _____ pinks and greens.

4 Can you _____ between the colour of these two paints? They look the same to me.

5 Octopuses can change colour to match their background and make themselves virtually _____.

6 The _____ of her left eye was so dark it was almost black.

7 The water was the most beautiful _____ of blue.

8 Most marine animals cannot _____ colours and only see in black and white.

ACTIVE VOCABULARY | Verbs ending in -ate

Certain verbs end with the letters -_ate_. Note how the word stress changes in these verbs according to the number of syllables:

• two syllables, stress on second syllable (e.g. cre**ate**)

• three syllables, stress on first syllable (e.g. _demonstr_**ate**)

• four syllables, stress on second syllable (e.g. app_reci_**ate**)

• five syllables, stress on third syllable (e.g. differ_enti_**ate**)

---

7 🔊 *32* Complete the sentences with the verbs from the box. Use a dictionary to help you if necessary. Listen and check. Then practise saying the sentences.

complicate congratulate cooperate estimate miscommunicate ~~vibrate~~

1 Don't forget to switch your phone to _vibrate_ mode when you go into the cinema.

2 My uncle came round to _____ me on passing my exams.

3 We _____ that your parcel will be delivered on Monday 4 February.

4 Sorry to _____ things, but we need to see your original birth certificate, not a copy.

5 Air traffic controllers simply cannot afford to _____ with pilots.

6 If the protesters _____ with police, then the demonstration should be peaceful.

8 ON A HIGH NOTE Write a paragraph describing a particularly colourful place, e.g. a fruit and vegetable market, a flower garden, a holiday resort, etc.

What colour are your eyes? Statistically, they are probably brown – like seventy-nine percent of people on the planet. If you have blue eyes, then you're among the eight to ten percent of the world's population, while around five percent of us have hazel eyes. If you're lucky enough to have green eyes, then you are part of an exclusive group which comprises just two percent of the human race. Extremely unusually, less than one percent of us have something called 'heterochromia' – a genetic condition in which one iris is a totally different colour to the other. Famous examples include actors Kate Bosworth, Jane Seymour and Dan Akroyd. Some people with heterochromia say that they enjoy the attention it brings, whereas others never get used to their different-coloured eyes and wear contact lenses to disguise them. Heterochromia may affect the way you look, but thankfully the condition doesn't usually affect the way you see. However, there are some genetic conditions that can have a radical effect on the way you perceive the world, particularly when it comes to your perception of colour.

A tiny group of people in the world have a condition called 'tetrachromacy'. In tetrachromacy, a variation in a single gene changes the way the eye develops, leading to the amazing ability to see colours that are invisible to others. To put that in perspective, an 'ordinary' eye can distinguish around one million shades of colour, whereas the eyes of a tetrachromat may be able to differentiate 100 million different shades! It is thought that the condition affects only women and in fact it has taken twenty years of research to prove that it exists at all.

It is almost impossible to appreciate what the world looks like to a tetrachromat, but the paintings of Concetta Antico, the only known tetrachromat artist, have given us a fascinating glimpse. As you might expect, her artwork is alive with colour, but her pictures of what she sees in the moonlight or at dawn are particularly interesting. As suggested by

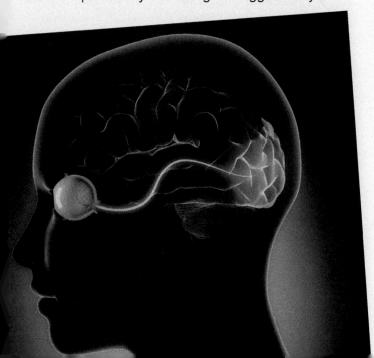

these night-time paintings, testing has shown that tetrachromats have enhanced vision in low light conditions. It's not all positive for Antico though – a simple trip to a colourful place such as fruit and vegetable market can be an overwhelming experience for her. She says her favourite colour is white because she finds it a welcome break from her world of vivid colour.

Another unusual genetic condition is synaesthesia. There are many different forms of the phenomenon, but basically it is a mixing of the senses that causes sounds, textures, flavours and shapes to be experienced with their own associated colours. For example, the sound of a cello may be blue, the taste of chocolate purple, the number 'one' green and Monday a pale shade of orange. Around four percent of the population is thought to have synaesthesia and over seventy variations have been recorded. Experiences vary from person to person and are not always associated with vision. As unlikely as it sounds, some people smell the time, while others taste music. There is a strong link between synaesthesia and artistic skill. Musicians Pharrell Williams, Kanye West and Lady Gaga all claim to have it, and it is thought that Russian author Vladimir Nabokov, artist Vincent van Gogh and jazz legend Duke Ellington were all synaesthetes too.

British composer, Nick Ryan, sees colours, shapes and textures that correspond to sound and music. He says it actually makes listening more enjoyable and, like Concetta Antico, he has produced artwork to try and help people appreciate what it is like to have his form of the condition. Together with digital artists, Ryan designed an audio-visual experience which was enjoyed by audiences in London as part of a festival organised by musician, Imogen Heap.

For years, scientists and philosophers have debated whether or not what we see is the same as what others see. Science has revealed that people with tetrachromacy and synaesthesia experience a very different world to the one that most of us open our eyes to every morning.

5E LISTENING AND VOCABULARY

1 🔊 **33** Listen to a radio programme about the history of sushi. Number the different generations of sushi in the order they are mentioned.

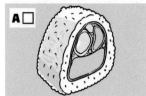
A ☐ inside-out roll

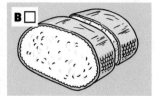
B ☐ second generation of sushi

C ☐ nare-sushi

D ☐ edo-mae

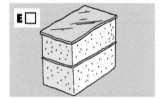
E ☐ eighteenth century

2 🔊 **33** Listen again and complete the sentences with no more than three words in each gap.

1 Sushi originated in _southern China_ 2500 years ago.
2 With the second generation of sushi, people ate the _____ rather than throwing it away.
3 _____ was used in the third generation of sushi to help make it last longer.
4 The fourth generation of sushi was the first kind of Japanese _____.
5 The inside-out roll was first invented during _____ in the USA.
6 There are now about _____ Japanese restaurants worldwide.

3 🔊 **34** Complete the extracts from the recording in Exercise 1 with the words from the box. Listen and check.

barrel ~~preserve~~ raw seaweed soy sauce vinegar

1 Sushi was born out of necessity, specifically the need to _preserve_ fish before fridges were invented.
2 Nare-sushi was basically fish rubbed with salt and left in _____ for several months.
3 The stuffed fish would be packed into a wooden _____, then weighed down with a heavy stone and left for a year.
4 OK, so preserved fish and rice, but still no _____, avocado or cream cheese!
5 Preservation with salt was no longer necessary, and the fashion for _____ fish slices really started.
6 These rolls have fish and other ingredients in the centre, surrounded by rice either with or without an outer layer of _____.

Pronunciation

4 🔊 **35** Read some sentences from the radio programme in Exercise 1. Find the stressed syllables in the underlined words. Listen and check.

1 I'm a massive fan, and <u>preferably</u> in huge quantities!
2 Sushi was born out of necessity, <u>specifically</u> the need to preserve fish before fridges were invented.
3 Skip forward to the twentieth century and <u>preservation</u> with salt was no longer necessary.

ACTIVE PRONUNCIATION
Suffixes that move word stress

The stress in some words changes position when a suffix is added to the word. Here are some examples:
- *-ity* (e.g. **ac**tive – ac**ti**vity)
- *-ic* (e.g. e**co**nomy – eco**no**mic)
- *-ble/-bly* (e.g. pre**fer** – **pre**ferable/**pre**ferably)
- *-ion* (e.g. in**form** – infor**ma**tion)
- *-al* (e.g. **sub**stance – sub**stan**tial)

Not all suffixes cause this change:
- *-ment* (e.g. de**ve**lop – de**ve**lopment)
- *-ly* (e.g. eco**no**mical – eco**no**mically)
- *-ance* (e.g. in**sure** – in**su**rance)

5 🔊 **36** Find the stressed syllable in the second word in each pair. Listen and check. Then practise saying the pairs of words.

1 <u>ge</u>nerous – gene**ro**sity
2 <u>pho</u>tograph – photographic
3 <u>spe</u>culate – speculation
4 <u>judge</u>ment – judgemental
5 <u>ac</u>cess – accessible

6 🔊 **37** Listen to these pairs of words. Tick the pairs which change the stress placement.

1 ☐ physical – physically
2 ☑ motivate – motivation
3 ☐ medicine – medicinal
4 ☐ punish – punishment
5 ☐ evolve – evolution

7 🔊 **38** Find the stressed syllables in the words in bold. Listen and check.

1 a **Unable** to sleep, I got up and made myself a cup of cocoa.
  b He blamed his parents for his **inability** to make friends.
2 a How can you **explain** that sort of behaviour?
  b She offered no **explanation** as to why she had left so suddenly.
3 a He is always ready to **accept** a challenge.
  b He wrote a letter of **acceptance** to the university.
4 a Through these lessons, students learn the basics of **science**.
  b We believe in investing in **scientific** research.

1 🔊 *39* Listen and repeat the phrases. How do you say them in your language?

SPEAKING
Asking and answering about preferences

ASKING ABOUT PREFERENCES

Which do/would you prefer? Tea **or** coffee?
What would you rather do? Eat out **or** stay in?

EXPRESSING GENERAL PREFERENCES

I **prefer** eating at home **to** going out to a restaurant.
I **don't like either of them.**
I **like** them both **equally.**
I **generally favour** savoury **over** sweet dishes.

MAKING A CHOICE

I'**d prefer to** have Chinese food **rather than** Indian.
I'**d prefer** Chinese food **rather than** Indian.
I'**d rather** have Chinese food.
I'**d sooner have** Chinese food **than** Indian.
Given the choice, I'd rather eat at home.
I'd **go for** fish and chips **any day/every time.**
I **have a preference for** Italian food.
I **have a slight preference for** eating Italian food.

GIVING SOMEONE ELSE THE CHOICE

It's **up to you.**
It's **your call.**
I'm **easy.**
Whatever/Wherever/ Whichever you prefer.

2 Put the words in order to make phrases that are useful for asking and answering about preferences.

1 rather / you / what / do / would / ?
What would you rather do?

2 both / equally / like / them / I
_____

3 choice / I'd / given / prefer / the fish / the
_____

4 go / a takeaway / for / any day / I'd
_____

5 have / slight / I / a / preference / savoury food / for
_____

3 Rewrite the sentences so that they mean the same and include the words in brackets.

1 I don't like this one or this one. (either)
I don't like either of them.

2 I'd prefer to order Chinese food. (sooner)
_____

3 I'd rather sit here than there. (prefer)
_____

4 I'd prefer you not to talk with your mouth full. (rather)
_____

5 I'd always rather cook than wash the dishes. (prefer)
_____

6 You decide. (call)
_____

4 🔊 *40* Complete the conversations with one word in each gap. Listen and check.

Lucy Which do you ¹p*refer*, Dom? Tea or coffee?
Dom Yes, please!
Lucy Oh, that's hilarious. Make a decision or make it yourself, funny man.
Dom ²W_____ you prefer. I like them both ³e_____.
Lucy OK … Here you go, Mr Comedian.
Dom Thanks. Urgh! What's this? It tastes awful.
Lucy I call it 'cof-tea' – half coffee, half tea. You did say it was my ⁴c_____.
Dom I suppose I deserved that.

Jane What would you ⁵r_____ do tonight, Beata? Stay at home or go out?
Beata I'd rather ⁶n_____ go out, to be honest. Do you fancy sofa, pizza, film?
Jane Oh. Well … actually … given the ⁷c_____, I'd ⁸s_____ go out.
Beata Oh – OK. I'm ⁹e_____. We can go out.
Jane How about … pizza and a film?
Beata So everything except the sofa?
Jane Exactly!

5 ON A HIGH NOTE Write a short conversation between two friends who are at the supermarket trying to decide what to buy for dinner.

Give brief details of where and when you went, and your overall impression.

Describe the event. Include information about what you did and saw.

Describe the positive aspects.

Write about any negative aspects.

Make recommendations.

MULTI-SENSORY CINEMA: *review by Claire Hewitt*

As advertised all over the city recently, Palm Shopping Centre's newest attraction is a multi-sensory cinema. My friend and I decided to **1**___. While it might not suit every kind of film, we found it extremely impressive and **2**___ watching our favourite superhero movie there.

A multi-sensory cinema appeals to all your senses. As well as the usual clear picture and the fabulous surround-sound, the seats in the cinema actually move and shake with the action. There are also some pretty unusual special effects such as scent, water and various highly entertaining weather effects. This means that when your favourite superhero is flying across the surface of water, you can actually smell the sea, and feel water and wind on your face.

What my friend and I **3**___ was how, after a few minutes, the effects really became part of the whole experience. It was utterly convincing and we felt like we were right in the centre of the action. Another seriously cool thing was how the effects made the scary moments in the film even more intense. When something suddenly touches your leg under your seat, or your seat unexpectedly drops, it really scares you! I was also **4**___ by the incredibly realistic weather effects. At one point in the film, there was a snowy scene and, unbelievably, snow actually fell in the cinema.

If I have **5**___, it's that a multi-sensory cinema is probably best suited to action or horror films only. For those who enjoy calmer, more dialogue-based films, this kind of cinema probably doesn't have much to offer. Also, ticket prices are quite high, but I guess that's to be expected.

All in all, I'd **6**___ a multi-sensory cinema to fans of action and horror films. By stimulating all your senses, it adds a whole new level of excitement to a familiar experience.

1 Read Claire's review and choose the best words to complete the sentences.

1 The review is generally *positive* / *negative*.

2 It's written in *a formal* / *an informal* style.

2 According to the writer, which kinds of film are best enjoyed in a multi-sensory cinema?

_____

3 Match phrases a–f with gaps 1–6 in the review.

a ☐ one criticism   **d** ☐ thoroughly enjoyed

b ☐ particularly liked   **e** ☐ blown away

c ☐ check it out   **f** ☐ definitely recommend

4 Choose the correct intensifiers to complete the extracts from the review. Then read the review again and check your answers.

1 While it might not suit every kind of film, we found it *completely* / *extremely* impressive.

2 There are some *pretty* / *utterly* unusual special effects.

3 ... and various *highly* / *totally* entertaining weather effects.

4 It was *super* / *utterly* convincing and we felt like we were right in the centre of the action.

5 Another *seriously* / *absolutely* cool thing was how the effects made the scary moments in the film even more intense.

6 I was also blown away by the *incredibly* / *completely* realistic weather effects.

7 Also, ticket prices are *absolutely* / *pretty* high, but I guess that's to be expected.

5 WRITING TASK **Write a review of an event, exhibition, museum or show.**

ACTIVE WRITING | A review

1 Plan your review.
- If possible, write about something you have actually experienced.
- Think about how you will describe what you did, saw and heard.
- Make notes about what you liked/didn't like about it.

2 Write your review.
- Use a lively, informal style.
- Use a range of adjectives and adjective intensifiers to emphasise your opinions.
- Give a clear recommendation at the end. It can be positive or negative.

3 Check that ...
- all the relevant information is there.
- there are no spelling, grammar or punctuation mistakes.

1 5A GRAMMAR AND VOCABULARY **Complete the sentences with the words and phrases from the box.**

colour-blind eyesight hearing loss ~~keen sense of smell~~
make out sensitive palate short-sighted tell them apart

1 Our dog has an extremely *keen sense of smell* and can detect sausages from a great distance.

2 Dancing with your head next to a nightclub speaker can result in _____.

3 A food taster needs to have a very _____.

4 If someone is _____, does it mean they see in black and white?

5 I'm _____ which means I can't see things in the distance, but I can read without glasses.

6 Helen's _____ is very poor, so she has to wear very thick glasses.

7 Without my glasses, I can't _____ what the sign says from here.

8 The twins are so similar that I find it very difficult to _____.

2 5B VOCABULARY **Choose the correct words to complete the sentences.**

1 The strong *stench / scent* of fish at the docks is overpowering as the boats unload their catch – some people find it disgusting.

2 The clouds were white and *fluffy / sticky*.

3 As you enter Marina Restaurant, the *mouth-watering / smelly* aroma of garlic fills the air.

4 My baby brother loves this *prickly / squishy* toy. It's so soft and makes some funny noises.

5 I scratched my hand on a *prickly / coarse* bush.

6 At this time of year, the gardens are filled with the subtle *scent / aroma* of wild flowers.

7 This particular blue cheese is a bit *smelly / smooth*, but I wouldn't say it *stinks / sizzles*.

8 The hedgehog is a *smooth / spiky* animal.

3 5D READING AND VOCABULARY **Complete the pairs of sentences with the correct form of the same word or phrase.**

1 a She was *put off* by the idea of swimming after seeing a crocodile in the water.

  b You'll be happy to hear we're going to *put off* the test until next week.

2 a Our _____ neighbours are lovely, but the couple who live two doors down aren't very friendly.

  b If you are bitten by a poisonous snake, you need _____ treatment.

3 a After the explosion there was _____ panic in the surrounding streets.

  b Simon started losing his sight when he was ten, and was completely _____ by the age of sixteen.

4 a The person who started this company had a _____ which has now become reality.

  b Gert has very little _____ in his right eye.

5 a I didn't _____ how late it was – I have to go!

  b Only a lucky few actually _____ their ambition of becoming astronauts.

6 a The police officers had to _____ the thieves on foot for a short distance.

  b We never wanted our only son to _____ a career in the army.

4 5E LISTENING AND VOCABULARY **Complete the text with one word in each gap.**

Tom and I couldn't be more different when it comes to our palates. I like ¹*mild* food, whereas for Tom, the spicier his food is, the better! He often says what I order is bland. For him, if it's not spicy, then it's not ²_____. He's a real fan of anything savoury, but I prefer ³_____ things. I would happily go straight to the dessert every time! For breakfast we usually have either peanut butter on toast or porridge. I like my peanut butter smooth, but of course Tom prefers it ⁴_____. There is one thing we both agree on though – we like our porridge watery and not ⁵_____ like cement!

5 5G WRITING AND VOCABULARY **Complete the sentences with the adjectives from the box, adding correct intensifiers. There are two extra adjectives.**

awful brilliant deafening exhausted frightening
hilarious ~~petrified~~ proud

1 Do I have to have an injection? I'm ¹*absolutely petrified* of needles!

2 He was a/an _____ child. He graduated at the top of his class.

3 When she finished speaking, the applause was _____ and she was _____ of herself.

4 If you feel _____ all the time, you should go to see a doctor.

5 The film was _____. It's a waste of time.

6 ON A HIGH NOTE **Write a short paragraph describing your preferences when it comes to food.**

1 For each learning objective, write 1–5 to assess your ability.

1 = I don't feel confident. 5 = I feel confident.

	Learning objective	Course material	How confident I am (1–5)
5A	I can use gerunds and infinitives to talk about different actions.	Student's Book pp. 64–65	
5B	I can talk about the senses.	Student's Book p. 66	
5C	I can use verbs with gerunds and infinitives to talk about different actions.	Student's Book p. 67	
5D	I can identify clues in a text and talk about disabilities.	Student's Book pp. 68–69	
5E	I can identify specific details in a podcast and talk about food and cooking.	Student's Book p. 70	
5F	I can ask and answer questions about preferences.	Student's Book p. 71	
5G	I can write a review.	Student's Book pp. 72–73	

2 Which of the skills above would you like to improve in? How?

Skill I want to improve in	How I can improve

3 What can you remember from this unit?

New words I learned and most want to remember	Expressions and phrases I liked	English I heard or read outside class

GRAMMAR AND VOCABULARY

1 Choose the correct words to complete the sentences.

1 I can't imagine living without my *short-sighted / eyesight*.

2 The only way to *tell the two houses apart / make the two houses out* is to go inside and see how they are decorated.

3 There was a truly *mouth-watering / keen* smell coming from the bakery.

4 If you leave your football boots wet like that, they'll *stink / stench* even more than usual.

5 Try our incredibly comfortable new range of *coarse / silky* underwear.

/ 5

2 Complete the sentences with one or two words in each gap.

1 My brother is *colour-blind*, so he can't tell the difference between colours.

2 _____ action is needed if we are going to halt climate change – there's no time to waste.

3 I don't like _____ boiled eggs, so I always boil mine for at least five minutes.

4 Jack's pizza was covered in chillies and was so _____ that it made him cry.

5 It's not pleasant to have such a keen _____ of smell when you live somewhere so polluted.

6 The tiny kitten's coat was white and _____.

/ 5

3 Complete the sentences with the correct forms of the words from the box.

apply	borrow	eat	go	have	~~think~~

1 I can't help *thinking* that I should have stayed at home.

2 We'd like to encourage you _____ for more than one summer job.

3 My sister wouldn't let me _____ her new hoodie.

4 I've lived in Spain for years, so I'm used to _____ a siesta in the afternoons.

5 It's too hot to have a full meal at this time of day – I'd rather _____ something light.

6 I'll never forget _____ to that restaurant for the first time.

/ 5

4 Complete the sentences with the correct forms of the words in brackets.

1 I met my friend in the street and we *stopped to chat* (stop/chat) for a few minutes.

2 Kenneth _____ (see/someone/fall over) their own dog this morning.

3 The kitchen _____ (need/clean), but I don't have time now. Will you do it?

4 Penelope _____ (regret/promise) to help now that she has seen how much there is to do.

5 We can't simply _____ (go on/burn) fossil fuels as if they are harmless.

6 I _____ (try/give up) sweets last month but I can't live without them.

/ 5

USE OF ENGLISH

5 Complete the sentences with the correct words formed from the words in bold.

There are lots of things that bother me about my flatmate, Justine. First of all, she thinks she's some kind of food expert and is always going on about how [1]*sensitive* (SENSE) her palate is. This is particularly annoying because she can't cook to save her life. She made some brownies, but they were so [2]_____ (STICK) that you couldn't really pick them up. Her cookies on the other hand are so [3]_____ (CRUNCH) that I actually fear for my teeth. The other really annoying thing is that she never listens properly to what I say. If I didn't know better, I'd say she suffers from some kind of [4]_____ (HEAR) loss, but in fact, she's just not that [5]_____ (INTEREST) in me. Finally, she wears too much of an extremely sweet and flowery perfume. The smell is completely [6]_____ (POWER) and stays in the flat for hours.

/ 5

6 Complete the second sentence using the word in bold so that it means the same as the first one. Use between two and five words, including the word in bold.

1 Please stop humming that tune all the time. **RATHER**
I'd *rather you didn't hum* that tune all the time.

2 My cat only allows me to tickle its belly. **LET**
My cat _____ except me tickle its belly.

3 Your parents didn't answer, even though we called them several times. **TRIED**
We _____ several times, but they didn't answer.

4 Halina doesn't usually eat bitter-tasting foods. **TENDS**
Halina _____ bitter-tasting foods.

5 Staying at home is the better option. **SOONER**
We _____ at home.

6 After the accident I no longer could do judo. (**STOP**)
After the accident I had to _____ judo.

/ 5

/ 30

6A GRAMMAR AND VOCABULARY

Modal and related verbs

1 ⭐ **Match the underlined modal verbs in sentences 1–10 with their functions a–g.**

1 ☐ You <u>have to</u> make your bed at a youth hostel.
2 ☐ You <u>must not</u> take room keys out of the hotel.
3 ☐ I <u>could</u> swim like a fish at the age of four.
4 ☐ If there's a fire, you <u>must</u> use the stairs, not the lift.
5 ☐ You <u>don't have to</u> switch on the light – it's automatic.
6 ☐ If you <u>can't</u> come on time, will you let me know?
7 ☐ We <u>weren't able to</u> deliver your parcel today because you weren't at home.
8 ☐ Children <u>may</u> only enter the place with an adult.
9 ☐ You <u>needn't</u> worry about noise – it's a quiet street.
10 ☐ You <u>ought to</u> book online, it's cheaper.

a permission
b lack of ability
c obligation and necessity
d prohibition
e duty and advice
f no obligation/no necessity
g ability

2 ⭐ **Choose the correct forms to complete the sentences.**

1 We only moved in a week ago and we've already *managed / forbidden* to get to know the neighbours.
2 Only local residents are *required / permitted* to park in the streets here.
3 You are *allowed / supposed* to sort your rubbish way more carefully than that, Helen.
4 The city has *succeeded / obliged* in reducing the crime rate significantly.
5 Glass is strictly *forbidden / permitted* in the swimming pool area.

3 ⭐⭐ **Rewrite the sentences so that they have the opposite meaning.**

1 We have to arrive exactly on time.
   We don't have to/needn't arrive exactly on time.
2 You mustn't wear jeans in the restaurant.
   _____
3 Customers may park here.
   _____
4 I couldn't find my glasses.
   _____

4 ⭐⭐ USE OF ENGLISH **Choose the correct words a–c to complete the text.**

VISITING THAILAND

There are certain things you ¹___ know before visiting Thailand. Thai people are often a lot more laid back than the average tourist, so you ²___ lose your temper and you ³___ raise your voice or shout at anyone in public. Thai people never point the soles of their feet at anyone or anything, so you ⁴___ never sit with your feet up on a table, for example. Men should have on a top of some sort, though they ⁵___ worry about this when at the beach. Everyone is ⁶___ to cover their shoulders and knees before entering a temple. Finally, remember that it is ⁷___ to say anything negative about the royal family because you can get into serious trouble.

1 a ought to	**b** don't have to	**c** are able to
2 a couldn't	**b** mustn't	**c** don't have to
3 a needn't	**b** couldn't	**c** shouldn't
4 a have to	**b** should	**c** could
5 a mustn't	**b** can't	**c** needn't
6 a required	**b** allowed	**c** forbidden
7 a permitted	**b** forbidden	**c** obliged

5 ⭐⭐ **Complete the sentences with the correct forms of *be able to* or *have to*.**

1 Unfortunately, we <u>weren't able to</u> see the new flat because they'd lost the key.
2 Good news! Gran _____ come next weekend.
3 We _____ pay for the garage; it was for free.
4 Tina? Sorry, I'm going to be late. I _____ find a parking space yet.
5 Don't worry! You _____ book the tickets. I'll take care of everything.

6 ★★ Complete the mini-conversations with the forms in bold.

HAVE TO / OUGHT TO / MUSTN'T / BE ABLE TO

Mina I ¹*mustn't* forget to collect that parcel from the post office today.

Salman You ²_____ write yourself a note.

Mina Would you ³_____ do it, Salman? You're nothing like as busy as me.

Salman Well, I suppose so, if I ⁴_____.

ALLOWED TO / MUST / REQUIRED TO / MAY

Kaia Am I ⁵_____ pay a deposit before I move in to my room?

Manager Yes, all students ⁶_____ pay two months' rent in advance.

Kaia And ⁷_____ I pay that with a credit card?

Manager No, sorry. I'm only ⁸_____ accept cash or a bank transfer.

HAVEN'T BEEN ABLE TO / SUPPOSED TO / COULDN'T / SUCCEEDED IN

Ludger You were ⁹_____ video call me, Scarlet. What happened?

Scarlet I ¹⁰_____ find your details, Ludger. Didn't you see my email?

Ludger I ¹¹_____ log on since yesterday. Something's wrong.

Scarlet Sometimes, I think technology has only ¹²_____ making life more complicated!

7 ★★★ USE OF ENGLISH Complete the second sentence using the word in bold so that it means the same as the first one. Use between two and five words, including the word in bold.

1 In Spain, you should eat an orange with a knife and fork. **SUPPOSED**

In Spain, you *are supposed to eat* an orange with a knife and fork.

2 You can't bring pets on the train. **PERMITTED**

Pets _____ on the train.

3 I was able to pick up the language quickly. **SUCCEEDED**

I _____ the language quickly.

4 In the UK, it isn't necessary to carry an ID card. **REQUIRED**

You _____ an ID card in the UK.

5 How many bags can I take on the aeroplane? **ALLOWED**

How many bags _____ on the aeroplane?

6 At my previous school, mobile phones were not allowed. **FORBIDDEN**

We _____ mobile phones at my previous school.

8 ★★★ Complete the notice with one word in each gap. Sometimes more than one answer is possible.

HOSTEL RULES

We hope you have a great stay here at the Travellers Rest Hostel. For your safety and comfort here are a few guidelines we ask you to follow.

1 Only paying guests are *allowed/permitted* in the kitchen, lounge and bedroom areas.

2 Use of portable audio speakers is completely _____ throughout the hostel.

3 All guests are _____ to keep noise to a minimum after 10 p.m.

4 Guests _____ leave the kitchen area clean and tidy after use. No exceptions!

5 Animals are not _____ in the hostel.

6 Guests _____ leave food behind when they check out of the hostel. Please put any unused food in our box for the homeless.

7 If you are not happy with anything at the hostel, you _____ tell a member of staff immediately.

8 If you aren't _____ to find a member of staff, please call +01 509 509 509.

ENJOY YOUR STAY!

9 ON A HIGH NOTE Write a paragraph about the things you are and aren't allowed to do at your school/college.

6B LISTENING AND VOCABULARY

1 🔊 *41* **Listen to a radio interview with a pupil at a boarding school and tick the topic that is NOT mentioned.**

1 ☐ international students   4 ☐ exams
2 ☐ independence   5 ☐ free time
3 ☐ homesickness

2 🔊 *41* **Listen again and choose the correct answers.**

1 What was the most important factor in Tilly's decision to go to boarding school?
   a The influence of her parents.
   b Her wish to experience a more independent lifestyle.
   c The non-academic opportunities that boarding school provides.

2 What does Tilly say about academic study at boarding school?
   a It's not as challenging as most people believe.
   b Success is respected by boarding school pupils.
   c Nobody manages to stay completely silent during evening study.

3 What kind of extra-curricular activities does Tilly prefer?
   a special interest groups
   b music lessons
   c sports and fitness

4 How does Tilly feel about being away from home?
   a It doesn't bother her.
   b It has made friendships more important.
   c It has made her closer to her parents.

5 What does Tilly say is the most important thing for boarders to do at weekends?
   a resting   b going home   c leaving the campus

Vocabulary extension

3 **Complete one listener's comment with the adjectives from the box, which you heard in the recording in Exercise 1. Use a dictionary to help you if necessary.**

diverse   extra-curricular   ~~marvellous~~   obligatory
rigid   strict

» What a(n) **¹*marvellous*** interview! I really enjoyed listening to Tilly. She made me realise I'm behind the times. I thought that the students at boarding school had to live according to very **²_____** rules with a lot of really **³_____** teachers shouting at the pupils. You know – the kind of thing we read about in novels where everyone has a(n) **⁴_____** cold shower every morning! And I was surprised to hear about how many **⁵_____** activities are offered to the students; I'd like to try canoeing or coding myself! It was really interesting to hear about the **⁶_____** range of nationalities among the students. Good luck, Tilly!

Pronunciation

4 🔊 *42* **Listen to some sentences from the radio interview in Exercise 1. What happens to the sounds /t/ and /d/ in the underlined phrases?**

1 Tilly, you board at a well-known school in Exeter, <u>don't you</u>?

2 How much of your time, <u>would you</u> say, is spent on academic study?

3 You mentioned how <u>important your</u> extra-curricular activities are.

4 You <u>get used</u> to it though, and I've found that it helps me to focus.

ACTIVE PRONUNCIATION
Assimilation of /t/ + /j/ and /d/ + /j/ sounds

When English speakers talk quickly, they do not always pause in between each word; they link different sounds and words together into connected speech. Sometimes two sounds blend together to form a completely new sound. This often happens with /t/ and /j/, which come together to become /tʃ/ (as in *choose*), and with /d/ and /j/ which become /dʒ/ (as in *jeans*).

• *I met_you.* (/t/ becomes /tʃ/)
• *He told_you.* (/d/ becomes /dʒ/)

---

5 🔊 *43* **Listen and notice how the sounds /t/ and /d/ change. Practise saying the words in isolation and in phrases.**

1 hold   hold you
2 did   did you
3 would   would you
4 meet   meet you
5 hit   hit you
6 get   get you

6 🔊 *44* **Tick the sentences in which the sounds /t/ and /d/ change in the underlined phrases. Listen and check. Then practise saying the sentences.**

1 ☐ <u>Would you</u> mind opening the window?
2 ☐ All the postmen <u>hate your</u> aggressive dog.
3 ☐ We <u>aren't open</u> yet!
4 ☐ <u>Act your</u> age!
5 ☐ <u>Did you</u> know his old roommate?

7 🔊 *45* **Read the sentences. Underline the phrases in which assimilation of the sounds from Active Pronunciation occurs. Listen and check. Then practise saying the sentences.**

1 I can't wait to meet your new neighbour.
2 What can I get you for the house-warming party?
3 Would you like to attend a boarding school?
4 We need your address to deliver your furniture.
5 You're prepared to share a room, aren't you?

6C GRAMMAR

Articles

1 ⭐ Cross out *the* where it is NOT necessary.

1 Have you ever been to the United States or ~~the~~ Canada?

2 You should spend less on the clothes and more on the food.

3 I don't really like the hot drinks like the tea or the coffee.

4 If I could live anywhere in the world, I would definitely choose somewhere in the Asia.

5 The moon shone down on the Mount Kilimanjaro that night.

6 The London Zoo is a very popular tourist attraction.

7 The sea in the Caribbean is the bluest sea I've seen since I was in the Thailand.

8 The fastest way to get to Manchester is to fly directly into the Manchester airport.

2 ⭐ What do the underlined words refer to? Choose *B* for a building or *I* for an institution.

1 Spending time in <u>hospital</u> is especially difficult for children.　　B / I

2 The <u>hospital</u> is an important landmark in our town.　　B / I

3 Matilda always loved <u>school</u>.　　B / I

4 Akash walks past the <u>school</u> every morning.　　B / I

5 Turn right when you see the front gates of the <u>university</u> and the garage is on your left.　　B / I

6 Mel isn't going to <u>university</u> immediately.　　B / I

7 I've always found the <u>prison</u> very scary with its high walls and barred windows.　　B / I

8 The thought of a year in <u>prison</u> was terrifying.　　B / I

9 Students go to <u>college</u> when they leave school.　　B / I

10 Dion's father works near the <u>college</u>.　　B / I

3 ⭐ Choose the correct options to complete the text.

I had never seen **1**a / the tourist attraction like **2**a / the one which we visited while on holiday in **3**the / Ø St Blazey – a small town in **4**the / Ø south of **5**the / Ø Cornwall, UK. The Eden Project is **6**a / Ø complex made up of enormous 'bubbles' called Biomes and **7**the / Ø huge outdoor gardens. Inside one of the Biomes there is **8**the / a world's largest indoor rainforest. The Eden Projects helps you understand how plants and **9**the / Ø people are connected. I would recommend it to anyone visiting **10**the / Ø area.

4 ⭐⭐ Complete the signs and notices with *a*, *an*, *the* or *Ø* (no article).

WELCOME TO **1**Ø BELGIUM.

2_____ STATUE OF LIBERTY IS CLOSED FOR MAINTENANCE TODAY.

Save **3**_____ Pacific Ocean!

Raspberries £3 **4**_____ kilo.

BELIEVE IN **5**_____ EUROPE!

6_____ IRISH STUDENTS DEMAND CHEAPER UNIVERSITY FEES!

We have **7**_____ best sandwiches in town.

THIS POST BOX IS EMPTIED TWICE **8**_____ DAY.

5 ⭐⭐ Complete the telephone conversation with *a*, *an*, *the* or *Ø* (no article).

Olga Hi, Theo! How are you? I hear you've moved into **1**<u>a</u> new flat. How is it?

Theo Olga! It's nice to hear from you. **2**_____ flat is great. My room is a bit small, but it's only €200 **3**_____ month, so I can't complain, and I've got **4**_____ really nice flatmates too. There's Cleo from **5**_____ USA and Arnau from **6**_____ Andorra.

Olga Err ... where?

Theo It's a little country in **7**_____ Pyrenees. Arnau says it's beautiful.

Olga It sounds like a real international community you've got in your flat. Where exactly is it?

Theo It's on **8**_____ Cambridge Lane, near **9**_____ university accommodation building. Would you like to come round for **10**_____ cup of tea and a look round?

Olga I'd love to. What number is it?

6 ON A HIGH NOTE Write a paragraph about a well-known city in your country.

1 Look at the photos and quickly read the article. In which paragraph can you read about each of the photos?

Photo A – Paragraph ___

Photo B – Paragraph ___

Photo C – Paragraph ___

2 Read the article again and match headings 1–4 with paragraphs B–E.

1 Cultural needs

2 A place to call your own

3 Personal hygiene

4 Temporary shelter

3 Read the article again and match questions 1–6 with paragraphs A–F.

In which paragraph does the author ...

1 ☐ describe a common negative attitude towards homelessness?

2 ☐ give an example of a scheme that helps homeless people survive when temperatures are low?

3 ☐ refer to the importance of feeling safe in your own home?

4 ☐ describe an initiative started by a person who had a first-hand experience in living on the streets?

5 ☐ give details of efforts to help homeless people feel less separated from the rest of society?

6 ☐ mention a country in which homelessness isn't a problem?

Vocabulary extension

4 Match the highlighted words from the text with the definitions.

1 Someone or something annoying. _nuisance_

2 Self-respect, feeling proud of yourself. _____

3 Protection from danger or the weather. _____

4 Plan or process to achieve an aim or solve a problem. _____

5 A way of dealing with a problem. _____

5 Complete the sentences with the words from Exercise 4.

1 It's hard to keep your _dignity_ when you're living on the streets.

2 The mosquitoes in this area are such a _____.

3 We found _____ from the rain in a shop doorway.

4 The government has begun a new _____ to tackle teenage homelessness.

5 The city's _____ to homelessness needs reviewing as the number of people without their own place is increasing.

ACTIVE VOCABULARY | Nouns ending in *-ness*

We can add the suffix *-ness* to an adjective to describe a state:

• homeless**ness** = the state of being homeless

• tired**ness** = the state of being tired

Sometimes spelling changes are necessary (e.g. *happy – happi**ness***).

---

6 Complete the sentences with nouns formed from the adjectives from the box. Use a dictionary to check spelling.

aware   conscious   dark   grumpy   ~~lonely~~   nervous   playful

1 Research shows that friendship is important and that _loneliness_ can cause ill-health.

2 This publicity campaign aims to raise people's _____ of common dangers around the home.

3 She lost _____ for a few moments after hitting her head on the cupboard door.

4 The best thing about our new puppy is its _____.

5 The prisoners were kept in cramped cells and almost total _____.

6 You could sense the students' _____ as they waited for the exam to begin.

7 In the end, his friends didn't want to hang out with him because of his regular bad moods and _____.

7 ON A HIGH NOTE Find out what programmes/schemes for the homeless are available in your area. Write a short paragraph about your findings.

Helping
the homeless

A Homelessness is a worldwide problem that affects almost all societies in countries both rich and poor. A 2017 report showed that the problem has reached crisis point in all European countries except Finland where the number of the homeless fell sharply. Although people who are unemployed or on a low-income are more likely to be affected, all sorts of people can end up living on the streets as a result of a wide variety of unfortunate circumstances. Governments attempt to tackle the problem with varying degrees of success. In many places charitable organisations and concerned individuals need to provide immediate relief from the hardship of a life without shelter. Some of the schemes and solutions proposed by such people show surprising creativity based on a good understanding of what is needed.

B ☐ To state the obvious, what homeless people require is somewhere to live and, ideally, feel at home. You only truly value the sense of security that comes from being able to lock your door behind you when you no longer have a door to lock. A number of schemes around the world try to provide long-term or permanent accommodation for those without homes of their own. In California for example, a kind-hearted builder has tackled the problem by using discarded materials to build compact temporary homes for the homeless. Gregory Kloehn's mobile homes all come on wheels and manage to combine responsible recycling with a charitable solution for people in need of a roof over their heads.

C ☐ Where it is not possible to provide permanent structures such as housing for the homeless, other short-term solutions are needed. Many homeless people become ill and some even lose their lives if they are forced to sleep outside during the cold months of winter. Michael Rakowitz, a New York artist, has come up with an ingenious solution that uses the heat given off by buildings in the city where he is based. His shelters are filled with hot air from the buildings' heating systems and provide warmth and cover for their owners.

D ☐ Cleanliness falls down the list of priorities when you don't know where you are going to sleep at night. Hygiene can return people's dignity, make them feel human again and reduce their sense of isolation. In San Francisco, a non-profit organisation called Lava Mae has converted buses and other vehicles into mobile shower units for the homeless. On the other side of the Atlantic, British hairdresser Josh Coombes offers free haircuts to homeless people on the streets. He also works with a generous vet who provides care and treatment to homeless people's dogs. Josh's aim was to inspire others to help and he has certainly succeeded as his initiative has now gone global.

E ☐ There ought to be more to life than just food and shelter, and having nowhere to live doesn't necessarily mean you lose interest in things like reading and music. In Sao Paulo, Brazil, a former builder who was homeless himself for many years began a 'bicycle library' – cycling round the city and lending books to homeless people. Robson Mendonça can carry 300 books on his bicycle and in his first year he made over 107,000 loans from his collection of 30,000 donated books. Back in the UK, in the city of Manchester, a scheme to encourage homeless people to get involved in the arts has helped them express themselves through poetry, photography and even opera. Participants have reported feeling an increased sense of purpose as a result.

F Homeless people are seldom respected in society. All too often, they are seen as a nuisance or as failures and are ignored, or looked down upon. Thankfully, individuals and organisations such as the ones mentioned above have taken a more understanding approach. Their generosity and their creativity have helped make a real difference to the lives of those who are trying to survive without a roof over their heads.

6E VOCABULARY | Household problems and solutions

1 ⭐ Match the two parts of the sentences.

1 ☐ Hello? Reception? Yes, I think the showerhead in our bathroom is

2 ☐ Every Christmas we spend ages trying to undo the tangled

3 ☐ Their beautiful new dining room table was ruined by a circular water

4 ☐ What kind of people would smash bottles and leave shattered

5 ☐ Well, of course a wool jumper will shrink

6 ☐ Once the screen on your phone becomes as

a if you wash it at 90 degrees!

b glass all over a children's playground?

c blocked because there's hardly any water coming out.

d stain from a glass that someone put down during the house-warming party.

e scratched as this, it's very difficult to make out any messages or pictures.

f leads of the Christmas tree lights.

2 ⭐ Choose the correct words to complete the sentences. In one sentence both answers are possible.

1 Always remember to switch off the electricity before you *replace / fix* a light bulb.

2 Please don't spill blackcurrant juice on anything as it's impossible to *mend / get rid of* the stains.

3 You should *repair / replace* your dishcloth every week as it gets full of bacteria.

4 Why *get rid of / do up* a perfectly good lamp when you could easily mend it with some superglue?

5 My uncle managed to *fix / repair* the vacuum cleaner, so we don't need to buy a new one.

6 Xiu knows how to *mend / replace* simple electric appliances like toasters and kettles.

7 We've decide to *do up / soak* my little sister's bedroom as a birthday present.

3 ⭐⭐ Replace the underlined parts with pronouns. Make any other necessary changes.

1 I'll wipe down <u>the table</u>.
I'll wipe it down.

2 We're doing up <u>the kitchen</u>.
_____

3 I came across <u>this ring</u> when I was vacuuming.
_____

4 The cushions don't go with <u>the sofa</u>.
_____

5 It's hard to keep up with <u>the cleaning</u>.
_____

6 Could you clear up <u>the broken glass</u>?
_____

7 When will they carry out <u>the repairs</u>?
_____

4 ⭐⭐ Complete the sentences with one word in each gap.

1 We're d<u>oing</u> up my bedroom and we need some m_____ tape so we can paint straight lines.

2 When you've finished making your lunch, take the d_____ and wipe d_____ the kitchen surfaces.

3 The best way to d_____ with stains and tough patches of dirt is to s_____ the item of clothing in warm water and soap.

4 I came a_____ this jar in the bottom of the freezer, but I'm not sure what's in it because I forgot to l_____ it.

5 My cat Edgar always chases the m_____ around when I try to m_____ up the kitchen floor.

6 Carefully p_____ up the bigger pieces of broken glass, then use the d_____ and brush to s_____ the rest up.

7 R_____ the surface with a soft cloth until all the fingerprints have completely disappeared.

8 The dishwasher has broken d_____ and I'm afraid if I open the door, water will flood out into the kitchen.

5 ⭐⭐⭐ Complete the note with one word in each gap. Sometimes more than one answer is possible.

Jobs for Julia

Hi, Julia. Thanks so much for offering to help out. You can do as many or as few of the following jobs as you want. No pressure!

- We need to get ¹<u>rid</u> of all the old bits of wood in the back yard somehow; either on a fire or at the rubbish dump.

- The ²_____ is blocked in the downstairs bathroom and the lock on the door is broken. I've bought a new lock of the same type, so could you ³_____ the broken one?

- The old BBQ in the back garden is really dirty and needs to be wiped ⁴_____. Plus, one of its legs is broken and needs to be ⁵_____ if possible.

- Before we repaint the kitchen, the edges of the cupboards need covering with masking ⁶_____.

- The lawn mower ⁷_____ down last week – not sure if you'll be able to ⁸_____ it, but you could have a look if you've got time.

Thank you so much! I will repay the favour.

G

6 ON A HIGH NOTE Write a note to someone describing five jobs that need doing around your house. These can be real or invented.

1 🔊 46 Listen and repeat the phrases. How do you say them in your language?

SPEAKING | Giving instructions

EXPLAINING WHAT TO DO

It's advisable to tidy your room at least once a week.

The first thing you do is make your bed.

When/Once you've done that, pick up all the clothes from the floor.

What you do is fold the clean clothes and put them away.

All you have to do is vacuum your room if you have a carpet.

The key/main thing to remember is to keep things in their proper places.

It's vital/essential that you only keep the things you really need.

Make sure the windows are clean.

The next step is to wipe down all the surfaces.

The way you do it is with a clean cloth and some cleaning fluid.

EXPLAINING WHAT NOT TO DO

Make sure you don't forget to empty the vacuum cleaner.

Be careful not to put everything into one bin.

Try to avoid getting distracted when you're cleaning.

I'd advise you not to take your smartphone into the room with you.

There's no need to use many cleaning products.

Whatever you do, don't use a dirty cloth.

FINISHING THE INSTRUCTIONS

And that's it.

And that's all there is to it!

---

2 Complete the leaflet about recycling with the words from the box.

---

essential it main not sure ~~thing~~

DOS AND DON'TS OF HOUSEHOLD RECYCLING

1 The first _thing_ you do is collect all your glass and metal containers, and wash them out quickly.

2 The _____ thing to remember is that the 'recycling triangle' symbol shows which items can be recycled.

3 It's _____ that you wrap broken glass in newspaper so the binmen don't cut themselves.

4 Make _____ you don't throw any food waste into the recycling bin.

5 Be careful _____ to get any newspaper or cardboard wet.

6 And that's all there is to _____!

3 Rewrite the sentences starting with the words given.

1 I switch off the electricity first.
What _I do is switch off the electricity first_.

2 You put the dirty clothes in the laundry basket.
All _____.

3 It works with solar power.
The way _____.

4 I cleaned the chair.
What _____.

5 You pick it up and it switches on automatically.
All _____.

6 You open it by pressing this button.
The way _____.

4 USE OF ENGLISH **Complete the conversation with one word in each gap.**

Dani Argh! I've never been able to use chopsticks.

Chen What you [1]_do_ is rest one on your ring finger and hold it with the lower part of your thumb.

Dani Like this?

Chen Yes, but there's no [2]_____ to hold it so tightly. Make [3]_____ your hand is relaxed. OK, and the next [4]_____ is to rest the second chopstick between your middle finger and your index finger, then hold it with the upper part of your thumb.

Dani OK, so like this?

Chen Yes, but try to [5]_____ holding it so tightly. The [6]_____ you do it is to rest it on your fingers and hold it with your thumb.

Dani OK.

Chen And once you've [7]_____ that, use your middle and index fingers to control the second chopstick and hold the food against the first one. And that's [8]_____!

Dani Thanks, Chen. And I guess it's [9]_____ to practise with something other than food?

Chen Well, I think it's best to practise with food, but I'd [10]_____ you not to start in public! Practise at home first. I know it seems difficult now, but you'll soon be able to pick up a single grain of rice.

Dani We'll see about that!

5 ON A HIGH NOTE **Write a short dialogue between two friends in which one is giving instructions to the other.**

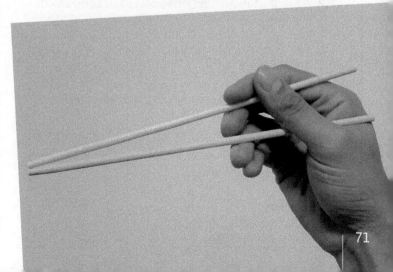

6G **WRITING** | A report

Report: Investing in our school

Aims

This report is [1]*intended* to identify areas for improvement to our school and make suggestions for how to achieve them. Seventy students [2]_____ in the survey.

A Classrooms

Many students [3]_____ a wish for coat hooks to be provided in classrooms. Several people also suggested that new flooring was needed in the science labs.

B Outdoor areas

Almost all the students were of the [4]_____ that the bike and scooter parking area is in need of renovation. Many [5]_____ that a roof to protect vehicles from heat and rain would be a welcome improvement.

C Canteen

[6]_____ the canteen, approximately three quarters of students are happy with both the space itself and the food on offer.

D Technology

Very [7]_____ students are satisfied with the strength of the wi-fi signal in the main school building. The current system is old and slow. A [8]_____ number of sixth-formers requested USB charging points be fitted in their common room.

E Eco-friendliness

The [9]_____ majority of students are satisfied with the school's efforts to be eco-friendly. However, over half the students agreed that the school should invest in more plants and trees to help reduce our carbon footprint.

Conclusion and recommendations

Taking everything into [10]_____, it appears that the priorities are to provide coat hooks in classrooms, improve the bike and scooter parking area, strengthen the wi-fi signal in the main building and invest in more plants and trees. With regard to USB charging points, I would recommend investigating the potential cost before making a decision.

Give your report a simple and concise title.

Begin with an introduction explaining the purpose of the report and how you obtained the information.

Use headings, and if appropriate, bullet points to make it easier to read.

Report the opinions of the people who were interviewed.

Use quantifiers to present statistics or report a survey.

Make a recommendation in the conclusion.

1 Complete the report with the words and phrases from the box.

consideration expressed felt few ~~intended~~ opinion regarding significant took part vast

2 Rewrite the sentences to make them correct. One sentence is correct.

1 We asked twenty club members and several them felt the prices were too high.
We asked twenty club members and several of them felt the prices were too high.

2 A handful the younger tennis players disagreed with the suggestion that the courts were old-fashioned.

3 All the women we spoke to said the changing rooms needed decorating.

4 The majority gym users would prefer not to have music playing in the gym.

5 Most the swimmers felt the water temperature was comfortable.

3 WRITING TASK **Write a report.**

During a work placement at a sports club you carried out a survey among members asking how to improve the club. Write a report about what needs to be improved and make suggestions.

ACTIVE WRITING | A report

1 Plan your report.
- Think of four or five areas of a sports club that might have appeared in the survey, e.g. the changing rooms.
- Think of some potential problems with these areas and how things could be improved.
- Decide how many people were involved in the survey and what your main recommendations will be.

2 Write your report.
- Use an impersonal, semi-formal style.
- Report people's opinions using quantifiers.
- Make recommendations in the conclusion.

3 Check that ...
- all the relevant information is there.
- there are no spelling, grammar or punctuation mistakes.

1 6A GRAMMAR AND VOCABULARY Complete the sentences with one word in each gap.

1 There are w<u>ay</u> more shops here than where we live.
2 Location is f_____ more important than anything else when choosing where to live.
3 House prices are ma_____ lower than they were last month.
4 Their flat is mi_____ more modern than ours, but not as big.
5 The second student room we looked at was c_____ more expensive than the first.
6 The area where we live is a l_____ older than this one.
7 The view from our balcony is n_____ near as nice as this.
8 The weather here is nothing l_____ as wet as in England.
9 Singapore is si_____ smaller than my country.
10 These stairs are a b_____ steeper than the ones at our house.

2 6B LISTENING AND VOCABULARY Complete the adverts with the words from the box.

down   home   ~~move~~   remotely   roots   settle   spaces

Are you the type of professional who is always on the **1** *move*? Do you prefer to work **2**_____ and not to be tied **3**_____ to one place? Our beautiful and well-equipped co-working **4**_____ could be exactly what you're looking for. See our list of locations here.

If you've just arrived in the UK and are looking to put down **5**_____, Homecoming UK's financial and legal advice could be just what you need. We can help you **6**_____ down without having to worry about your legal and financial status. Call and talk to us today.

When you travel the world, you can't take all your **7**_____ comforts with you, but you can take one of our high-quality travel pillows. Make sure you're comfortable wherever your journey takes you.

3 6D READING AND VOCABULARY Replace the underlined parts with the words from the box.

airy   ~~compact~~   densely-populated   excess
medium-sized   vast

1 I don't know how a family of four manages to cram into this <u>tiny</u> space. *compact*
2 Our old house had a <u>huge</u> garden. _____
3 The flat we are buying is <u>neither small nor large</u>. _____
4 With all the windows open the kitchen was light and <u>fresh</u>. _____
5 I wouldn't want to live anywhere as <u>full of people</u> as Tokyo. _____
6 We use the spare room to keep our <u>extra</u> clothes and books in. _____

4 6E VOCABULARY Choose the correct words to complete the sentences.

1 We can't afford a new washing machine, but maybe your dad would be able to ___ the old one?
   a fix   b remove   c label
2 Kevin remembered to switch off the electricity before he ___ the light bulb.
   a rubbed   b replaced   c decorated
3 The bathroom was dirty and the showerhead was ___.
   a tangled   b shattered   c blocked
4 Claire I'm really sorry, but I've ___ your yellow jumper in the wash.
   a shrunk   b scratched   c soaked
5 Can you pass me the ___, so I can wipe the kitchen surfaces?
   a mop   b dustpan and brush   c dishcloth
6 I can tell you've been decorating because there's ___ stuck to your shoe.
   a dirt   b masking tape   c a water stain
7 It's time we ___ this awful carpet and bought a new one.
   a got rid of   b dealt with   c came across

5 6E VOCABULARY Complete the sentences with *up* or *down*.

1 Please remember to wipe *down* the gym equipment after you've finished using it.
2 Will you please pick _____ your dirty clothes!
3 If you spill sugar on the floor, sweep it _____ or we'll have ants everywhere.
4 Nick's car broke _____ on the motorway.
5 My parents did _____ my little sister's bedroom for her birthday.
6 If you don't mop _____ the water on the bathroom floor, someone is going to slip and break a bone.

6 ON A HIGH NOTE Write a short paragraph describing how you could make your room or home cleaner, tidier and more organised.

1 For each learning objective, write 1–5 to assess your ability.

1 = I don't feel confident. 5 = I feel confident.

	Learning objective	Course material	How confident I am (1–5)
6A	I can use modal and related verbs to talk about obligation, necessity, prohibition, advice, ability or permission.	Student's Book pp. 78–79	
6B	I can understand fast speech and talk about mobile lifestyle.	Student's Book p. 80	
6C	I can use articles to talk about general and specific things.	Student's Book p. 81	
6D	I can identify specific details in an article and talk about houses and space.	Student's Book pp. 82–83	
6E	I can talk about household problems and solutions.	Student's Book p. 84	
6F	I can give instructions.	Student's Book p. 85	
6G	I can write a report.	Student's Book pp. 86–87	

2 Which of the skills above would you like to improve in? How?

Skill I want to improve in	How I can improve

3 What can you remember from this unit?

New words I learned and most want to remember	Expressions and phrases I liked	English I heard or read outside class

GRAMMAR AND VOCABULARY

1 Replace the underlined parts with the words from the box with a similar meaning. There are two extra words.

a lot   decorating   marginally   removing   repair
replace   ~~significantly~~   spacious

1 The exam was <u>considerably</u> more challenging than Ellis had expected. *significantly*

2 My parents are <u>doing up</u> the kitchen this week, so we're eating takeaway every evening. _____

3 Do you know anyone who can <u>fix</u> hi-fi equipment? _____

4 First we'll <u>change</u> the front door, then later we'll do the windows. _____

5 The white paint is <u>miles</u> cheaper than the coloured ones. _____

6 The living room is pretty <u>large</u> for such a small house. _____

/ 5

2 Complete the sentences with one word in each gap.

1 Your room is nothing *like* mine – yours is big and airy, mine is small and cosy.

2 The small coffee is too small and the large one too big, so I'll take a _____-sized one, please.

3 I can't imagine being tied _____ to one place for the rest of my life.

4 Make sure you sweep all that broken glass _____.

5 My parents and I used to be on the _____ and never lived in the same place for long.

6 It's time we got _____ of this awful carpet.

/ 5

3 Choose the correct words to complete the sentences.

1 I *could / was able to* sell the tickets for the concert we couldn't go to.

2 You *need to / may* travel by train I'm afraid because there are no flights.

3 Passengers *may not / need not* enter this zone.

4 It is *forbidden / required* to remove stones, shells, plants or animals from the beach.

5 Fa was *managed / supposed* to complete her application by yesterday, but she missed the deadline.

/ 5

4 Complete the diary entry with *a*, *the* or *Ø* (no article).

I definitely don't want to live in [1]<u>*the*</u> country; it's too quiet. I'd rather live in [2]_____ busy town by the sea. I'm thinking of somewhere in Europe, perhaps on the coast of [3]_____ Mediterranean. [4]_____ south of France would probably be the best choice as I already speak some French. I studied it at [5]_____ university. Also, it's not far from [6]_____ Alps and I love mountain climbing.

/ 5

USE OF ENGLISH

5 Complete the second sentence using the word in bold so that it means the same as the first one. Use between two and five words, including the word in bold.

1 Finding a flat was much easier than I had expected. **NOWHERE**

Finding a flat was *nowhere near as difficult* as I had expected.

2 Pour salt on the red wine stain. **WHAT**

_____ salt on the red wine stain.

3 Do we have to attend lessons on a Saturday? **OBLIGED**

_____ lessons on a Saturday?

4 Food and drinks aren't permitted in the taxi. **ALLOWED**

You _____ or drink anything in the taxi.

5 You needn't go as fast as the other runners. **HAVE**

You _____ up with the other runners.

6 The Greens got a good price for their house. **MANAGED**

The Greens _____ their house for a good price.

/ 5

6 Choose the correct words a–d to complete the text.

Hi, Khalid. Just got back from Edinburgh where Dad and I finally [1]___ to find some accommodation for my first year at [2]___ uni. I've got a lovely [3]___ room in a big house near the centre. At £120 [4]___ week, it's definitely not cheap, but it's in a great location, so we decided to [5]___ it. I can't believe I'll be living there in six weeks!

1 a could	**b** had	**c** managed	**d** allowed
2 a some	**b** a	**c** the	**d** Ø
3 a confined	**b** spacious	**c** cramped	**d** populated
4 a a	**b** the	**c** an	**d** Ø
5 a get rid of	**b** come across	**c** do up	**d** go with

/ 5

/ 30

7A GRAMMAR AND VOCABULARY

Reported speech

1 ⭐ Read the reported statements and choose the correct forms to complete the sentences in direct speech.

1 She asked what the government had been thinking when it changed the law.

'What *was the government thinking / has the government been thinking* when it changed the law?'

2 He said we should stand up for important things.

'We should *have stood / stand* up for important things.'

3 He asked us whether we believed in civil rights.

'*Did you / Do you* believe in civil rights?'

4 She said young people had taken to the streets and protested.

'Young people *have taken / took to* the streets and protested.'

5 He said that their protest would change the world.

'Our protest *will / would* change the world.'

2 ⭐ Choose the correct forms to complete the news report.

Pupils at Sleaforth School went on strike yesterday to rally against climate change. Our reporter asked student representative, Amy Read why **¹***had pupils / pupils had* joined the strike. Amy said that they **²***are / were* extremely angry about the state of the planet and **³***have / had* decided to stage a protest after hearing about similar actions taking place around the world **⁴***the week before / last week*. Interviewed in front of the school, Amy said students had gathered **⁵***here / there* to wave placards in the hope of putting pressure on the government to declare a climate emergency. She asked why **⁶***adults weren't / weren't adults* doing more about deforestation and fossil fuels, and said that young people **⁷***will / would* never forgive them if they **⁸***carried / carry* on destroying the planet.

3 ⭐⭐ Read the text in Exercise 2 again and complete the interview in direct speech with one or two words in each gap.

Reporter Amy, why **¹***have you* joined the strike?

Amy We **²**_____ extremely angry about the state of the planet. We **³**_____ to stage a protest after hearing about similar actions taking place around the world **⁴**_____. We have gathered **⁵**_____ to wave placards in the hope of putting pressure on the government to declare a climate emergency. Why **⁶**_____ doing more about deforestation and fossil fuels? We **⁷**_____ forgive them if they **⁸**_____ destroying the planet despite clear warnings.

4 ⭐⭐ Complete the sentences with *asked*, *said* or *told*.

1 The police officers *asked* me whether I was eighteen years old.

2 The security guard _____ us not to come any closer or he would call the police.

3 The fire-fighters _____ we had to stay behind the barriers.

4 The conductor _____ if he could see our tickets.

5 The driving instructor _____ you that you needed to slow down.

6 The doctor _____ I was very lucky to be alive.

5 ⭐⭐ USE OF ENGLISH Choose the correct words a–c to complete the text.

I met a guy at the climate demonstration last week. He looked a bit confused, so I asked him **¹** ___ I could help him. He said that he wanted to know what we **²** ___. I explained that we **³** ___ against the destruction of the environment. Then he told me that he **⁴** ___ on a demonstration before and asked me if he **⁵** ___ join in. I told him that I was sure that it **⁶** ___ be alright. I asked him what **⁷** ___. He frowned and told me he **⁸** ___ Nelson Mandela Smith!

1 **a** that	**b** why	**c** if
2 **a** asked	**b** wanted	**c** wants
3 **a** protested	**b** protest	**c** were protesting
4 **a** wasn't	**b** hadn't been	**c** hasn't been
5 **a** can	**b** will	**c** could
6 **a** will	**b** would	**c** could
7 **a** his name was	**b** was his name	**c** his name is
8 **a** had been called	**b** was called	**c** called

6 ⭐⭐ **Complete the reported questions. Only change the tenses if necessary.**

1 'Why are you lobbying for change?'
He asked us _why we were_ lobbying for change.

2 'Were you at the protest yesterday?'
She wanted to know if I _____.

3 'What slogan will you be chanting?'
She's just asked us _____ chanting.

4 'How many people took to the streets last week?'
He asked how many people _____.

5 'Is it safe to protest in your country?'
She asked us _____ country.

6 'How long have you been preparing this banner?'
He wanted to know _____ banner.

7 'Are you keen on protests?'
She often asks me _____ keen on protests.

7 ⭐⭐⭐ **Report the comments and questions. Only change the tenses if necessary.**

1 'Could I ask you a few questions here and now?'
He asked _if he could ask me a few questions there and then_.

2 'They have been trying to put pressure on the government.'
She said _____.

3 'We and a few other friends staged a protest last week.'
They say _____.

4 'Politicians need to be honest.'
He said _____.

5 'Protesters might have to wait in long queues.'
She said that _____.

6 'Stop what you are doing right now!'
She ordered us _____.

7 'It had been a successful day of action.'
They said _____.

8 ⭐⭐⭐ **Report the sentences. If it's possible to report them in two ways, write both answers.**

1 'People are getting really upset about this issue.'
She said that people _were getting really upset about that issue_.

2 'This march is really amazing.'
She says that _____
_____.

3 'I love going on protest marches.'
She said that she _____
_____.

4 'The march has been a great success.'
She says that the march _____
_____.

5 'There will probably be a general election soon.'
She said that there _____
_____.

9 ⭐⭐⭐ **Use the prompts to report the conversation.**

Last week ...

Faye Are you going to the protest this afternoon, Tom?

Tom I'm not sure, but I might. Who else will be there?

Faye Asia and Jarek will be going because they love marches and they wouldn't miss it for the world. Kinga can't make it because she has an exam tomorrow.

Tom Did you tell Kara about it?

Faye Yes, I did.

Tom In that case, I've made up my mind. I'm definitely going to come.

1 Faye asked Tom whether _he was going to the protest that afternoon_.

2 Tom replied that _____.

3 Then he asked _____.

4 Faye told him that _____.

5 But she said that _____.

6 Tom wanted to know if _____.

7 Faye said _____.

8 Tom said he _____.

10 ON A HIGH NOTE **Imagine a short interview between a journalist and a celebrity who is involved in a protest. Report the questions asked and the answers given.**

The journalist asked the activist whether she thought the climate crisis was the biggest problem facing the human race now. She said ...

7B VOCABULARY | Social issues

1 ⭐ Match the two parts of the sentences.

1 ☐ Families living in **relative**
2 ☐ My family and I were victims of **hate**
3 ☐ The question of how to deal with **juvenile**
4 ☐ It can be difficult for victims of **domestic**
5 ☐ How can children be helped to escape from **modern**
6 ☐ Police are attempting to crack down on **organised**
7 ☐ A great deal of **institutional**
8 ☐ Scandinavian firms are to reach **gender**

a **slavery** in clothing and footwear factories?
b **delinquency** is a difficult one.
c **violence** to speak out.
d **racism** happens in criminal justice systems.
e **poverty** often can't afford access to the Internet.
f **crime** groups in the south of the country.
g **equality** standards for pay and promotion.
h **crime** targeted at foreigners living in this block of flats.

2 ⭐⭐ Complete the sentences with the social issues in bold from Exercise 1.

1 *Modern slavery* is not so much about owning people, but more about exploiting people.
2 Making violent threats against someone online because of their race or gender is an example of a _____.
3 _____ can be seen in the US legal system where African American criminals are treated more harshly than white American criminals.
4 Families living on less than 50 percent of the average income are described as living in _____.
5 Women have been fighting for _____ for centuries, yet society is still not fair.
6 With so many young teenagers committing multiple crimes, _____ is a real problem in our cities.
7 The classic example of a(n) _____ group is the Sicilian Mafia.
8 Tragically, you never know behind which front doors _____ is happening.

3 ⭐⭐ Choose the correct words to complete the newspaper headlines.

> Students ¹*rebellion / rebel* after being taught wrong book and failing English exam.

> Prime Minister cancels ²*equal / equalise* pay plans.

> Climate protesters rally against ³*expansive / expansion* of regional airport.

> University entrance requirements highly ⁴*discriminatory / discrimination* according to investigation.

> ⁵*Oppression / Oppressive* government claims victory in 'joke' elections.

> Academics still being ⁶*persecution / persecuted* by government authorities.

4 ⭐⭐ USE OF ENGLISH Complete the text with the correct words formed from the words in bold.

University Equality Policy

At this university, we reject any and all ¹*discrimination* (**DISCRIMINATE**) based on race, gender, religion or sexuality. We believe in ²_____ (**FREE**) of speech and will never accept any ³_____ (**PERSECUTE**) of individuals based on their ⁴_____ (**PERSON**) beliefs. Should anybody feel they have suffered ⁵_____ (**VICTIM**) because of their race, lifestyle or beliefs, an ⁶_____ (**INVESTIGATE**) will be carried out and sutiable disciplinary action will be taken.

5 ⭐⭐ Find and correct one mistake in each sentence.

1 A well-known ⟨organised violence⟩ group boss was arrested in London this morning.
   organised crime
2 Knife-crime among fourteen to eighteen-year-olds is fuelling juvenile slavery statistics.
   _____
3 The oppress of free journalism is a worrying development in our country.
   _____
4 It is no longer possible to justification the production of single-use plastics.
   _____
5 Zero-hour contracts are seen by many as an exploitation form of employment.
   _____

6 ON A HIGH NOTE Write a short news report based on one of the headlines in Exercise 3.

1
🔊 *47* **Listen to Part 1 of a radio programme. What is the main topic of the phone-in? Choose the correct answer.**

a coping with hot weather

b improving society

c encouraging creativity

2
🔊 *48* **Listen to Part 2 of the programme. Match speakers 1–4 with ideas a–g which most closely match what the speakers say. There are three extra ideas.**

Speaker 1 ☐
Speaker 2 ☐
Speaker 3 ☐
Speaker 4 ☐

This idea ...

a recognises the power of individual actions.

b would encourage people to clean up their local environment.

c could help solve two social problems at the same time.

d has the potential to make street artists' lives easier and safer.

e would help to control population growth.

f would allow people to use their talents to earn money legally.

g combines voluntary work with commercial advantage.

Vocabulary extension

3
Complete the collocations in bold, which you heard in the recording in Exercise 1, with the correct forms of the words from the box.

angle ~~blue-sky~~ bright share prove

1 The committee says we need some *blue-sky* **thinking** in order to find new ideas for charity day.

2 Does anyone have any _____ **ideas** for Mika's surprise party?

3 To find a solution I think we need to **look at the problem from a different** _____.

4 Please _____ **your thoughts** on what you think went wrong.

5 His parents said he wasn't working hard enough and his terrible exam results have _____ **them right**.

4
Match the collocations from Exercise 3 with their definitions.

1 Tell someone your opinions/ideas. *share your thoughts*

2 Creative ideas not limited by old views. _____

3 Clever suggestion. _____

4 Think about something in a different way. _____

5 Show that someone is/was correct. _____

Pronunciation

5
🔊 *49* **Listen to some sentences from the radio programme in Exercise 2, focusing on the underlined syllables. Can you hear any extra sound there?**

1 We have a long tradition of <u>pa</u>vement collection back home – home is Australia in <u>case</u> you couldn't <u>tell</u>!

2 Instead of relying on TV <u>ta</u>lent shows to find new performers, the opportunity to prove what you can do in front of an audience and raise a bit of <u>cash</u> at the same <u>time</u> could be open to everyone, you know.

ACTIVE PRONUNCIATION | Aspiration

We sometimes add an extra puff of air after /p/, /t/ and /k/ before we move on to the next sound. This happens only if

• the sound is at the beginning of a stressed (or the only) syllable.

• the sound is immediately followed by a vowel (e.g. *pʰaper, cʰar, tʰouch*).

6
🔊 *50* **Listen and repeat the words which include aspiration. The aspirated sounds have been underlined.**

/pʰ/	/tʰ/	/kʰ/
<u>p</u>oor	<u>t</u>alent	<u>c</u>urrent
<u>P</u>olish	<u>t</u>ime	<u>c</u>apital
un<u>p</u>opular	re<u>t</u>urn	oc<u>c</u>ur
im<u>p</u>ortant	po<u>t</u>ential	un<u>c</u>ommon

7
🔊 *51* **Tick the words where the underlined sounds include aspiration. Listen and check. Practise saying the words.**

1 ☐ vi<u>t</u>amins
2 ☑ re<u>p</u>air
3 ☐ <u>d</u>rop
4 ☐ lo<u>c</u>ation

5 ☐ <u>t</u>ortoise
6 ☐ <u>c</u>lock
7 ☐ me<u>ch</u>anic
8 ☐ <u>c</u>omputer

8
Look again at the words in Exercise 7 which do NOT include aspiration. Match them with reasons a–c below.

a ☐☐ unstressed syllable

b ☐ at the end of a syllable

c ☐ followed by a consonant

9
Underline the syllables which include aspiration.

1 This is a direct consequence of your petition.

2 He's so cowardly he wouldn't even commit a petty crime.

3 We should take action and push for further development.

10
🔊 *52* **Listen and check. Then practise saying the sentences.**

7D READING AND VOCABULARY

1

You are going to read an article about oline trolls. Put paragraph headings a–e in a logical order. Then read the article quickly and check your ideas.

- **a** ☐ Why do online trolls do what they do?
- **b** ☐ Who can help?
- **c** ☐ What is a troll?
- **d** ☐ How should you react to an online troll?
- **e** ☐ Will trolls ever stop trolling?

2

Read the article again and complete the sentences with no more than three words in each gap.

1 The term 'troll' has changed from its original meaning and now refers to *anonymous individuals* who bully others.
2 Trolls are motivated by _____ and the need for attention.
3 As trolls usually feel _____, they try to make their life meaningful by hurting others.
4 You need to have _____ and the ability to think ahead in order to deal with trolls.
5 If you respond to online trolls, you will probably face _____.
6 Victims of online bullying should first talk to _____.
7 It is against the law to threaten someone with _____ online.
8 Those receiving violent threats online can inform either the police or _____.

3

Read the article again and choose the correct answers.

1 What is the writer emphasising in Paragraph 1?
- **a** The way technology leads to changes in language.
- **b** The typical victims of online trolls.
- **c** The geographical origins of the word 'troll'.
- **d** The similarities between old and new meanings of the word 'troll'.

2 In Paragraph 2, the writer says that online trolls
- **a** are treated as celebrities by some people.
- **b** seek attention of any kind.
- **c** are often lonely.
- **d** like to write about their experiences on the Internet.

3 Why is it illogical to respond to online trolls?
- **a** It is exactly what they want you to do.
- **b** It goes against human nature.
- **c** It shows a lack of self-control.
- **d** It is copying their negative behaviour.

4 Why does the writer recommend joining support communities to victims of online bullying?
- **a** They report illegal threats to the police.
- **b** They put victims in touch with each other.
- **c** They provide secure Internet services.
- **d** They also support friends and family of victims.

Vocabulary extension

4

Match the words to make adjective-noun phrases from the text.

1 ☐ sensible	**a** attack
2 ☐ attention	**b** approach
3 ☐ human	**c** individual
4 ☐ golden	**d** nature
5 ☐ anonymous	**e** seeker
6 ☐ personal	**f** rule

5

Complete the sentences with the correct forms of the phrases from Exercise 4.

1 Police would like to thank the *anonymous individuals* who reported last night's robbery at the local bank.
2 I think the most _____ to cyberbullying is to just shrug it off, but not everybody is able to do that.
3 It is _____ to judge other people based on their appearance, but that doesn't make it right.
4 It's OK to disagree with somebody on social media, but you mustn't make _____ on other users.
5 My mum believes that people who appear on reality shows are mostly just _____.
6 The _____ of safe Internet use is never to give away personal information such as your address.

ACTIVE VOCABULARY | Prepositional phrases

A prepositional phrase is a group of words which includes a preposition (e.g. *at*, *in*, *about*) and a noun, gerund or clause. Prepositional phrases are usually used to give more information about a verb or a noun.

*Those who are suffering **at the hands of** trolls … .*

6

Replace the underlined phrases with the highlighted prepositional phrases from the text.

1 You are in danger of freezing to death if you get lost in the mountains in winter.
   at risk of
2 I may seem confident, but I'm actually quite shy when it comes to my real personality.
   _____
3 When my brother is bored and has nothing to do, he gets very annoying.
   _____
4 A bodyguard must keep his or her client safe whatever happens.
   _____
5 How can anyone be so intelligent and also make such poor choices in life?
   _____
6 Many innocent pets suffer because of the harmful actions of irresponsible owners.
   _____

7

ON A HIGH NOTE Write a short message offering advice to a friend who is being bullied online.

DON'T FEED THE TROLLS!

In the days before the Internet, the word 'troll' had two different meanings. As a noun, 'a troll' was an ugly, bad-tempered creature that appeared in Scandinavian fairy tales like those written by the Brothers Grimm. As a verb, 'to troll' means to fish using a line pulled slowly behind a boat. On the end of the line is the bait – a worm or something similar – which is there to tempt the fish. Perhaps it's easy to see why the word 'troll' has changed over time to describe anonymous individuals who, from the darkness of their bedrooms, 'fish' for victims by deliberately insulting and attacking people in online forums. Online trolls seek out politicians, celebrities, vloggers and, of course, ordinary people like you and me. Their favourite target is anyone who they can mock for being different to them in terms of image, ethnicity, beliefs or opinions.

A man who was once a troll himself, wrote about his experiences online and explained that there are two main reasons for a troll's behaviour. The first is boredom. Trolls lack stimulation in their everyday lives and so seek satisfaction by attempting to humiliate and harm others. They are often insecure at heart, so having someone respond to their hurtful attacks, brings a bizarre kind of meaning to their lives. As the ex-troll pointed out, he wouldn't have been trolling if he had had anything better to do with his time. As well as being at a loose end, these people desire attention. They want people to react to them regardless of whether the response is negative. They are happy to be hated, as long as they are being replied to and written about.

Dealing with online trolls requires self-control and thinking ahead. It is human nature to want to respond when someone makes a personal attack on you, but remember why it is that trolls troll. They are attention seekers, so by engaging with them we are actually giving them exactly what they want. Don't feed the trolls! If you had rats in your house, you wouldn't leave food out for them, so it's worth applying the same logic to these malicious online pests. Shrug them off and avoid becoming the fish that takes the bait! Instead, leave them starved of attention. If engagement is still tempting, think what the probable result will be. They are unlikely to change either their minds or their behaviour, so arguing with them will simply put you at risk of suffering further abuse. A more sensible approach is this: delete, block, report, move on. Adopt this plan and stick to it at all costs.

Those who are suffering at the hands of trolls or because of online bullying can seek help in various ways. The first place to turn for support might be friends and family. Talking to someone we trust, and who loves us and all the positive things about us, can be of great help. There are also support communities which exist to help victims of online bullying and abuse from trolls. As numerous victims writing online have reported, visiting these organisations' websites and joining the conversations there has allowed them to stay informed and at the same time to hear positive stories from people dealing with similar issues. Victims should also remember that any threats of violence made online are illegal and can be reported to Internet service providers, or the police.

Given the size of the online community and the anonymity that the Internet allows, it is unlikely that the problem of trolls will ever disappear completely. For now perhaps the best we can do is starve them of the attention they seek by following the golden rule: don't feed the trolls!

7E GRAMMAR

Reporting verbs

1 ⭐ **Put the words in order to make sentences.**

1 promised / the police officer / she / would / that / investigate the matter

The police officer promised that she would investigate the matter.

2 was due next lesson / the teacher / the students / reminded / their homework / that

_____

3 to collect / Natalia / agreed / from school / her sister

_____

4 his dog / at strangers / Ivan / to bark / approaching the house / encouraged

_____

5 the doctor / much more exercise / getting / advised

_____

6 for / apologised / waking / Ghulam / the baby

_____

7 insisted on / her original birth certificate / Miko / bringing / the secretary

_____

8 about / warned / the farmer / the bull in the field / the walkers

_____

2 ⭐ **Match sentences in direct speech a–h with reported sentences 1–8 from Exercise 1.**

a ☐ 'I'm afraid we need to see the original, not a copy.'

b ☐ 'Be careful! There's a bull in the field up there.'

c ☐ 'You really should walk, run or swim more.'

d ☐ 'Don't forget to hand in your essays next lesson.'

e ☐ 'I'll look into this for you, Madam.'

f ☐ 'OK, I'll pick her up, Mum.'

g ☐ 'Oh, I'm so sorry I woke her up!'

h ☐ 'Good boy! You protect the house.'

3 ⭐⭐ **Choose the correct words to complete the sentences.**

1 Helen agreed ___ Mohammed was discriminated against.

   a that   **b** to   **c** she

2 The man at the information desk advised ___ to leave our phone number.

   a that   **b** we   **c** us

3 Miguel offered ___ lend Penny his car for the weekend.

   a to   **b** for   **c** he would

4 The politician denied ___ gifts from industry representatives.

   a to receive   **b** receiving   **c** about receiving

5 The musician objected ___ playing only his hits at the concert.

   a that   **b** to   **c** for

6 Police praised the teenager ___ saving the man's life.

   a on   **b** of   **c** for

4 ⭐⭐ **Complete the conversation with the correct forms of the verbs in brackets. Add any other necessary words.**

Clare What's wrong, Mark?

Mark I've fallen out with an old friend and she refuses **1** *to forgive* (forgive) me.

Clare Oh, dear. What happened?

Mark Well, she used to have a fiancé I didn't like so when she said he wasn't her fiancé anymore, I jumped straight in and admitted **2** _____ (never/be) fond of him and I congratulated her **3** _____ (make) the right choice.

Clare So? What's wrong with that?

Mark Well, she explained **4** _____ (get) married in July!

Clare Oh no!

Mark Obviously, I regretted **5** _____ (open) my big mouth so I apologised **6** _____ (say) what I'd said and reminded her **7** _____ (promise) to invite me to her wedding if she ever got married.

Clare What did she say?

Mark She accused me **8** _____ (be) insensitive. I don't think she'll ever forgive me.

5 ⭐⭐⭐ **Rewrite the sentences in reported speech using a suitable reporting verb.**

1 'I wish I hadn't bought white trainers.'

Guy *regrets/regretted buying white trainers*.

2 'I will cook for you on Saturday.'

Elisabeta _____.

3 'I was wrong.'

Anna _____.

4 'Why don't we have a party?'

Reginald _____.

5 'Amy is so rude.'

Kenny _____.

6 ON A HIGH NOTE **Choose five of the reporting verbs from this lesson and use them to report things that people have said to you recently.**

7F SPEAKING

1 🔊 *53* Listen and repeat the phrases. How do you say them in your language?

SPEAKING | Expressing and challenging opinions

EXPRESSING YOUR OPINION

- **Strong opinion**

  It goes without saying that animal rights are extremely important.

  I really think/don't think that it's an important issue.

  Without a shadow of a doubt, animals need more protection in law.

  Frankly, I think it's obvious that we need to do more to protect animals.

- **Less strong opinion**

  My impression is that online abuse are not punished properly.

  I'm of the opinion that we need more severe punishments.

  As far as I'm concerned, online abusers should be punished.

- **Counter opinion**

  It's a good idea in principle, but is it actually possible to police the Internet?

  I can see where they're/you're coming from, but I'm not sure that's the best solution.

- **Tentative opinion**

  I'm no expert, but I don't believe these protests will change anything.

  I tend to think (that) these protests won't change anything.

  I'm inclined to think (that) we need to come up with a different type of protest.

CHALLENGING SOMEBODY ELSE'S OPINION

That's debatable, isn't it?

You're entitled to your opinion, but I don't agree with you.

Are you saying that we have to change our diet completely?

---

2 Match the two parts of the sentences.

1. ☐ Without a shadow of
2. ☐ Frankly, I think it's
3. ☐ It's a good idea in
4. ☐ That's debatable,
5. ☐ I can see where
6. ☐ I'm no expert,
7. ☐ You're entitled

a principle, but it may be difficult to achieve.

b obvious that he isn't suitable for the position.

c to your opinion, but I'm entitled to disagree with you!

d isn't it? I'm not sure many people will agree with you.

e you're coming from, but I don't think it's so simple.

f a doubt, the government should address this issue.

g but don't we already pay enough tax?

3 Find the missing words and rewrite the sentences.

1. I really don't that school uniforms are a good idea.
   I really don't think that school uniforms are a good idea.

2. You're entitled your opinion, but don't make up facts.
   _____

3. My impression that people should be more tolerant.
   _____

4. I'm the opinion that schools should only provide healthy meals for their students.
   _____

5. I'm expert, but I'm not sure waving placards does much good.
   _____

6. As far I'm concerned, a small fine is not a strong enough deterrent.
   _____

7. It goes saying that police officers should never break the law.
   _____

4 USE OF ENGLISH Complete the mini-conversations with one word in each gap.

Haruki Without a ¹*shadow* of a doubt, vandals that spray graffiti should be made to clean it as a punishment.

Gemma I'm ²_____ to think the same, Haruki, but the difficult bit is catching them.

Aarav I ³_____ to think that the laws designed to protect animals are not strong enough. I mean, I'm of the ⁴_____ that harming an animal is no different to harming a person.

Anika That's ⁵_____, isn't it? I mean we kill over 150 billion animals every year for food.

Aarav Well, I can see where you're ⁶_____ from, but as far as I'm ⁷_____, food production is different.

Anika I'm not sure the animals would agree, Aarav.

Lucas It ⁸_____ without saying that petrol and diesel cars should be banned. Electric cars are the future of transport.

Flora Well, I'm no ⁹_____, but I think that depends on how the electricity is generated, doesn't it? If it's done by burning high-carbon fuels, then what's the point?

Lucas Are you ¹⁰_____ that electric cars are a waste of time?

Flora No, you're not listening properly, Lucas. I'm saying it depends on how the electricity is produced.

5 ON A HIGH NOTE Write a short dialogue about banning free speech online. Make speakers express and challenge opinions.

Give your article a catchy title.

Make sure the introduction clearly defines what the article is about.

Hold the reader's attention in the introduction with a surprising fact or statistic, a short anecdote or a rhetorical question.

Make sure each body paragraph has a clear topic.

The conclusion should return to the main idea from the introduction.

Leave the reader with something to think about. Consider using the words from the title again, making a suggestion, giving a personal opinion or asking a question.

FOOD (TRUCKS) FOR THOUGHT!

1 Did you know that half of all mental health conditions that affect adults begin by the age of just fourteen? No wonder the World Health Organisation believes in engaging **1**_with_ young people to raise awareness about mental health issues. This is one of the reasons why they hold World Mental Health Day every year on 10 October. This year our city participated **2**_____ the day by organising a special event called 'Food (trucks) for thought'. My friends and I went along to check it out.

2 As well as the usual joggers and dog-walkers in City Park last Saturday, one sunny corner was filled with food trucks and chattering youngsters. There was music, mouth-watering smells, and most importantly, the buzz of conversation – not about the latest TV blockbuster, but about mental health and how to cope **3**_____ the stresses of life. As part of the event, information points had been set up alongside the trucks by mental health organisations. There were presentations, competitions and plenty of experts on hand to offer advice. Everywhere you looked, people were relaxing and eating and relating **4**_____ each other on a wide range of topics from dealing **5**_____ stress at school to combating social media addiction.

3 What we really liked was the mix of entertainment and serious information. Understandably, topics such as depression or self-harm can be very difficult to talk about, but the relaxed atmosphere of the event helped people connect **6**_____ each other and open up.

4 All in all, my friends and I felt the day offered a practical demonstration of how awareness raising can promote important discussion. Judging by the numbers who attended, many of us are concerned about ourselves, others, or perhaps just mental health in general. Hopefully, the organisers will go ahead **7**_____ the event in future years as there was certainly as much interesting food for thought as there was delicious food for lunch!

1 Read the Writing task and the article. Then match paragraphs 1–4 of the article with statements a–e.

You recently took part in an event which was held in order to raise awareness about an issue that is important for young people. Write an article in which you describe the event and what it achieved.

This paragraph ...
a ☐ states the topic of the article.
b ☐ begins with a rhetorical question.
c ☐ describes the event mentioned in the task.
d ☐ offers a final thought.
e ☐ describes what the event achieved.

2 Read the article again and complete it with one dependent preposition in each gap.

3 WRITING TASK Write your own article answering the task from Exercise 1.

ACTIVE WRITING | An article

1 Plan your article.
• Think of an issue that affects young people and could be the subject of an awareness raising campaign.
• Think of a catchy/interesting title for your article.
• Decide how you will describe the event and what you liked about it.
• Think about what the event achieved overall.

2 Write the article.
• Use a chatty, conversational style including rhetorical questions and one or two exclamation marks.
• Make sure each paragraph has a clear topic.
• Return to the main topic in the conclusion.

3 Check that ...
• you have correctly used any verbs with dependent prepositions.
• there are no spelling, grammar or punctuation mistakes.

1 **7A GRAMMAR AND VOCABULARY Complete the text with one word in each gap.**

> Over twenty thousand people took to the **¹**_streets_ yesterday to rally **²**a_____ the government's attempts to control the media. Protestors waved **³**p_____ and chanted the **⁴**s_____ 'Free media! Free speech!'. The recent jailing of several well-known journalists has caused a public **⁵**o_____ and already led citizens to stage several **⁶**p_____ recently. Opposition politicians are lobbying for **⁷**c_____ and putting further **⁸**p_____ on the government to release the journalists.

2 **7B VOCABULARY Complete the sentences with one word in each gap.**

1 Progress is being made on g_ender_ e_quality_, but there is still a lot to be done to empower women.

2 The p_____ of migrant workers by greedy employers continues.

3 D_____ v_____ involves physical or psychological abuse and control of a partner.

4 When neither parent is earning, children face the consequences of r_____ p_____.

5 This policy results in the v_____ of the poor, the sick and the disabled.

6 The number of h_____ c_____ reported by minorities increases after terrorist attacks.

7 Fifty-four people have been arrested in a police operation to disrupt o_____ c_____.

8 Forcing immigrants to work for nothing is an example of m_____ s_____.

3 **7C LISTENING AND VOCABULARY Complete the pairs of sentences with the words in bold.**

1 **TEST / PROVE**

a We have to _test_ all the new equipment before we let the students use it.

b Scientists are now able to _____ that black holes actually exist.

2 **OVER / ABOVE**

a There are _____ 100 bridges in the city of Wroclaw, Poland.

b _____ us now is the famous glass pyramid of the Louvre Museum.

3 **IN THE END / AT THE END**

a _____ of a long day's work in the fields, the fruit pickers shared a simple meal.

b They booked a table for seven, but _____ only four people came.

4 **EVADE / AVOID**

a The killer managed to _____ capture for over twenty-three years.

b I try to _____ the supermarket at weekends.

5 **ROSE / RAISE**

a There have been many unsuccessful schemes to _____ the Titanic from the sea bed.

b The drone _____ slowly into the sky.

4 **7D READING AND VOCABULARY Complete the sentences with the words from the box.**

fat-shaming humiliated malicious misjudged
mocked multi-talented rethink ~~shrugged~~

1 They _shrugged_ off their manager's aggressive tone and got on with the job.

2 You spread that _____ gossip about Ben because you wanted to hurt him.

3 _____ somebody because of their weight is a cruel thing to do.

4 Our group isn't getting many new members; I believe we should _____ our strategy.

5 The girls _____ the boys when they beat them 4–2 at football.

6 I think I _____ Greg when I first met him because he's actually a very pleasant man.

7 Men are sometimes _____ for crying in public.

8 She's a singer, dancer and actress – what a _____ girl!

5 **7G WRITING AND VOCABULARY Complete the sentences with one preposition in each gap.**

1 We need to discourage people _from_ using plastic products.

2 Members of the public must not interfere _____ police business.

3 If I could wish _____ anything, it would be a world filled with kindness.

4 Many families are struggling to get by _____ minimum wage earnings.

5 Hundreds of protesters gathered yesterday to demonstrate _____ violence.

6 A large number of homeless people are struggling _____ addiction.

7 Charlie's been banned _____ driving for a year.

8 The prime minister relates the rise in crime _____ an increase in unemployment.

9 The police don't usually like to intervene _____ disputes between family members.

10 We are here to campaign _____ child labour.

6 **ON A HIGH NOTE Choose one social issue from your country that you are concerned about. Write a short paragraph explaining what could be done to tackle the problem.**

1 For each learning objective, write 1–5 to assess your ability.

1 = I don't feel confident. 5 = I feel confident.

	Learning objective	Course material	How confident I am (1–5)
7A	I can use reported speech to talk about what someone else said.	Student's Book pp. 94–95	
7B	I can talk about social issues.	Student's Book p. 96	
7C	I can identify specific details and talk about social issues in films.	Student's Book p. 97	
7D	I can understand complex and compound sentences in articles.	Student's Book pp. 98–99	
7E	I can use reporting verbs to summarise what someone said.	Student's Book p. 100	
7F	I can express and challenge opinions.	Student's Book p. 101	
7G	I can write an article.	Student's Book pp. 102–103	

2 Which of the skills above would you like to improve in? How?

Skill I want to improve in	How I can improve

3 What can you remember from this unit?

New words I learned and most want to remember	Expressions and phrases I liked	English I heard or read outside class

GRAMMAR AND VOCABULARY

1 Complete the sentences with the words from the box.

delinquency oppressing ~~placards~~ slogans stance streets

1 Some of the protesters were waving some very funny *placards*.
2 It's time the people took a _____ against extremism and hatred in this country.
3 We've decided to take to the _____ to show our support for endangered animals.
4 Shouting _____ is not going to help when what we need is real action now.
5 Juvenile _____ is extremely common in this grey and depressing concrete-filled neighbourhood.
6 The government has been accused of _____ free speech.

/ 5

2 Complete the sentences with one word in each gap.

1 The boxer was mocked *for* crying during his retirement speech.
2 Am I supposed to just shrug _____ the fact that you've spent all our savings?
3 We should put pressure _____ the government to pass laws protecting the environment.
4 School pupils are rebelling _____ the strict new uniform rules.
5 His poor eyesight prohibited him _____ becoming a pilot.
6 A lot of people demonstrated _____ plans to expand the runway at the local airport.

/ 5

3 Report the comments and questions. Only change the tenses if necessary.

1 My wife and I are trying to eat fewer calories.
He says *he and his wife are trying to eat fewer calories*.
2 What time did you arrive here yesterday?
She asked _____.
3 Be quiet and pay attention!
He ordered us _____.
4 We had been preparing for the party all week.
They said _____.
5 The weather is always great on our island.
She says _____.
6 Direct action can make governments change their plans.
She said _____.

/ 5

4 Rewrite the sentences in reported speech using the words in brackets.

1 'Black doesn't suit you.' (agree)
Gabriela *agreed that black doesn't/didn't suit me.*
2 'I'll give you a lift in my new car.' (offer)
Abel _____.
3 'I'm not sharing a tent with Paulo.' (object)
Francisco _____.
4 'I simply will not walk in the rain.' (refuse)
Hugo _____.
5 'Well done for passing your test, Carmen.' (congratulate)
Larissa _____.
6 'Kelly, you should come up with a different solution.' (advise)
Noah _____.

/ 5

USE OF ENGLISH

5 Complete the sentences with the correct words formed from the words in bold.

Fair-fight International is a non-profit [1]*organisation* (ORGANISE) which offers free legal advice to those who need it. We help victims of [2]_____ (INSTITUTION) racism and those suffering because of gender [3]_____ (EQUAL) in the workplace. We fight for victims of modern [4]_____ (SLAVE) and families or individuals living in relative [5]_____ (POOR). If you have been [6]_____ (VICTIM) in some way or have suffered discrimination, but cannot afford legal help, visit our website at **www.ffifree4u.org**.

/ 5

6 Choose the correct words a–d to complete the text.

The fall out between musicians Kim Simmons and Missy Galore continues this week after Simmons caused a public [1]___ by tweeting a racist insult about Galore. Simmons [2]___ that she had been intentionally racist and refused to apologise [3]___ the tweet. She said she didn't regret [4]___ the message, but has since been banned [5]___ Twitter.

1 a change   b outcry   c pressure   d defence
2 a denied   b evaded   c reminded   d promised
3 a on   b with   c for   d against
4 a post   b to post   c the post   d posting
5 a from   b with   c against   d of

/ 5

/ 30

Digital perspectives

8A GRAMMAR AND VOCABULARY

The passive

1 ⭐ **Rewrite the sentences in the passive.**

1 This German company manufactures hybrid engines.

Hybrid engines *are manufactured by this German company*.

2 By 2025, you could embed a chip like this in your wrist.

By 2025, a chip like this _____.

3 Researchers are researching racial bias in facial recognition software.

Racial bias in facial recognition software _____.

4 Over two million people have downloaded this 'body tracking' app.

This 'body tracking' app _____.

5 An insect caused the malfunction.

The malfunction _____.

6 Somebody was regularly hacking into celebrities' smartphones.

Celebrities' smartphones _____.

7 Burglars had triggered sensors in the device when they broke in.

Sensors in the device _____.

8 The smart device will alert owners if their dog steps outside the yard.

Owners _____.

9 Most people are going to use wearables in the near future.

Wearables _____.

10 You should update the software in your fitness tracker regularly.

The software in your fitness tracker _____.

2 ⭐⭐ **Complete the sentences with *by* or *with*.**

1 The first real smartphone was created *by* a company called IBM.

2 Our household appliances are made _____ only the highest quality materials.

3 The original smartwatch was designed _____ the inventor, Steve Mann.

4 A device this simple can be operated _____ a young child.

5 The controversial sculpture was made _____ electronic waste.

6 Your pet can be tracked _____ selecting 'live tracking' mode.

3 ⭐⭐ **Complete the sentences with the correct forms of *to be*.**

1 The burnt appliance could *be* smelled in every room of the house.

2 Has he ever _____ asked to hack into a bank's computer system before?

3 The facial recognition software is going _____ updated for the new model.

4 This device is dangerous and shouldn't _____ used by anyone under the age of sixteen.

5 I _____ asked for my password every single time I wanted to log in.

6 You should all have _____ given a four-digit code. Does everyone have it?

7 The leaking batteries were found _____ the cause of the malfunction.

8 Have you got any insect spray? I really don't fancy _____ eaten alive by mosquitoes.

4 ⭐⭐ **Complete the sentences with the correct passive forms of the verbs from the box.**

call up   employ   invite   ~~persuade~~   sell   tell

1 I regret *being persuaded* to buy this phone. I shouldn't have listened to that sales assistant.

2 I would really like _____ by one of the giant tech companies once I graduate.

3 Do you ever complain about _____ at home by people trying to sell you things?

4 Young people don't need _____ how to use new devices, they just know instinctively.

5 The new phone implants are going to _____ in all kinds of shops.

6 The head teacher congratulated them on _____ to take part in the science fair.

5 ★★ Complete the letter with the correct passive forms of the verbs in brackets.

Dear Sir or Madam,

I am writing to complain about one of your company's smartwatches, which **1** _was given_ (give) to my son for his birthday last week. Firstly, it **2** _____ (wrap) in large amounts of unnecessary plastic packaging. Don't you think your products **3** _____ (should/pack) in a more eco-friendly way? Secondly, the watch clearly **4** _____ (not check) before **5** _____ (sent) from your factory, as the all-important charging cable **6** _____ (not include). Could a cable please **7** _____ (sent) to us as soon as possible? We would appreciate it if this **8** _____ (could/do) without unnecessary plastic packaging.

Yours faithfully,
Marjorie Baggins

6 ★★ Complete the mini-conversations with the correct passive forms of the verbs in brackets.

At home ...

Martin Everyone knows you risk getting into trouble for downloading films illegally.

Rachel Do you know of anyone who **1** _has been caught_ (catch)?

Martin Well no, but I'm still worried about **2** _____ (track) online, so I never do it.

In a department store ...

Salesman All our large household appliances can **3** _____ (find) on the second floor, sir.

Damian Thank you. And if I find what I need, can I arrange for it **4** _____ (deliver)?

Salesman Certainly, though you **5** _____ (charge) a small fee for home delivery unless you spend over £500.

On the phone ...

Mia Hi, Randal. Where are you?

Randal Mia! I overslept again. I'm on the way, but could you tell the boss something, like er ... like my car **6** _____ (break into) last night or something?

Mia I don't appreciate **7** _____ (ask) to make excuses for you, Randal.

Randal I know, I'm sorry. Just one more time? Please?

Mia One last time, Randal, and I expect **8** _____ (take) somewhere nice for lunch today as a thank-you.

Randal It's a deal. Wherever you want.

7 ★★★ USE OF ENGLISH Complete the second sentence using the word in bold so that it means the same as the first one. Use between two and five words, including the word in bold.

1 I expect that the courier company will deliver the parcel by four o'clock this afternoon. **DELIVERED**
I expect the _parcel to be delivered_ by four o'clock this afternoon.

2 The teacher said we mustn't use our phones during the exam. **TOLD**
We _____ use our phones during the exam.

3 The fridge will automatically order more milk before you run out. **ORDER**
More milk _____ by the fridge automatically before you run out.

4 We ought to recycle old devices to avoid waste. **SHOULD**
Old devices _____ to avoid waste.

5 The main material in this device is plastic. **MADE**
This device _____ plastic.

8 ★★★ Complete the advert with the correct active or passive forms of the verbs in brackets.

The Dingdong Smart Doorbell

1 _is manufactured_ (manufacture) at our factory in Portugal and to date over 10,000 Smart Bells **2** _____ (sell) throughout Europe. Hans Klingel, the famous tech engineer, **3** _____ (design) this state-of-the-art device. So, what's so special about the Dingdong Smart Doorbell? You **4** _____ (can/answer) your door from anywhere with your smartphone. Incredible but true! The on-board camera **5** _____ (can/use) to see who's at your door.
You can even let visitors into your home when you're not there if you want. To activate this function, the Smart Doorbell needs **6** _____ (pair) with one of Dingdong's smart locks. What **7** _____ (you/wait) for? Buy one now! Only £39.99 while stocks last!

9 ON A HIGH NOTE Write a short paragraph explaining some of the functions of a pair of 'smart shoes'. Use several examples of passive structures.

1 🔊 54 **Listen and repeat the phrases. How do you say them in your language?**

SPEAKING | Describing trends

INTRODUCING DATA

The graph illustrates/In this graph, we can see sales of smartphones over a six-month period.

DESCRIBING CHANGES OVER TIME

The number of online customers **increased/rose slightly.**

Sales of fitness trackers grew/went up sharply.

Users of smart clothing items declined/decreased steadily.

The number of online customers **went down gradually.**

Sales of fitness trackers dropped dramatically.

The number of online customers **stayed the same.**

Sales of fitness trackers remained steady.

There is a slight increase/rise in the number of sales.

There was a sharp/steady growth in the number of users.

There has been a gradual decrease/fall in the number of customers.

There will be a dramatic drop/decline in the number of fitness trackers sold.

SUMMARISING DATA

Overall, the trend in this season **is upwards/downwards.**

Between 2013 and 2018, sales of smart household appliances grew.

During the period shown on the graph, sales of smart household appliances went up.

It is noticeable that sales of smart household appliances dropped over the last six months.

---

2 **Match statements 1–6 with graphs a–f.**

1. ☐ The number of users went up sharply.
2. ☐ The number of users declined gradually.
3. ☐ The number of users dropped dramatically.
4. ☐ There was a steady rise in the number of users.
5. ☐ The number of users stayed the same.
6. ☐ Overall, the trend in users is upwards.

3 **Complete the sentences with one word in each gap.**

1. The nighttime temperature r*emained* steady throughout August.
2. The club's membership numbers s_____ the same last month.
3. O_____ , the trend in sales of men's beauty products is upwards.
4. Between 2018 and 2020, there was a g_____ drop in the number of malfunctions experienced by users.
5. During the p_____ shown on the graph, sales figures dropped slightly.
6. It is n_____ that there was no change in the markets last week.
7. The graph i_____ electricity usage over a twenty-four-hour period.
8. In this graph, we can s_____ data relating to the number of IoT devices sold last year.

4 **Complete the second sentence so that it means the same as the first one.**

1. The number of electronic cars produced increased slightly that year.
   There *was a slight increase in the number of electronic cars produced that year*.
2. There has been a sharp decline in the insect population this year.
   The insect population _____.
3. Battery-life will rise dramatically over the next five years.
   There _____.
4. Sales of CDs are expected to fall significantly.
   There _____.
5. There was a steady growth in production of wearable devices over the last three years.
   Production of _____.
6. The price of wireless speakers will decrease as the market develops.
   There _____.

5 **Complete the description of a graph with the words from the box.**

dramatic during gradually ~~graph~~ growth risen

In this **1**_graph_, we can see that the number of people using voice-activated devices to go online has **2**_____ sharply again this year. When they were first introduced, sales of such devices increased **3**_____. Then, **4**_____ the period 2016–2018 **5**_____ remained steady before taking off again in 2019. Experts predict there will be further **6**_____ increases next year as prices drop and the range of products expands.

6 ON A HIGH NOTE **Go online and find a graph which gives data over time on something that interests you. Write several sentences describing the trends and summarising the data.**

1 ★Complete the crossword.

```
            ¹C   ²O
      ³L       ⁴H        ⁵O
⁶F ⁷U  N  C  T  I  O  N  A  L  I  T  Y
⁸B
                    ⁹G
```

Across

6 Everything a computer or piece of software can do.

8 Make a copy of information held on a computer or other device.

9 Small problems or faults that prevent something from working well.

Down

1 The ability for one piece of equipment or software to be used with another.

2 Not in use any more because something newer has been invented.

3 Newest or most modern.

4 Deal with something.

5 No longer fashionable.

7 Change for something newer or better.

2 ★Choose the correct words to complete the sentences.

1 Very few of our new laptops have CD drives as CDs are virtually *obsolete / dated*.

2 This shop is full of clever little *gadgets / glitches* that make excellent presents.

3 The fashions and haircuts from early episodes of the sitcom *Friends* look very *dated / obsolete* now.

4 Household *appliances / devices* such as dishwashers and freezers are on sale this weekend.

5 If I need to make notes quickly, I still prefer a good *outdated / old-fashioned* pen and paper.

6 The app is designed to work on handheld *gadgets / devices* rather than laptops.

3 ★★Complete the sentences with one word in each gap.

1 Can your phone h<u>andle</u> hi-res music files?

2 U_____ to *Virustrap* for just €1.99 per month.

3 Sales of the formerly o_____ audio-cassette have grown steadily in the last year.

4 The app is really poor, so expect to suffer through plenty of bugs and g_____.

5 This phone has a s_____ -of-the-art camera, better than any other currently on the market.

6 I used to have to remember to b_____ up my files, but these days it happens automatically.

7 The phone company said that it would fix the c_____ problems with its latest model.

8 The cheaper tablets are OK for doing the basics, but they don't have the f_____ of the best models.

4 ★★Complete the mini-conversations with the words in bold. There is one extra word in each group.

LATEST / OUTDATED / UPGRADE / HANDLE

Tina Are you still using those ¹*outdated* old headphones, Magid?

Magid Sure! I mean, there's nothing wrong with them. I'm not the kind of person who has to have the ²_____ model of everything.

Tina Well, I know, but you love dance music so much that it seems a shame not to have headphones that can ³_____ the bass better.

Magid Well, it is my birthday next month – if you know what I mean!

GADGETS / STATE-OF-THE-ART / DATED / COMPATIBILITY

Tedra Have you thought about ⁴_____?

Kosmo What do you mean?

Tedra Well, if you switch brands of gaming console none of your old games will work.

Kosmo Hmm. You're right. But all my games are so ⁵_____ now that it probably doesn't matter. Games are my thing. I've saved up the money myself, so I'm going to invest in a ⁶_____ console.

BACK UP / BUGS / UPGRADE / APPLIANCES / OLD-FASHIONED

Felicity This laptop is full of ⁷_____ – something goes wrong every ten minutes!

Iain Make sure you ⁸_____ your work then. You really don't want to lose your project.

Felicity Oh, I will. Don't worry. To be honest, I think it's time for a(n) ⁹_____ – this one is nearly ten years old.

Iain Well, yes, it looks kind of ¹⁰_____, and it weighs a ton!

5 ON A HIGH NOTE Imagine you can choose one state-of-the-art technological device. Write a paragraph explaining what you would choose and why.

8D READING AND VOCABULARY

1 **Look at the photos and read the article quickly. What do you think would be the best title for the article?**
- **a** Ray Kurzweil and his incredible inventions
- **b** Predicting the future using artificial intelligence
- **c** The man who sees the future

2 **Read the article again and match headings A–G with paragraphs 1–6. There is one extra heading.**
- **A** A series of accurate predictions
- **B** A man of many talents
- **C** Future forecasts are often wrong
- **D** Incredible future
- **E** Reasons to be rational
- **F** Say hi to machine-human hybrids
- **G** What's around the corner?

3 **Read the text again and choose the correct answers.**
1. Why does the writer use the example of the millennium bug in Paragraph 1?
   - **a** To emphasise how technology can help us predict the future.
   - **b** To illustrate how difficult it is to predict the future accurately.
   - **c** To suggest we are better at predicting the future now than twenty years ago.
   - **d** To explain how damaging and costly poor predictions can be.
2. What does 'stockpiled' mean in line 14?
   - **a** Collected a supply of something for use in the future.
   - **b** Bought something at a very high price.
   - **c** Threw something out because it was out of date.
   - **d** Waited a long time for something to be delivered.
3. The main purpose of Paragraph 2 is to
   - **a** list the jobs held by Ray Kurzweil.
   - **b** give examples of Kurzweil's many inventions.
   - **c** highlight Kurzweil's ability to make accurate predictions.
   - **d** illustrate how famous Kurzweil is.
4. According to the author, what does Kurzweil sometimes get wrong?
   - **a** What will happen with computer technology.
   - **b** Exactly when his predictions will happen.
   - **c** How machine language will develop.
   - **d** In what ways our day-to-day lives will change.
5. What does 'that' refer to in line 63?
   - **a** People will need to pass the Turing Test.
   - **b** Machines will become as intelligent as humans.
   - **c** Machines will become more intelligent than humans.
   - **d** People will live in a world of virtual reality.
6. In Paragraph 6 the writer aims to
   - **a** reassure worried readers.
   - **b** make a recommendation.
   - **c** convince sceptical readers.
   - **d** issue a warning.

Vocabulary extension

4 **Match the highlighted words and phrases from the text with the definitions.**
1. No longer happens or exists. *a thing of the past*
2. Guess something without any evidence. _____
3. Ability to predict the future. _____
4. What will happen to someone in the future. _____
5. Idea that claims to be scientific, but is not. _____
6. Develop or progress. _____
7. The time when something happens. _____
8. People who claim to be able to predict the future. _____

5 **Complete the sentences with the correct forms of the words and phrases from Exercise 4.**
1. Don't let other people tell you what to do. You are in control of your own *destiny*!
2. My cousin went to see a _____ and was told she would become famous one day.
3. I refuse _____ about my exam results and would rather just wait and see.
4. I can't wait for the day when passwords become _____ – I can never remember mine!
5. Artificial intelligence is _____ so quickly that laws regarding safety can't keep up.
6. He had the _____ to sell his computer before something serious went wrong with it.
7. The _____ of the storm meant huge delays to all the morning flights at the airport.
8. Don't trust all the health advice you find online. There is a lot of false information and _____ out there.

ACTIVE VOCABULARY | Suffix *-fold*

We can add the suffix *-fold* to any number word to make an adverb or adjective meaning 'a particular number of times' (e.g. two**fold**, thousand**fold**).

The resulting words are often used with the words *increase* (n/v) or *decrease* (n/v).

*We'll be able to **increase** our intelligence a **billionfold**.*

---

6 **Complete the sentences using the suffix *-fold* and the information in brackets.**
1. Sales of our natural language interface device have increased *fivefold* (by 5 times) in the last year.
2. There was a _____ (by 3 times) decrease in the number of visitors after the price of tickets was put up.
3. The number of users has decreased _____ (by 2 times) since last week.
4. Since last month, there has been a _____ (by 20 times) increase in the value of the company.

7 ON A HIGH NOTE **Write a paragraph predicting how technology might make life easier for students and teachers in the future.**

08

1 ☐ The idea of predicting the future has always fascinated the human race. This desire to speculate has sometimes led us to trust in pseudo-science or to believe fortune-tellers who were probably more
5 interested in our money than our destiny. On a bigger scale, there have been some spectacular failures in our efforts to predict the future. Take for example the global panic created by the 'millennium bug'. This was the prediction that at midnight on the first of January
10 2000, computers around the world would crash and cause anything from financial catastrophe to a nuclear meltdown! Governments issued warnings, scientists searched for solutions and worried members of the public stockpiled food and medicine in fear of
15 possible future shortages. Then, at midnight … nothing happened.

2 ☐ Obviously, it is incredibly difficult to predict the future, … unless your name is Ray Kurzweil. Kurzweil is an American author, entrepreneur, futurist and
20 inventor. He has twenty honorary doctorates and has received honours from three U.S. presidents. Described as 'the ultimate thinking machine', he is the inventor of technologies such as the scanner and a reading machine for the blind. However, Kurzweil is perhaps
25 most famous for the accuracy of his predictions about the future of technology. If you accept that his timing was not always exact, an astonishing eighty-six percent of them – including the ability of computers to beat humans at chess, the rise of the Internet, and the
30 invention of VR headsets – have come true.

3 ☐ The list of predictions that Kurzweil has got right is incredible. Highlights include his 1990 forecast that by 2010, computers would be able to answer questions by accessing information wirelessly via the Internet.
35 As we all know, that one certainly came true! Nine years later he predicted that by 2009 we would be able to talk to our computers and give them commands. While his timing may have been slightly inaccurate, the technology was in the early stages of development by
40 2009 and in today's world, natural language interfaces are everywhere. Again in 1999, Kurzweil said that computer displays would be built into glasses to allow for augmented reality, and in 2005, he used his incredible foresight to predict real-time translation.

45 **4** ☐ So going back to where we started, what fascinating predictions can Kurzweil provide for tomorrow's world? Well, first there's good news for us all in terms of health. Kurzweil predicts that within the next ten years or so, 'nano-bots' will begin to play an
50 important role in medicine. These tiny robots could help advance medical science to the stage where many of today's diseases become a thing of the past. Next, when it comes to transportation, Kurzweil sees roads filled with self-driving cars which are so safe that we will no
55 longer be allowed to drive ourselves. And then there are his longer-term predictions, and that's where things begin to get a lot more bizarre.

5 ☐ Kurzweil's most talked-about forecast concerns the moment at which technology is expected to become
60 more intelligent than humans. He believes that by 2029, artificial intelligence will be able to pass the 'Turing Test', which means it will have achieved the same level of intelligence as humans, and soon after that machine intelligence will begin to advance beyond ours. Virtual
65 reality will start to feel 100 percent real by the 2030s and by the end of that decade we will be able to copy our consciousness electronically. Rather terrifyingly, Kurzweil believes that by the 2040s, artificial intelligence will be a billion times more capable
70 than us. He also says that by 2045, we will be able to increase our own intelligence a billionfold by linking our biological brains to artificial intelligence.

6 ☐ If these awe-inspiring predictions sound like science fiction to you, it's worth remembering three
75 things. Firstly, how unbelievable his past forecasts would have sounded when he made them. Secondly, the ever-increasing rate at which technology is advancing. And thirdly, his incredible and proven eighty-six percent accuracy rate in predictions. One thing is for sure, you'll
80 certainly be hearing more about Kurzweil and his mind-blowing predictions in the future.

8E LISTENING AND VOCABULARY

1 🔊 **55 Listen to a radio interview about photo-sharing apps. Choose two issues discussed on the show.**

a amount of time users waste on these apps

b impact of these apps on users' mental health

c the chances of becoming famous through these apps

d impact of these apps on tourist attractions

2 🔊 **55 Listen to the interview again and choose the correct answers.**

1 What did Lara like most about being an influencer?

a modelling work   c additional money

b free products   d attention of others

2 Lara gave up being an influencer because she

a felt stressed about maintaining her popularity.

b realised it was taking up too much of her time.

c felt it was distracting her from her education.

d worried about the effect it had on her followers.

3 How does Lara feel now about her former role?

a ashamed   c proud

b stressed   d worried

4 Lara advises those who may be worried by the issues discussed in the interview to

a delete their photos.

b follow other people instead of influencers.

c uninstall photo-sharing apps.

d only follow people you know personally.

5 According to the presenter, the main problem caused by tourists taking photos at famous sights is the

a increased queuing time.

b impact on the environment.

c fact that views are being spoiled.

d fact that all the photos are the same.

Vocabulary extension

3 **Match the adjectives from the box, which you heard in the recording in Exercise 1, with their definitions.**

appealing   endless   envious   ~~influential~~   upbeat

1 Able to change what people do or think. *influential*

2 Attractive or interesting. _____

3 Positive and cheerful. _____

4 Wanting something that someone else has. _____

5 In large quantities or for a long time. _____

4 **Complete the sentences with the adjectives from Exercise 3.**

1 I find the architecture of the city *appealing*.

2 He's very _____ and should act responsibly.

3 I'm _____ of people who learn Maths easily.

4 My piano teacher was very _____ about my progress, which made me feel great.

5 I've done _____ revision, so I should pass my exams with good grades.

Pronunciation

5 🔊 **56 Read some sentences from the interview in Exercise 1. Are the two underlined letters *a* in each sentence pronounced the same or differently? Listen and check.**

1 Our next guest used to be an influential photo-sharing app star.

2 ... but in actual fact it was deceptive because it was all manufactured.

3 The apparent positive aspect is part of the problem.

ACTIVE PRONUNCIATION | The letter *a*

The letter *a* can be pronounced in many ways and the spelling of a word is not always a clear guide to its pronunciation. Two common ways of pronouncing *a* are:

- /æ/ like in *cat, jam* (with a very open mouth)
- /ɑː/ like in *start, father* (at the back of the throat; this sound is also slightly longer)

---

6 🔊 **57 Listen to these pairs of words. Tick the word you hear first.**

1 ☑ bark   ☐ back

2 ☐ heart   ☐ hat

3 ☐ parking   ☐ packing

4 ☐ art   ☐ at

5 ☐ harm   ☐ ham

6 ☐ aunt   ☐ ant

7 ☐ part   ☐ pat

8 ☐ hard   ☐ had

7 **Write the words you ticked in Exercise 6 in the correct place in the chart.**

/æ/ cat	/ɑː/ start
	bark

8 🔊 **58 Listen and repeat the pairs of words from Exercise 6.**

9 🔊 **59 Read the sentences aloud. Can you pronounce the words with the underlined letter *a* correctly? Listen and check. Then practise saying the sentences.**

1 Actually, there are massive problems in the city with both traffic jams and parking.

2 The acrobat's manager handles his contracts and travel plans.

3 My aunt was alarmed by the fast cars going past our garden.

UNIT VOCABULARY PRACTICE > page 97

8F GRAMMAR

Impersonal passive structures

1 ⭐ **Study patterns a–c and match them with sentences 1–6.**

a *It* + passive + *that* clause
b subject + passive + *to*-infinitive
c subject + passive + perfect infinitive

1 ☐ The designer is known to have been heavily influenced by early Japanese computers.

2 ☐ It is thought that the city's schools will be completely paperless within fifty years.

3 ☐ 5G mobile networks are expected to greatly improve Internet connection speeds.

4 ☐ It was once believed that guided missiles would be used to deliver post.

5 ☐ The company is estimated to have sold nearly ten million handsets in the last ten years.

6 ☐ Sales of the company's main product were reported to be steady.

2 ⭐ **Choose the correct forms to complete the sentences.**

1 It *is* / *was* said that high-speed rail travel would cause people to stop breathing.

2 Over half a million passwords are thought *to be* / *to have been* stolen in the hack.

3 It has often been *remarked* / *remarking* that the world was a simpler place before the Internet.

4 *The Internet* / *It* is thought that there are over 1.5 billion websites today.

5 It *is being* / *was* revealed that personal data had been collected illegally by the company.

6 The hacker is thought to *be* / *being* a man in his thirties living somewhere in southern Germany.

3 ⭐⭐ **Put the words in brackets in order to complete the sentences.**

Amazing facts
ABOUT THE INTERNET

The Internet ¹*is thought to have contained* (thought / to / is / have contained) 5 million terabytes of data in 2010. ² _____ (is / it / that / expected) by 2020, there will be 40 billion terabytes of data online.

Of the nearly 2 billion websites ³ _____ (to / exist / believed) today, it is estimated that less than 200 million are actually active.

Instagram users ⁴ _____ (to / are / reported) upload 95 million photographs every day. Rather sadly, ⁵ _____ (said / is / it / that) 70% of them are never looked at by anyone.

The first email ⁶ _____ (known / have / is / to / been / sent) by a programmer called Ray Tomlinson. Unfortunately, ⁷ _____ (not / is / known / it) what the message was as Tomlinson can't remember!

4 ⭐⭐⭐ **Complete the sentences with the correct impersonal passive forms of the words in brackets. Sometimes more than one answer is possible.**

1 It *is often remarked* (often/remark) that too much screen time is bad for your eyes.

2 IT graduates _____ (expect/pay) a high wage as soon as they graduate.

3 Five people _____ (believe/injure) in yesterday's accident.

4 It _____ (claim) that wi-fi signals are harmless to birds and insects.

5 I _____ (never/expect/do) this in my last job.

5 ⭐⭐⭐ **Rewrite the sentences using impersonal passive structures.**

1 Experts thought this new invention would revolutionise the way we communicate.
It *was thought that this new invention would revolutionise the way we communicate*.

2 Reports say the cause of the problem is a glitch in the software.
The cause of the problem _____.

3 The company thinks that over 40,000 cars have been affected by the malfunction.
Over 40,000 cars _____.

4 We expect the new model to sell very well indeed.
The new model _____.

5 Research has found that we send nearly 210 billion emails every day.
We _____.

6 People claim that technology has cost us our privacy.
It _____.

6 ON A HIGH NOTE **Use impersonal passive structures to report six opinions or beliefs about teenagers.**

8G **WRITING** | A for-and-against essay

Summarise the topic of the essay using your own words.

Outline both points of view which you are going to discuss.

In the first main paragraph, give arguments in favour of the situation.

In the second main paragraph, give arguments against the situation.

In the conclusion, summarise the main points of the essay and offer your opinion.

[1]In recent years, it has become more and more common for those suffering from minor illnesses and injuries to look for advice online. [2]While some people feel this is a helpful development, others consider the practice to be unsafe.

In times of ill-health, people have always asked advice from non-professional sources such as friends or family. Arguably, consulting the Internet is no different and there may be clear benefits to doing so. Simple medical problems can often be handled easily at home with online help. If people are able to diagnose and treat their own minor conditions, medical professionals may have more time to focus on those with more serious problems. Another positive aspect of online advice is that it may lead to a faster return to health, and therefore less disruption to work and life.

[3]In spite of these potential benefits, a major disadvantage of consulting the Internet for medical advice is the trustworthiness of the information provided. It is widely agreed that a significant amount of online advice is poor or even dangerous. Of course, some websites are operated by professional health care providers. Nonetheless, misinformation is common, especially on public forums. Even though contributors to these forums may be well-meaning, they are not usually medically trained and are not held responsible for the guidance they give. [4]Many people are of the opinion that following this kind of amateur advice could make a medical condition worse or lead to unnecessary worry because of a wrong diagnosis.

[5]In conclusion, it is clear that medical information on the Internet should be used with caution. Although online advice may help people to treat themselves, there is significant danger of the spread of misinformation and of making someone's health worse rather than better. [6]In my considered opinion, unless a source is completely trustworthy, it is better to consult a professional.

1 Read the essay. Match phrases a–f with underlined parts 1–6 from the essay with a similar meaning.

a ☐ Whereas
b ☐ It is argued by many people that
c ☐ Nowadays it is extremely common
d ☐ Despite
e ☐ As far as I'm concerned
f ☐ It seems sensible to conclude that

2 Read the essay again and complete the advice with *Do* or *Don't*.

1 *Don't* include a title.
2 _____ use a formal style.
3 _____ give your own opinion in the introduction.
4 _____ use the same wording as the task to summarise the topic.
5 _____ introduce and evaluate arguments on both sides of the debate.
6 _____ use a variety of structures to present contrasts.
7 _____ use some impersonal passive structures.

3 WRITING TASK Read the topic and write your for-and-against essay.

Nowadays many people use the Internet to shop for everything from food to holidays. Write an essay presenting the advantages and disadvantages of this practice.

ACTIVE WRITING | A for-and-against essay

1 Plan your essay.
• Make a note of some possible arguments for and against online shopping.
• Think about how you will summarise the topic in your own words.

2 Write the essay.
• Use a formal style.
• Use impersonal passive structures where possible.
• Include phrases of contrast where possible.

3 Check that …
• you have considered both sides of the argument.
• there are no spelling, grammar or punctuation mistakes.

UNIT VOCABULARY PRACTICE

1 8A GRAMMAR AND VOCABULARY **Complete the sentences with the correct forms of the words in brackets.**

1 You can unlock your phone using the selfie cam and the facial *recognition* (recognise) software.

2 A _____ (function) at a nuclear power plant is a very serious problem.

3 The _____ (sense) in the car allow it to park itself without the driver's help.

4 All _____ (house) appliances will be connected to the Internet of Things.

5 The history of _____ (wear) technology began hundreds of years ago with the watch.

2 8A GRAMMAR AND VOCABULARY **Complete the sentences with one word in each gap.**

1 The microchip carries a unique number and is e*mbeded* under the skin of your dog's neck.

2 The government's secret database was h_____ into over the weekend.

3 This device will a_____ your doctor if your blood pressure drops to a dangerously low level.

4 The heating in the house can be controlled using a s_____ device such as a phone or tablet.

5 Smart clothing makes it possible to t_____ your body's fat and water content.

3 8B SPEAKING AND VOCABULARY **Choose the correct words to complete the text.**

The graph illustrates the sales of our product – the tracking undies. They became immediately popular, and between 2016 and 2019 their sales **1**dropped / increased steadily from fifty thousand a year to around seventy thousand a year. Overall, it's a(n) **2**upward / downward trend: sales are predicted to continue to **3**rise / decrease slightly to around seventy-five thousand a year in 2021 before **4**growing / declining more **5**sharply / steadily between 2021 and 2023 to a hundred thousand a year. We expect a gradual **6**decline / growth starting in 2025 so we need a new product by 2022.

4 8C VOCABULARY **Complete the online review with the words from the box.**

compatibility   device   handle   ~~latest~~   outdated
state-of-the-art   upgrade

The **1***latest* smart speaker from Target-tech was released just yesterday. The Room-fill 2.0 is a **2**_____ piece of equipment for those looking to **3**_____ their **4**_____ audio speakers with a conveniently portable **5**_____. The speaker boasts excellent **6**_____ with any computer, tablet, TV or smartphone. It is also able to **7**_____ high volumes with no impact on its excellent sound quality.

5 8D READING AND VOCABULARY **Replace the underlined parts with the correct forms of the phrasal verbs from the box.**

~~break off~~   eat away at   end up   fit in with   go through
hold down

1 People stopped what they were doing to watch the beautiful sunset. *broke off*

2 We travelled across Europe and finished in Krakow. _____

3 I've never experienced the break-up of a serious relationship. _____

4 I wasn't like the other kids at school. _____

5 Gina managed to do her job for six months before it got too much and she quit. _____

6 Jasmine's poor exam results reduced her confidence. _____

6 8D READING AND VOCABULARY **Complete the sentences with the words from the box.**

~~hypersensitivity~~   meltdown   neurotypical   overload
overwhelming

1 Legend says vampires suffer from *hypersensitivity* to light.

2 Derek covered his eyes due to the sensory _____ he experienced in the street.

3 '_____' is a word used by autistic people to describe people who do not have autism.

4 The menu is so large that many customers find it _____ and prefer to ask for a recommendation.

5 Frustration, anxiety, stress and depression together can lead to what some people call an emotional _____.

7 8E LISTENING AND VOCABULARY **Complete the text with the words from the box.**

curate   ~~deceptive~~   enhance   features   flattering
flaws   superficial

Appearances can be **1***deceptive*. Most of the photos in magazine adverts have been digitally altered to **2**_____ how the models look and present a more **3**_____ picture of their physical attributes. Spots, wrinkles and other **4**_____ in their skin may have been removed just like their body shapes and facial **5**_____ may have been changed significantly. On a **6**_____ level, this may result in a more beautiful image, but looking deeper, these 'fake' images may in fact be harmful to the young people viewing them. Some young men and women make huge efforts to **7**_____ a model-like image on their social-media feeds, but what they are aiming for might be unachievable without digital alterations and lead to low self-esteem.

8 ON A HIGH NOTE **Write a paragraph about an old or outdated gadget or device you own and give details of what you would like to replace it with.**

1 For each learning objective, write 1–5 to assess your ability.

1 = I don't feel confident. 5 = I feel confident.

	Learning objective	Course material	How confident I am (1–5)
8A	I can use the passive to talk about actions.	Student's Book pp. 108–109	
8B	I can describe trends and talk about the Internet of Things.	Student's Book p. 110	
8C	I can talk about technology and gadgets.	Student's Book p. 111	
8D	I can identify specific details in a text and talk about virtual reality.	Student's Book pp. 112–113	
8E	I can understand fast speech and talk about taking selfies.	Student's Book p. 114	
8F	I can use impersonal passive structures to talk about beliefs and opinions.	Student's Book p. 115	
8G	I can write a balanced for-and-against essay.	Student's Book pp. 116–117	

2 Which of the skills above would you like to improve in? How?

Skill I want to improve in	How I can improve

3 What can you remember from this unit?

New words I learned and most want to remember	Expressions and phrases I liked	English I heard or read outside class

Self-check

08

GRAMMAR AND VOCABULARY

1 Choose the correct words to complete the sentences.

1 My computer crashed last night – thank goodness I'd *backed up / held down* my files.
2 I'm going to *end up / break off* from studying and make some lunch in a minute.
3 Nobody is perfect – we all have our *attributes / flaws*.
4 Kerry found that meeting her father for the first time was a(n) *overwhelming / flattering* experience.
5 A serious *functionality / malfunction* with the city's water system means no water for the next three hours.

/ 5

2 Complete the sentences with one word in each gap.

1 My granddad still has bits of metal e*mbeded* in his leg after fighting in the war.
2 At the museum of o_____ technology we display technology that is no longer used by society.
3 Are you sure you have the l_____ version of the software installed?
4 A w_____ of anxiety hit Karin when she realised it was 4 a.m. and Maxwell still wasn't home.
5 This is such a f_____ picture of you; it makes you look even more beautiful than usual.
6 This browser is d_____ and doesn't function as fast as the latest versions.

/ 5

3 Complete the sentences with the correct forms of *to be*.

1 Spectators are required *to be* quiet while the game is in progress.
2 I don't enjoy _____ watched while I eat.
3 Any malfunctions should _____ picked up by the sensors and shown on this screen.
4 Old devices and appliances _____ recycled here free of charge until recently.
5 Our smartwatches have _____ designed and built by Swiss professionals for the last six years.
6 The new gadget produced by this company isn't _____ sold in Europe.

/ 5

4 Rewrite the sentences using impersonal passive structures.

1 They think that the device exploded during the flight.
It *is thought that the device exploded during the flight*.
2 At first, they reported that the killer was innocent.
At first, it _____.
3 Experts have claimed that a bird caused the accident when it flew into the engine.
A bird _____.
4 Cyber police revealed that hackers had accessed the bank's security system.
Hackers _____.
5 We know that the students are safely back at school.
The students _____.
6 In 1916, people thought that cinema would never become popular.
In 1916, it _____.

/ 5

USE OF ENGLISH

5 Complete the online post with one word in each gap.

Statistics show that there is a steady growth ¹*in* the number of household appliances we buy. What makes me furious is that so many perfectly good devices such as fridges and washing machines end up ²_____ thrown away simply because the owners prefer to have the latest model. ³_____ is often claimed that this is normal in our modern, consumer society. People say I should calm ⁴_____ and accept that there is nothing I can do personally, but the general lack of concern for the environment is eating ⁵_____ at me and I feel something ⁶_____ to be done to raise awareness of the issue. That's why I've started this social media group.

/ 5

6 Complete the sentences with the correct words formed from the words in bold.

Space Captain Varanessi realised that the door of her ship wouldn't open because the ¹*facial* (FACE) recognition software had stopped working. It was meant to have been ²_____ (GRADE) during the last service at Home Station AZ-57. The ship's old computer was virtually obsolete compared to the ³_____ (LATE) models and to keep flying she needed a system with much better ⁴_____ (FUNCTION). It was often remarked that ⁵_____ (DATE) ships such as hers were 'accidents waiting to happen' and she worried that the risk to her crew was going up ⁶_____ (DRAMA) with every passing day.

/ 5
/ 30

99

09 Highs and lows

9A GRAMMAR AND VOCABULARY

Conditionals

1 ⭐ Match the two parts of the sentences.

1 ☐ Unless you're very well-off,
2 ☐ Viola wouldn't run out of cash every month
3 ☐ You can live on very little
4 ☐ If money grew on trees,
5 ☐ My parents wouldn't be as well-off as they are
6 ☐ If you hadn't received an inheritance,

a if she didn't splash out every time she went shopping.
b you'll need to borrow money to buy a house.
c you might actually have needed to work for a living.
d if I'd gone to a costly private school.
e I wouldn't have had to work so hard all my life.
f if you manage your finances carefully.

2 ⭐ Match types of conditionals a–f with sentences 1–6 from Exercise 1.

a ☐ Zero conditional: a situation that the speaker considers always or generally true.
b ☐ First conditional: a situation that the speaker considers likely to happen in the future.
c ☐ Second conditional: a hypothetical or improbable situation in the present or future.
d ☐ Third conditional: a hypothetical situation in the past.
e ☐ Mixed conditional: the present consequences of a hypothetical past situation.
f ☐ Mixed conditional: the effects of a hypothetical present situation on the past.

3 ⭐ Read the sentences. Then choose the correct words to complete explanations a and b.

1 If video games weren't so costly, I'd buy a new one every month.
   a Video games *are / aren't* costly.
   b I *buy / don't buy* a new one every month.
2 If Snoopy had entered the Surf Dog competition, he would definitely have won.
   a He *entered / didn't enter* the competition.
   b He *won / didn't win*.
3 If you don't buy the car today, it will be more expensive tomorrow.
   a You are *recommended / not recommended* to buy the car today.
   b The car costs *more / less* today than it will tomorrow.
4 If we were affluent, we would've bought a big flat.
   a We *are / aren't* affluent.
   b We *bought / didn't buy* a big flat.
5 If Anastasia's business had been more lucrative, she wouldn't be trying to sell it.
   a Anastasia's business *was / wasn't* lucrative.
   b She *is / isn't* trying to sell it.

4 ⭐⭐ Complete the sentences with the phrases from the box. There are three extra phrases.

---
cancel   don't struggle   'll pick you up   weren't
weren't struggling   ~~would have to~~   wouldn't be feeling
wouldn't need   you will cancel
---

1 If we spent more on society and less on defence, fewer people <u>would have to</u> live in hardship.
2 If we'd eaten breakfast, we _____ so hungry now.
3 If our house hadn't been burgled, I _____ a replacement passport.
4 I _____ at 6 p.m. outside the shopping centre unless I hear differently.
5 If we _____ for money, I'd have bought my fiancée a nicer ring.
6 _____ your bank cards immediately if you lose your wallet.

100

5 ★★ Complete the mini-conversations with the correct forms of the verbs in brackets. Use short forms where possible.

David If you weren't so cute, I **1**_wouldn't have rescued_ (not rescue) you from the dog shelter, right?

Boomer Woof!

Ashley If I **2**_____ (pass) my exams, I would be at university now.

Lucy True, but at least you are earning money rather than getting into debt.

Marcus Don't you know what to do?

Lisa Marcus, if I knew what to do, I **3**_____ (not ask) for your help.

Alma I thought you were one of those unusual people who don't like chocolate.

Will If I **4**_____ (not like) chocolate, I wouldn't have made chocolate cake, would I?

Jarvis If I was richer, I **5**_____ (donate) some money to help the poor people affected by the last hurricane.

Thabo I guess you could donate some goods instead.

Yang If you **6**_____ (not be) so extravagant during your last shopping trip, you'd have enough money left to go out this weekend.

Pierre I know, I know! Could I borrow £20?

6 ★★ USE OF ENGLISH Choose the correct words a–c to complete the text.

1 a aren't   **b** weren't   **c** wouldn't be
2 a 're   **b** 'd   **c** 'll
3 a unless   **b** as   **c** when
4 a buy   **b** bought   **c** 'd buy
5 a mightn't   **b** might   **c** will
6 a would be   **b** is   **c** will be

7 ★★★ Complete the sentences with *unless*, *if* or, where possible, *when*.

1 _Unless_ you pay me back right now, I'm going to tell Mum and Dad.

2 You'll laugh _____ I tell you what happened to me yesterday.

3 _____ you don't feel like going then don't go!

4 Don't bother making coffee for me _____ you're making one yourself.

5 _____ I told you a secret, would you be able to keep it?

6 _____ the clock strikes midnight, the race will begin.

8 ★★★ Use the prompts to write conditional sentences. Use short forms where possible.

1 Jerry went to hospital straight away. He didn't become seriously ill.

If Jerry hadn't gone to hospital straight away, he'd have become seriously ill.

2 Sara visited Spain and loved it. She is learning Spanish now.

_____

3 Mina is extremely tall. She can reach the top cupboard in the kitchen.

_____

4 I didn't study hard. I don't have an offer for a place at university.

_____

5 Rebekah doesn't like heights. We didn't go up the Eiffel Tower.

_____

6 Hagen didn't have his hair cut. He looks scruffy.

_____

9 ON A HIGH NOTE Write a paragraph explaining how your life would have been different if you'd grown up in a different country.

LAMP-SHOP
SPECIAL OFFER!

The Adjusta-Lamp Pro is the best smart desk lamp on the market. Believe us, if they **1**___ so great, we wouldn't have installed them as standard in our own offices! Adjusta-Lamp Pro is available now at a bargain price. If you miss this offer, you **2**___ regret it. Why? Because **3**___ we say bargain, we mean BARGAIN! If you **4**___ this lamp at any other shop, it would cost at least £99, but we're proud to offer it for just £59!

Place your order now as stocks are running out fast! In fact, if we'd known how popular this lamp was going to be, we **5**___ have offered it at such a low price!

24-hour delivery guaranteed – if you'd ordered last night, it **6**___ sitting on your desk right now! Don't wait another day. Order right away!

9B LISTENING AND VOCABULARY

1 🔊 *60* **Listen to four people talking about apologising and complete the notes with one word in each gap.**

1 Speaker 1 has fallen out with his *sister*.
2 Speaker 2 lives in _____.
3 Speaker 3 used to be a _____.
4 Speaker 4 gossiped about a _____.

2 🔊 *60* **Listen again. What does each person say about apologising? Match speakers 1–4 with sentences a–g. There are three extra sentences.**

Speaker 1 ☐   Speaker 3 ☐
Speaker 2 ☐   Speaker 4 ☐

a Apologies are not always welcome.
b If you overuse the word 'sorry', it loses its meaning.
c Apologies are necessary for society to function properly.
d Feelings of guilt can be reduced by apologising.
e If someone apologises, you ought to forgive them.
f Consider apologising even for things that aren't your fault.
g Apologise for small things before they cause greater conflict.

Vocabulary extension

3 🔊 *61* **Complete the sentences, which you heard in the recording in Exercise 1, with the verbs from the box. Listen and check.**

acknowledge admitting learned make offer take

1 It's not easy to *acknowledge* your mistakes and say sorry.
2 In most situations she is incapable of _____ that she's wrong.
3 Her 'shortcut' actually took twice as long, but did she _____ the blame or _____ an apology?
4 So when I saw him recently in a coffee shop, I decided to try and _____ amends.
5 You could say that the experience was a blessing in disguise because I _____ some important lessons.

4 ON A HIGH NOTE **Write a short note to a friend apologising for something you said or did that upset them.**

Pronunciation

5 🔊 *62* **Listen to some sentences from the recording in Exercise 1. Then hum the intonation of the underlined phrases to trace how the voice rises and falls.**

1 <u>Just yesterday</u>, we were driving around looking for this shop she wanted to go to.
2 <u>To be honest</u>, apologising is kind of like a habit in Taiwan, and I think it makes it less genuine.
3 <u>Before long</u>, it had spread and I spent forty-eight hours feeling awful and then decided I couldn't stand it anymore.

ACTIVE PRONUNCIATION
Intonation in adverbial phrases

English intonation has a pattern which falls and rises again within one phrase. We can use this fall-rise tone in adverbial phrases.

• *actually* (æk\tʃʊə/li)
• *in my opinion* (ɪn maɪ\ə'pɪn/jən)
• *to be honest* (tə bi 'ɒn\ɪst/)

6 🔊 *63* **Listen to some more adverbial phrases and repeat, paying particular attention to the fall-rise intonation pattern.**

1 Actually, …   3 To tell you the truth, …
2 On the whole, …   4 As you know, …

7 🔊 *64* **Look at the short text and listen. Find the phrases that follow the fall-rise tone pattern. Read the text aloud.**

Recently, I've been feeling much better. To be perfectly honest, it's the best I've felt for a long time. It's hard to say what's happened, but in my opinion it's all down to positive thinking.

8 🔊 *65* **Work with a partner. Practise reading the dialogue. Then listen and check.**

Adam Have you got any interesting plans for summer?
Ben <u>Actually</u>, we aren't doing anything special this year. Travelling is so expensive.
Adam <u>If you ask me</u>, it's OK to splash out from time to time.
Ben <u>To tell you the truth</u>, that's what I told my family, but I couldn't change their minds.
Adam <u>In my opinion</u>, it's worth going away even if it's just for a couple of days.

9C **VOCABULARY** | Chance and risk

1 ⭐ Complete the puzzle with the missing parts of the binomials. What is the mystery binomial?

		³					⁸
			⁴				
¹U	²			⁵	⁶	⁷	
P			and				
S							

1 ___ and downs
2 ___ and take
3 ___ and go
4 ___ ___ or leave it
5 ___ and then
6 safe and ___
7 ___ or less
8 sooner or ___

The mystery binominal is _____.

2 ⭐⭐ Replace the underlined parts with the binominals from Exercise 1.

1 Wherever my cat has disappeared to, I just hope he'll come home <u>with no problems</u>. *safe and sound*

2 Visitors to the museum can <u>select</u> from over 100 arcade games from the 80s and 90s. _____

3 Don't be too hard on yourself. After all, most people fail at something <u>at some point</u>. _____

4 Like every business we have our <u>good and bad times</u> but generally we are successful. _____

5 I can't sell it for less than £100. That's my lowest price – <u>accept it or don't</u>. _____

6 <u>Compromise</u> is the recipe for success in a long-term relationship. _____

7 We are <u>almost</u> finished here so I can meet you in about half an hour. _____

8 I told him <u>immediately</u> that if he lied to me again, our friendship would be over. _____

9 It was <u>uncertain</u> whether the rescue team would be able to save the man in the cave. _____

3 ⭐⭐ What does the word *chance* mean in the sentences below? Choose *O* for opportunity, *P* for possibility, *R* for risk or *L* for luck.

1 If I had the chance to try skydiving, I'd take it. O / P / R / L

2 The chances are we'll win the match unless Scoggins gets injured. O / P / R / L

3 This is your chance to show what a superb singing voice you have. O / P / R / L

4 The lost manuscript was found by chance during renovations at the museum. O / P / R / L

5 There's a chance we'll have to cancel the BBQ if the weather is really bad. O / P / R / L

6 I discovered this dish by chance when I added salt instead of sugar. O / P / R / L

7 There's almost no chance you'll win the game. O / P / R / L

4 ⭐⭐ Complete the sentences with *chance*, *risk*, *luck* or *opportunity*. Sometimes more than one answer is possible.

1 The <u>risk</u> of injury or even death is very high for base-jumping wing-suit flyers.

2 You've won three games in a row now – what _____!

3 It's already 10 p.m. so there is very little _____ of me staying awake for a whole film.

4 Given the _____, I'd love to take a sports car out for a drive.

5 The country simply must grab this _____ to host the next Olympic Games.

6 By _____ I looked down and saw that I'd dropped my keys.

7 Don't miss this once in a lifetime _____ to meet your favourite TV stars face-to-face!

5 ⭐⭐⭐ Complete the mini-conversations with suitable binominals.

Kerem I was worried about you Azize! I'm so glad you are home ¹*safe and sound*.

Azize I said I'd be back by 9 o'clock and it's ... ten past so I'm ² _____ on time.

Fidel The neighbours were arguing again last night.

Eduardo Hmm, that sucks. I suppose every couple have their ³ _____.

Fidel I guess it's true what they say about compromise; a successful relationship requires plenty of ⁴ _____.

Ryu I'm making omelettes, if you want one.

Satoshi Omelettes, huh? Not very exciting. How about something else?

Ryu It's omelettes or nothing, ⁵ _____.

Satoshi Hmm. Omelettes would be lovely, thanks.

Clive You really need to wear a helmet when you're on your bike, Lenny. ⁶ _____ you're going to injure yourself. It's only a matter of time!

Lenny I know, but I can't afford to buy one this month. I'll get one soon.

9D READING AND VOCABULARY

1 Look at the photos of Ellie Simmonds. Who do you think she is? What might she have taken a gap year from? Read the introduction to the article and check your ideas.

2 Read the text again and match headings A–F with paragraphs 1–6.
  A Taking risks
  B Finding my global community
  C The search for anonymity
  D Finding a new direction
  E Overcoming my fears
  F Learning the kindness of strangers

3 Read the article again and choose the correct answers.
  1 What do you think would be the best title for the article?
    a How my gap year taught me who I am.
    b How I learned to love the sea on my gap year.
    c How my gap year helped me become a champion.
    d My gap year: a welcome break from fame.
  2 What does Ellie say about being a traveller in Paragraph 1?
    a Having a foreign accent doesn't help you make friends.
    b It's easy for a famous person to travel abroad anonymously.
    c Locals are more honest with you because you're a stranger.
    d People are curious about you because you are an outsider.
  3 How did Ellie feel when the Thai man helped her across the road?
    a She was annoyed by his assumptions.
    b She was embarrassed by the situation.
    c She misunderstood his intentions.
    d She understood his reasons.
  4 Why does Ellie say she wants to go into teaching?
    a Because she loves children and wants to go to university.
    b Because she feels she has a valuable lesson to teach children.
    c Because she plans to end her swimming career.
    d Because that's what her parents want her to do.
  5 Why does Ellie refer to herself as 'just Ellie' in Paragraph 6?
    a Because she felt more confident of herself after her trip.
    b Because she wasn't travelling in connection with her swimming career.
    c Because she was travelling alone for most of the trip.
    d Because she left her friend in Vietnam.

Vocabulary extension

4 Match the highlighted words from the text with the definitions.
  1 Walked around without a specific purpose. _wandered_
  2 Appear or become known. _____
  3 Person who does not belong to a group. _____
  4 Put in prison. _____
  5 People who are the same age or have the same job/social position, etc. _____
  6 Careful because you are worried someone/something may be harmful. _____

5 Complete the sentences with the words from Exercise 4.
  1 When I first started at my new school, I felt like an _outsider_, but now I have lots of friends.
  2 The famous singer was _____ for two months after being caught avoiding taxes.
  3 It's better not to lie because the truth will almost always _____ in the end.
  4 Teenagers usually choose to spend their free time with their _____.
  5 We _____ around the affluent part of the city and saw some rather extravagant architecture.
  6 Ken is _____ of splashing out on designer clothes and shoes.

ACTIVE VOCABULARY | Suffix -ist

The suffix -ist can be added to certain nouns to describe a person who practises or is concerned with something, or who holds certain beliefs.
  • A **psychiatrist** is someone who practices psychiatry.
  • A **socialist** is someone who believes in socialism.
  • A **gold medallist** is someone who has won a gold medal.

---

6 Complete the definitions with the correct nouns ending in the suffix -ist. Use a dictionary to help you if necessary.
  1 A _novelist_ is someone who writes novels.
  2 An _____ is someone who holds extreme beliefs.
  3 A _____ is someone who is concerned with language and linguistics.
  4 A _____ is someone who owns and/or rides a motorcycle.
  5 An _____ is someone who is concerned with the economy.
  6 A _____ is someone who makes it to the final of a competition.
  7 A _____ is someone who believes in the system of capitalism.
  8 An _____ is someone who believes in protecting the natural environment.

7 ON A HIGH NOTE Write a short comment to post after the text you read about Ellie Simmonds. Give your reaction to the text and your opinion of what you read.

UNIT VOCABULARY PRACTICE > page 109

Ellie Simmonds, the Paralympic swimming gold medallist, took a solo trip around the world which tested her spirit and helped her realise how life after swimming might be. Here she describes her experiences.

...

I love airports. The moment I step into one, I know that I'm heading off on an adventure. Usually, I'm on my way to compete somewhere. For most of my life, I've been focused on my swimming routine: waking at 5.30 a.m. to swim from 6 a.m. until 8 a.m., going straight to school until 3 p.m. and then directly back to the pool to train for two more hours. Through swimming, I get to go to loads of amazing places, but I often see little more than the hotel, the airport and the swimming pool. Just over a year ago, right after the Rio Paralympics, I packed my bag for a different type of trip. I wanted to get away, consider my options for the future and be a normal, anonymous twenty-one-year-old. I visited nine countries over the course of the year, working and backpacking, mainly alone, but also meeting up with friends. Looking back, a few themes emerge.

1 ☐ The first thing that happened on my gap year was that I was upgraded. The charming flight attendants recognised me and moved me to first class for my flight from London to San Francisco. Once there, I just walked and spent my days people-watching. One day in a café, a woman sat down and started telling me all about her son, who had just been jailed. I think my UK accent gave her a sense of privacy. If I was American, she probably wouldn't have opened up to me in the same way. This is one of the privileges of being a traveller: your outsider status gains you access to people's lives.

2 ☐ A few years ago I did a TV documentary in Mozambique about swimming with dolphins and I met the free-diving expert and ocean conservationist, Hanli Prinsloo. This year we went to Mexico together, and swam with whale sharks. A few months later, I met her again in Cape Town and we surfed. I used to be very wary of the sea, and it's only recently – and largely thanks to these experiences – that I stopped feeling afraid.

3 ☐ When I was in Thailand on my own, I wandered down back alleys that I probably shouldn't have – it was quite scary. It was wonderful to explore, but I felt like I was jumping into people's lives, and possibly invading their space. I also went to Vietnam with a friend and we took an overnight train. Was that a dangerous thing for two young women to do? That's hard to say, but we didn't run into any problems, except for some very smelly toilets, which we had no choice but to use!

4 ☐ While I was in Canada, I travelled to Ontario, for the Seventh World Dwarf Games, where I was part of the British football team. We trained for a few days in preparation for the competition, and I'm so glad I did it. If I hadn't gone, I wouldn't have all these new friendships with people from the dwarf community across the world. I met people from India, Russia, America – everywhere.

5 ☐ I spent more time alone this year than I ever have before, which can be isolating, but it can also help you to realise how friendly the world is. While in Bangkok, a Thai man helped me across the road. I was standing on a street corner and he decided that I needed help to cross the street. Of course, I didn't: I have achondroplasia, a common cause of dwarfism, but I'm perfectly capable of getting about on my own. Still, he was trying to be kind. Neither of us could actually make ourselves understood, but I said 'thank you' and he smiled.

6 ☐ Visiting schools everywhere from Cape Town to Shanghai, and meeting children wherever I went, has convinced me that I'd like to go into teaching. There's so much pressure on children – from social media, from their peers, from their parents – telling them what they should look like, how they should feel about things. Once I retire from swimming, I'd love to go to university and become a primary school teacher. I'd like to guide children into being comfortable with who they are, and not feel they have to try to change themselves. I have often visited places as an ambassador for Paralympics GB, and I'm really proud of that. But on this trip, I wasn't a gold-medal winner, I was just Ellie, and, to my surprise, that gave me huge confidence. I would recommend a gap year to anyone who wants to learn more about themselves and their place in the world.

9E GRAMMAR

wish/if only, past modals

1 ⭐ Choose the correct options to explain the meaning of the sentences in bold.

1 **I wish I could stop biting my nails.**

   The speaker *can* / *can't* stop biting their nails.

2 **If only Agnes knew how I felt about her.**

   Agnes *does* / *doesn't* know how the speaker feels about her.

3 **They needn't have bought a ticket.**

   The speaker is talking about someone who *did* / *didn't* buy a ticket.

4 **It was sunny so we didn't need to wear our raincoats.**

   The speakers *did* / *didn't* wear their raincoats.

5 **I should have asked if the boy needed help.**

   It was a good idea to ask if the boy needed help, *so the speaker did* / *but the speaker didn't*.

6 **Omar could have given Millie a lift into town.**

   Millie *did* / *didn't* get a lift into town from Omar.

2 ⭐⭐ Complete the sentences with the correct forms of the verbs in brackets.

1 I wish I ___*knew*___ (know) what questions they plan to ask during the English oral exam.

2 If only I _____ (walk) to school yesterday instead of going by bike.

3 You needn't _____ (buy) that new charging cable but I guess it's good we've got a spare one.

4 We didn't need _____ (bring) our waterproof jackets afterall.

5 I wish I _____ (can be) at the world cup finals last month and seen my country win.

6 Looking back, perhaps I _____ (should not say) anything, but I did so it's too late now.

7 We wish you _____ (stop) complaining and just get on with your work.

8 You _____ (should tell) me you were vegetarian – I've made beef burgers.

3 ⭐⭐ Complete the second sentence using the correct forms of the underlined verbs.

1 I wish I <u>were</u> luckier.

   I wish I ___*had been*___ luckier the last time I bought a lottery ticket.

2 If only I <u>could afford</u> to buy a new scooter.

   If only I _____ to buy a new scooter for my sister's last birthday.

3 I wish <u>you'd been</u> here to watch me perform yesterday.

   I wish you _____ here to watch me perform now.

4 If only we<u>'d known</u> where you were, we'd have come to get you.

   If only we _____ where you are, we would come and get you.

5 You <u>should probably see</u> a doctor immediately.

   You _____ a doctor as soon as it happened.

4 ⭐⭐⭐ Complete the dialogue with the correct forms of the words in brackets. Use short forms where possible.

Alvin Did you read about that guy who unlocked that safe in Canada?

Bart Er ... what? Is this a joke?

Alvin No! I read it online – it's a true story. He was visiting a museum in Alberta and there was this safe there that nobody had been able to unlock for 40 years. Anyway, he tried a random combination and opened it first time!

Bart Wow. Lucky guy. If only he ¹___*'d visited*___ (visit) earlier!

Alvin Ha! I wish I ² _____ (be) that lucky.

Bart So what was inside?

Alvin Well, he probably ³ _____ (need not bother) to be honest because there were just a couple of old documents.

Bart What a shame! If only it ⁴ _____ (be) something more exciting or mysterious there.

Alvin I guess they ⁵ _____ (could give) a prize, or something for cracking the code.

Bart It sounds like he ⁶ _____ (should buy) a lottery ticket instead – I mean if you're going to have a lucky day, you might as well win something.

Alvin True enough.

5 ON A HIGH NOTE Write a paragraph mentioning two things you regret doing and two things you regret not doing.

1 🔊 66 Listen and repeat the phrases. How do you say them in your language?

SPEAKING | Discussing advantages and disadvantages

A major advantage of travelling solo **is that** it's cheaper than travelling with family or friends.

One minor argument for travelling solo **is that** it pushes you out of your comfort zone.

Another obvious benefit of travelling solo **is that** you will get to know yourself better.

The first possible good point about travelling solo **is that** you will make a lot of new friends.

One potential positive aspect of travelling solo **is that** you get to choose your own route.

One significant argument against travelling solo **is that** it might not be safe.

Another possible disadvantage of travelling solo **is that** there's nobody to share the experience.

A potential downside to travelling solo **is that** you can't share the travelling expenses.

The first possible drawback of travelling solo **is that** it's difficult to book a single room.

Another obvious negative aspect of travelling solo **is that** you have to carry all your luggage alone.

A significant minus point of travelling solo **is that** you have nobody to help you make decisions.

SUMMING UP YOUR ARGUMENTS/GIVING YOUR OPINION

On first consideration, this seems like a good reason for travelling solo.

Ultimately, there are arguments on both sides. However, I prefer to travel with a friend.

Having looked at both sides of the argument, I think that travelling with others is more satisfying.

Having looked at both sides of the argument, I believe that travelling alone is best.

Although some people might disagree, I can't help feeling that travelling solo could get lonely.

---

2 Match the two parts of the sentences.

1. ☐ Having looked at both sides
2. ☐ Although some people might disagree,
3. ☐ Ultimately, there are
4. ☐ Another significant minus
5. ☐ The first major

a arguments on both sides.
b I can't help feeling we made a poor decision.
c point of living in the city centre is the noise.
d advantage of going vegetarian is the benefit to health.
e of the argument, I believe you are correct.

3 USE OF ENGLISH Complete the second sentence using the word in bold so that it means the same as the first one. Use between two and five words, including the word in bold.

1 A major negative aspect of nuclear power is the potential for an accident. **DRAWBACK**

A major _drawback of nuclear power_ is the potential for an accident.

2 Another significant minus point of winter sports is the damage they cause to mountain environments. **ARGUMENT**

Another significant _____ is the damage they cause to mountain environments.

3 Initially, this seems like a forward-thinking solution to the problem. **CONSIDERATION**

_____, this seems like a forward-thinking solution to the problem.

4 Another obvious downside to studying overseas is the need to leave friends and family behind. **ASPECT**

Another obvious _____ is the need to leave friends and family behind.

5 Ultimately, there are pluses and minuses to using speed bumps to try and reduce the number of road accidents. **ARGUMENTS**

Ultimately, there are _____ of the debate about using speed bumps to try and reduce the number of road accidents.

4 USE OF ENGLISH Complete the mini-conversations with one word in each gap.

Marsha A possible good point [1]_of_ this university is the city centre location.

Alexi Well, [2]_____ first consideration, this seems like it would be a plus, but there are also drawbacks to urban campuses.

James A major argument [3]_____ zoos is that the animals have no freedom.

Laura Although some people might disagree, I can't [4]_____ feeling that not having to worry about hunting or being hunted is a potential positive aspect [5]_____ living in a zoo.

Kylie Having looked [6]_____ both sides of the argument, I believe that school uniforms are actually a very good idea.

Zac Well, ultimately there are arguments [7]_____ both sides, but I agree that the pluses outweigh the minuses.

Veronica A potential downside [8]_____ asking people to sort their rubbish into five categories rather than three is that it will put them off recycling.

Eric You see, I don't think recycling should be a matter of choice. One major advantage [9]_____ making it a legal requirement is that people are forced to do it.

5 ON A HIGH NOTE Write a short dialogue in which you continue one of the conversations from Exercise 4.

Use a suitable greeting to begin your letter.

In the opening paragraph, say why you are writing.

In the main body, convince the reader why you deserve to win the competition or be chosen as an applicant.

Use more formal linkers to add ideas.

Mention any relevant qualifications.

Use emphatic structures to make your points stronger.

Give details of any relevant experience you have (work experience or hobbies) and say why it is relevant and what skills you developed.

Close with a suitable phrase and a sign-off that complements the greeting you used to open your letter.

Dear [1]Sir/Madam,

I am writing [2]to apply for the job of Euro-grounds campsite host – French Alps, which was advertised recently on your website.

I [3]have always been fascinated by French culture and it has been my lifelong ambition to work in the great outdoors of the French Alps. I am a keen walker and cyclist and have a great interest in mountain environments and their plants and animals. If I got this job, I would enjoy sharing my knowledge with campsite guests.

Working as a campsite host would appeal to me enormously for several reasons. As previously mentioned, I love the outdoors and am a keen camper myself. As such, the setting up, cleaning and maintenance of Euro-grounds' tents and caravans would come naturally to me. [4]In addition, according to friends and colleagues, I'm a sociable and easy-going person and I'm sure I would really enjoy welcoming guests to the site and chatting with them during their stay.

I [5]have studied French at B2 level, and feel confident that my language skills would enable me to interact meaningfully with local staff and suppliers. Furthermore, I do have some experience of solving holiday-makers' problems after working at my aunt and uncles' guest house during school holidays. [6]Amongst my other duties there, I was [7]responsible for the front desk during the busy morning shifts. If I was chosen to work for Euro-grounds, I could draw on this experience and would welcome the chance to learn more about customer service in the tourism industry.

I've attached my CV. If you require any further information, please do not hesitate to contact me.

I look forward to hearing from you.

[8]Yours faithfully,

Marcel Bongers

1 Read the letter and tick the things Marcel can offer.
  1 ☑ a foreign language
  2 ☐ an interest in the outdoors
  3 ☐ a qualification in tourism
  4 ☐ an outgoing personality
  5 ☐ experience in a similar job

2 Match underlined words and phrases 1–8 from the letter with their counterparts a–h.
  a ☐ in charge of   **e** ☐ gained a qualification in
  b ☐ with reference to   **f** ☐ am passionate about
  c ☐ Yours sincerely   **g** ☐ Mr Koos
  d ☐ As part of my role   **h** ☐ Moreover

3 WRITING TASK Write a letter of application for a summer job as a tour guide for young foreign visitors to your city. Mention your language skills and any other relevant experience or qualifications.

ACTIVE WRITING
A competition entry / A letter of application

1 Plan your letter.
  - Consider why you deserve to be given a chance at this job.
  - Make some notes about suitable skills and experience that would help you with this position.
  - Think about what you can say to persuade the reader that you are a strong candidate for the vacancy.

2 Write the letter.
  - Use a formal/semi-formal writing style including formal linkers to add ideas.
  - Use emphatic structures to make your points stronger.
  - Make sure the sign-off at the end of your letter matches the greeting at the beginning.

3 Check that …
  - all the relevant information is there.
  - there are no spelling, grammar or punctuation mistakes.

UNIT VOCABULARY PRACTICE

1 9A GRAMMAR AND VOCABULARY **Complete the extract from a city guide book with one word in each gap.**

Panta Vella is an old and ¹affluent area of the city where the inhabitants either have very ²l_____e careers or else large ³i_____es from their wealthy parents. Residents here are more than ⁴w_____–_____f; they can afford to ⁵s_____h out on expensive cars, prestigious private schools and ⁶c_____y designer clothes. Meanwhile, less than a kilometre away in Las Gidunas, hundreds of families live in ⁷h_____p, unable to put ⁸a_____e any money at the end of the month. Such contrasting circumstances are common in this country.

2 9B LISTENING AND VOCABULARY **Choose the correct words and phrases to complete the sentences.**

1 I'd like to remind you that there is a lot *in disguise / at stake* in today's auditions.

2 There has been a further *masterstroke / setback* for the unlucky climbers stuck on K2.

3 I've *flourished / messed up* my signature on my new debit card and I don't know what to do.

4 It can take many years for students to *pay off / put aside* their student loans.

5 I'm *getting nowhere / messing up* with my homework, so I think I'll go to bed and carry on tomorrow.

6 After forgetting Mel's birthday, Omar made a *vain / mixed* attempt to apologise – with flowers from the petrol station.

7 The foreign secretary has made yet another diplomatic *blunder / flop*, this time by insulting the Dutch royal family.

8 Being famous as a child was a *blessing in disguise / mixed blessing* which made some dreams come true and ruined others.

3 9C VOCABULARY **Complete the text messages with one word in each gap.**

You can ¹*pick* and choose from the chocolate bars in the fridge, but leave one for me.

Just to let you know, we've arrived ²_____ and sound in Paris.

The guy offered £100 for the bike – take it or ³_____ it. So I took it.

I've ⁴_____ or less finished my homework so you can come over.

Try not to worry. Every relationship has its ups and ⁵_____ .

I'm sure your spare keys will turn up ⁶_____ or later.

4 9C VOCABULARY **Complete the sentences with *chance*, *luck*, *opportunity* or *risk*.**

1 Base jumping is not worth the *risk* in my opinion.

2 Your mum and I met by _____ at a friend's party.

3 Finding a parking space so easily was a real piece of _____ .

4 Given the _____, what would you like to do as a career?

5 9D READING AND VOCABULARY **Complete the mini-conversations with the correct verb forms.**

Lena What's up, Gracie?

Gracie I'm tired. The stress of revising is ¹*taking* its toll on me.

Lena How about we ²_____ your mind off it with a walk to the ice cream place?

Gracie Now that is a good idea. A double chocolate chip with extra syrup might just be enough to ³_____ me going.

Euan I haven't ⁴_____ a clue what to do with my gap year.

Roma Well, why don't you ⁵_____ your options carefully, and if you're still not sure, maybe you should drop the idea altogether and go straight to uni.

Marie We ⁶_____ through such an ordeal at the hospital in Tokyo. No one spoke English!

Lewis But presumably you managed to ⁷_____ yourself understood in the end?

Marie Well, eventually, though I must have looked like a bit of an idiot. I ⁸_____ no choice but to use mime.

Lewis I wish I'd seen that!

Marie Hmm well. I just ⁹_____ it for granted that someone there would speak English.

Mr Cox We're back! How was our little man, Belinda? Did he wake up?

Belinda He did, but we read a story and he soon fell asleep again.

Mr Cox Stories usually ¹⁰_____ the trick. But just one? Sounds like you ¹¹_____ off lightly. He usually wants three or four before he'll go to sleep.

6 ON A HIGH NOTE **Write a paragraph about the last time you took a risk. What happened? Was everything OK in the end?**

1 **For each learning objective, write 1–5 to assess your ability.**

1 = I don't feel confident. 5 = I feel confident.

	Learning objective	Course material	How confident I am (1–5)
9A	I can use mixed conditionals to talk about present effects of a hypothetical situation in the past.	Student's Book pp. 124–125	
9B	I can identify specific details in a recording and talk about failure and success.	Student's Book p. 126	
9C	I can talk about chance, risk, opportunity and luck.	Student's Book p. 127	
9D	I can identify events in a narrative news story.	Student's Book pp. 128–129	
9E	I can use *I wish/If only/should/need/could* to talk about present and past regrets.	Student's Book p. 130	
9F	I can discuss advantages and disadvantages.	Student's Book p. 131	
9G	I can write a competition entry / a letter of application.	Student's Book pp. 132–133	

2 **Which of the skills above would you like to improve in? How?**

Skill I want to improve in	How I can improve

3 **What can you remember from this unit?**

New words I learned and most want to remember	Expressions and phrases I liked	English I heard or read outside class

GRAMMAR AND VOCABULARY

1 Complete the extract from a short story with one word in each gap.

Uma was looking for a way to take her **¹**_mind_ off the fact that yet again, she had **²**_____ nowhere with her efforts to find a job. She decided to splash **³**_____ on having her nails done at the nail bar. There were hundreds of designs and colours to pick and **⁴**_____ from, but Uma went with black and sharp to match her mood. She couldn't really afford them, but the attention certainly **⁵**_____ the trick and, slowly but **⁶**_____, helped her foget about the frustrating day.

/ 5

2 Find and correct one mistake in each sentence.

1 I earn so little that it's very difficult to put money (inside) for unexpected expenses. _aside_

2 The storm was actually a blessing on disguise as it refilled the dry streams overnight. _____

3 The group were very pleased to be back at the hostel safe or sound. _____

4 Having concerned my options, I'm going to apply to three different universities. _____

5 The soldier had no choice but waiting in the darkness for morning to come. _____

6 A few serious masterstrokes haven't discouraged Kelly from following her dream and becoming a lawyer.
_____

/ 5

3 Choose the correct forms to complete the sentences.

1 If only I _had backed up / would back up_ my documents!

2 I _shouldn't / couldn't_ have been so rude, but I lost my temper.

3 We _didn't need to make / needn't have made_ a meal because we were still full from lunch.

4 I wish you _would have washed / would wash_ your hands more thoroughly.

5 If only I _had have done / had done_ some homework yesterday instead of leaving it all for today.

/ 5

4 Choose the correct words to complete the sentences.

1 If Majid ___ forgotten to buy a lottery ticket last week, he would be a millionaire now.

  a hadn't   **b** had   **c** has

2 If Gary ___ so critical of other people, he might have had more friends at school.

  a isn't   **b** wouldn't be   **c** wasn't

3 ___ Sahar gets eight hours' sleep, she can't concentrate during classes.

  a Unless   **b** If   **c** When

4 If I give my dog a bone, he ___ with happiness.

  a jumped   **b** jumps   **c** would jump

5 When you ___, text me to let me know.

  a arrived   **b** will arrive   **c** arrive

/ 5

USE OF ENGLISH

5 Complete the text with one word in each gap.

The male human started talking in a **¹**_vain_ attempt to make **²**_____ understood. The service robot behind the counter clearly didn't have a **³**_____ what he was talking about. The man had lived on this strange planet for six months, but still had to go **⁴**_____ this ordeal every time he was asked to report to the authorities. He decided to **⁵**_____ and see what happened for another month, but if things went on like this much longer, he **⁶**_____ have to consider moving on again.

/ 5

6 Complete the second sentence using the word in bold so that it means the same as the first one. Use between two and five words, including the word in bold.

1 It wasn't necessary for you to buy me a present. **NEEDN'T**

You _needn't have bought_ me a present.

2 If you don't go to the party, I'm not going. **UNLESS**

I'm not going to the party _____ too.

3 I'd love to have a better understanding of Maths, but I don't. **WISH**

I _____ a better understanding of Maths, but I don't.

4 I really regret sending Polly that email. **ONLY**

If _____ Polly that email.

5 It wasn't a good idea to tell him about the money. **SHOULDN'T**

I _____ about the money.

6 Having no money for food, she didn't have any other choice but to beg for some in the street. **NO**

Having no money for food, she _____ but to beg for some in the street.

/ 5

/ 30

111

10 Culture vulture

10A GRAMMAR AND VOCABULARY

Past modals of speculation

1 ⭐ Choose these parts of the sentences that refer to the past.

1 This ivory comb *might have been made / might be made* for a member of the Dutch royal family.

2 These enormous footprints *can't have belonged / can't belong* to a human.

3 Solid circular earrings like this *must be / must have been* extremely unusual.

4 These bronze coins *may have been used / may be used* to pay soldiers.

5 The pharaoh *must have been wearing / must be wearing* this golden mask during burial.

6 These pointed wooden swords *might be used / might have been used* for practising.

2 ⭐ Choose the most suitable answers to replace the underlined parts in the sentences below.

1 <u>It's possible that the map was</u> drawn by Portuguese sailors.

   a The map must have been   **b** The map can have been
   c The map might have been

2 <u>I'm pretty sure that it was not</u> very accurate compared to today's maps.

   a It must not have been   **b** It can't have been
   c It may not have been

3 <u>I assume the owner</u> used it to navigate across the oceans.

   a The owner would have   **b** The owner might have
   c The owner can have

4 Its creator <u>was quite possibly</u> an explorer.

   a must have been   **b** may well have been
   c would have been

5 <u>It's possible that it wasn't</u> the original but a copy.

   a It couldn't have been   **b** It can't have been
   c It might not have been

6 My assumption is that other navigation tools <u>were used</u> together with the map.

   a would have been used   **b** may have been used
   c might have been used

7 Obviously, in those days, navigators <u>were unable to use</u> GPS because it hadn't been invented.

   a couldn't have used   **b** may well not have used
   c might not have used

3 ⭐⭐ Complete the second sentence with *must/might/can't/would have been* so that it means the same as the first one.

1 It's possible it was a king's helmet.
It *might have been* a king's helmet.

2 I'm sure that it wasn't an ordinary soldier's helmet.
It _____ an ordinary soldier's helmet.

3 The helmet was most likely the most important part of his equipment.
The helmet _____ the most important part of his equipment.

4 I think we can assume that it was very expensive.
It _____ very expensive.

5 I'm sure that it wasn't from this country.
It _____ from this country.

6 I'm sure it was even more beautiful when it was new.
It _____ even more beautiful when it was new.

4 ⭐⭐ Match evidence a–f with sentences 1–6 from Exercise 3.

a ☐ The gold and jewels would have been shinier.

b ☐ It's made of solid gold with costly jewels.

c ☐ A regular soldier could never have afforded such a thing.

d ☐ It has what looks like a royal symbol on the front.

e ☐ The part of the body which needs most protection is the head.

f ☐ No one in this country had the skills to make it at the time.

5 ★★ Complete the mini-conversations with the correct continuous modal forms of the words in brackets.

Max	I saw Dan going into the shopping centre at 10 p.m. last night.
Leo	He **¹** *must have been doing* (must/do) some late night shopping.
Max	He **²**_____ (can't/shop). All the shops are closed at that time.
Leo	True. He **³**_____ (might/go) to see a film. The cinema is open until very late.

Victoria	I thought Kendra seemed really tired today.
Polly	She **⁴**_____ (must/revise) until late at night. She's got an exam on Friday.
Abdul	Our neighbour was standing out in his garden in the middle of the night last night.
Tariq	That's weird. He **⁵**_____ (may/watch) the stars or the planets or something.
Abdul	He **⁶**_____ (couldn't/look) at the stars. It was cloudy all night.

6 ★★ Complete the mini-conversations with the correct forms of the verbs in brackets.

DJ	On the line is retired archaeologist, Professor Douglas Hole. Doug, you **¹** *must have been teased* (must/tease) about your name over the years?
Doug	I think I **²**_____ (may well/hear) every joke it's possible to make, but at least people remember me! Actually, I used to know a family called 'Paine' and one of them was a doctor.
DJ	Dr Paine? Ha ha, that **³**_____ (can't/be) easy for him!

TV Host	Welcome back viewers! Here we go with round two of the mystery object quiz 'What on Earth!' Ready teams? What on Earth ... was this unusual thing and what was it used for? Kiera?
Kiera	Well, we think it **⁴**_____ (might/use) to repair socks, you know as part of a sewing kit. So, a Victorian mother, let's say, **⁵**_____ (would/fix) holes in her children's' socks and this thing **⁶**_____ (would/put) inside the sock to make it easier for her to mend the hole.
TV Host	Interesting idea. Thank you, Team A. Now, Team B? What's your explanation?

7 ★★★ USE OF ENGLISH Complete the second sentence using the word in bold so that it means the same as the first one. Use between two and five words, including the word in bold.

1 I'm sure it was made of bone. **MUST**
It *must have been made of* bone.

2 I'm sure they weren't perfectly geometric. **CAN'T**
They _____ geometric.

3 I'm assuming that this part was the lid. **WOULD**
This _____ the lid.

4 It's quite likely that this was spherical when it was first made. **MAY**
This _____ when it was first made.

5 It's possible that this curved part was shaped by human hands. **MIGHT**
This curved part _____ by human hands.

6 I assume that these beige sections were originally brightly-coloured. **WOULD**
Originally, these beige _____ brightly-coloured.

8 ★★★ Complete the sentences with suitable modal verbs and the correct forms of the verbs in brackets.

1 Nobody knows exactly what this hollow tube *might have been used for* (use for).

2 The owner _____ (shock) when she found out how much the vase was worth because she stood there with her mouth wide open.

3 We _____ (never/find) the ancient temple without the help of the helicopter.

4 In all likelihood, this pocket-size diary _____ (belong to) a young woman from a wealthy family.

5 The man in this photograph _____ (try) to light a fire as you can see him blowing on the dry grass.

6 These footprints _____ (leave) by any kind of creature we know as they are simply too big.

7 The treasure found near Broadshore Beach yesterday _____ (bury) by pirates as similar pirate treasure was found nearby last year.

9 ON A HIGH NOTE Write a paragraph speculating about a mysterious object you found on a beach. Give some evidence for your speculations.

10B LISTENING AND VOCABULARY

1 🔊 *67* **Decide if the statements about karaoke are true or false. Then listen to Part 1 of a podcast and check your answers.**

1 ☐ Karaoke was invented in China.
2 ☐ The worldwide value of the karaoke business is almost 1 billion dollars.
3 ☐ Karaoke is only popular in Asia.

2 🔊 *68* **Listen to Part 2 of the podcast and complete the sentences with no more than three words in each gap.**

1 The English translation of karaoke is 'empty *orchestra*'.
2 Karaoke became popular throughout Japan in _____.
3 Westerners tend to be more _____ about singing in public than the Japanese.
4 Research seems to show that _____ helps people connect.
5 There are around _____ young, single people in China.
6 Many young Chinese people sing karaoke as a way to relieve _____.

3 🔊 *68* **Listen again to Part 2 and answer the questions.**

1 What kind of musician was Daisuke Inoue? *a drummer*
2 What might a committed karaoke fan employ an expert to do for him/her? _____
3 What's unusual about the format of one part of James Corden's talk show? _____
4 The researchers at which institution found that karaoke could help people bond? _____
5 In which public places can mini-karaoke booths be found in China? _____
6 What audio equipment can you find in a mini-karaoke booth? _____
7 What do people often do with the songs recorded in the mini-karaoke booth? _____

Vocabulary extension

4 **Are these adjectives, which are related to sound and music, positive (P) or negative (N)? Use a dictionary to help you if necessary.**

1 ☐ ear-splitting   5 ☐ out of tune
2 ☐ in tune   6 ☐ monotonous
3 ☐ piercing   7 ☐ melodic
4 ☐ tuneless   8 ☐ tuneful

5 **Choose the correct words to complete the text.**

> The first person who sang karaoke this evening must have been practising because her voice was ¹*melodic / tuneless* and she sang every note ²*out of tune / in tune*. That's more than can be said for the next guy who couldn't possibly have been given a single singing lesson in his life. His voice was ³*tuneless / tuneful* and so loud it was ⁴*monotonous / ear-splitting*! Halfway through, his girlfriend joined in, and she had such a high and ⁵*tuneful / piercing* voice that my friend and I decided it was time to leave.

Pronunciation

6 🔊 *69* **Look at some sentences from the podcast in Exercise 2. What sound disappears from the underlined parts when the modal forms are contracted? Listen and check.**

1 He <u>must have</u> / <u>must've</u> been pleased to see his idea spread all over Japan during the 1980s.
2 Researchers have suggested that collective music-making <u>may have</u> / <u>may've</u> evolved in humans to encourage social bonding between whole groups of people.

ACTIVE PRONUNCIATION
Contracted forms of past modals

When using past modal forms, speakers of English often reduce *have* by omitting the /h/ sound.

• *might have* → *might've* /ˈmaɪtəv/
• *would have* → would've /ˈwʊdəv/

---

7 🔊 *70* **Listen to these pairs of past modals. Tick the one you hear first.**

1 ☐ must have   ☑ must've
2 ☐ should have   ☐ should've
3 ☐ might have   ☐ might've
4 ☐ could have   ☐ could've
5 ☐ would have   ☐ would've

8 🔊 *71* **Practise saying the pairs of past modals from Exercise 7. Listen and check.**

9 🔊 *72* **Read the sentences aloud. Listen and check.**

1 This ivory comb might've belonged to a member of the Dutch royal family.
2 Solid circular earrings like this must've been extremely unusual.
3 These bronze coins may well 've been used to pay soldiers.
4 These enormous footprints can't 've been left by a human.

10C GRAMMAR

Reduced adverbial clauses

1 ⭐ Find the subject of each participle clause.

1 Having had guitar lessons for years, (Paco) amazed Mercedes with his playing.
2 Standing in front of the painting, Helen and Fiona instantly recognised it as a masterpiece.
3 Frank added more blue paint to the mix, creating a darker shade of green.
4 Clearly impressed by the sculpture, the child stood with his mother and stared.
5 Realising Kyle had a wonderful voice, the record company executive signed him immediately.
6 Having been to the latest exhibition at the National Gallery, I'm afraid we don't recommend it.
7 Having added the final touches to Erika's costume, Jasmine took a step back to admire it.

2 ⭐ Match the two parts of the sentences.

1 ☐ Having done stand-up comedy for years,
2 ☐ Feeling nervous about the singing competition,
3 ☐ The actor began to improvise,
4 ☐ Knowing how excited Lily was,
5 ☐ Isobel joined the writing class,
6 ☐ Having read the poem many times before,
7 ☐ Not knowing how to speak German,
8 ☐ Having never met before,

a her father decided not to cancel the trip.
b Clark knew the words by heart.
c Emily knew hundreds of funny jokes.
d never having written a story or poem in her life.
e the musicians needed time to get to know each other.
f Erin bit her nails until they bled.
g Philip couldn't help with the translation.
h having forgotten his lines.

3 ⭐⭐ Complete the sentences with the adverbial clauses from the box.

After having had   ~~Having forgotten~~   Knowing
Never having been   Not wanting to offend   Thinking
Wanting

1 *Having forgotten* to plug in my phone, I woke to find the battery dead.
2 _____ how difficult Annabelle can be, I prepared myself for an argument.
3 _____ to impress his new teacher, Edward put up his hand every time she asked a question.
4 _____ to London, the twins were very excited about their upcoming trip.
5 _____ he was doing the right thing, Barry let Meg's cat out of the flat.
6 _____ breakfast, they packed the car and set off on holiday.
7 _____ anyone, Sian decided to keep her opinion to herself.

4 ⭐⭐⭐ Replace the underlined parts with participle clauses.

1 <u>Because she thought</u> her driving lesson started at 4 p.m. instead of 5 p.m., she had to wait an hour at the driving school. *Having thought*
2 <u>I had met her before, so</u> I didn't bother introducing myself properly. _____
3 <u>Because he felt</u> it would be a bad idea to be tired, he went to bed early the night before his exam. _____
4 The little girl used a naughty word, <u>which left</u> her parents open-mouthed. _____
5 <u>After I had been</u> to the gym, I showered and had some lunch. _____

5 ⭐⭐⭐ Complete the text with participle clauses using the verbs in brackets.

Tell us who you are proud of and why ...

molly_girl14

1*Having grown up* (grow up) during the late 60s and early 70s, my mum is proud to have been a 'hippy'. She grew her hair very long and wore brightly-coloured clothes, **2**_____ (leave) her conservative parents rather shocked! **3**_____ (know) that the hippy movement stood for love and tolerance, she became a passionate campaigner for peace and equality. **4**_____ (take part) in many marches, debates and protests, she had a wide network of contacts. In her thirties, **5**_____ (feel) she might make a good politician, she ran for election. She succeeded for the first time in 1985, **6**_____ (go on) to represent her local community in parliament for twenty-three years.

6 ON A HIGH NOTE Imagine you are old and looking back on your life. Write a short description of what happened to you beginning with the words below.

Having grown up in ...

10D READING AND VOCABULARY

1 Quickly read the text. What do you think would be the best title for the article?

a How a computer managed to write a bestseller

b Could an algorithm help you write a bestseller?

c The secrets behind James Patterson's success

2 Read the article again and match questions 1–6 with paragraphs A–F.

In which paragraph does the author …

1 ☐ point out that the algorithm fails to give particularly innovative insights?

2 ☐ explain what publishers need to do to be successful?

3 ☐ reveal what motivated Archer to create the algorithm with Jockers?

4 ☐ give examples of the determination required to succeed as an author?

5 ☐ indicate what the inventors of the algorithm intend to do with it?

6 ☐ suggest what type of experience could help a writer produce a bestseller?

3 Read the article again and answer the questions.

1 How much does the average UK writer earn?
£12,000

2 What does the writer suggest about the publishers who rejected Stephen King and Judy Blume?
_____

3 What did Jody Archer do before writing *The Bestseller Code*?
_____

4 How accurate is Archer and Jockers' algorithm?
_____

5 According to the algorithm how should a best-selling novel start?
_____

6 Why are journalists more likely than other writers to produce bestsellers?
_____

7 What criticism of inexperienced authors does Archer offer?
_____

Vocabulary extension

4 Make collocations from the text, using the words from the box.

a complete a painful a smash disappear give up
rise ~~the next~~

1 *the next* big thing ☐
2 _____ experience ☐
3 _____ flop ☐
4 _____ hit ☐
5 _____ hope ☐
6 _____ to the top ☐
7 _____ without a trace ☐

5 Are the collocations in Exercise 4 related to success (S) or failure (F)? Which phrase could be used for both (B)? Write S, F or B in Exercise 4.

6 Complete the sentences with the correct forms of the collocations from Exercise 4.

1 The author's first book disappeared *without a trace*.

2 The young British writer quickly _____ after his novel won a major prize.

3 Being rejected twenty times was a very _____.

4 Could this seventeen-year-old writer become _____ in young adult fiction?

5 Friends who read and enjoyed my first book told me not to _____.

6 The fact that your second book was a _____ must have been hard for you.

7 Her _____ children's book sold half a million copies this Christmas!

ACTIVE VOCABULARY | *Nothing/Anything but …*

- Use *nothing but* before a noun, infinitive without *to*, or -ing form to mean 'only'.

  *She received **nothing but** rejections from publishers for two years straight.*

- Use *anything but* before adjectives to emphasise that something is not true.

  *It seems that writing or spotting best-selling novels is **anything but** easy.*

7 Complete the sentences with *nothing but* or *anything but*.

1 I'd like to thank you for being *nothing but* kind towards me and my family.

2 It's done _____ rain since we got here. Where's the sun?

3 I read that this was a good restaurant, but I'm afraid it's been _____ good today.

4 In my opinion, boxing is _____ entertaining. I can't stand violent sports.

5 Vicky's parents were extremely proud after the teacher had _____ praise for her.

6 The doctor was _____ friendly which, understandably, made the patient feel even worse.

8 ON A HIGH NOTE Choose one of the topics below.

1 Read Paragraph D again and write the first paragraph of your own book.

2 Do research on your favourite author. Find out how he/she started his/her career and write a short paragraph about it.

A What does it take to write a best-selling novel? It's a multi-million pound question that those in the publishing industry have worked hard to answer over the years. Clearly, a writer's talent is vital, along with a good imagination, plenty of creativity and a great deal of dedication. Publishers must be willing to spend vast amounts of money on marketing and promotion and think carefully about things like timing and distribution. Many authors dream of the recognition and high earnings that go along with writing a bestseller, but in all likelihood, that dream will not become a reality. Even if you get your book published, there is still no guarantee of success. Several million books are published each year and the vast majority of them disappear without a trace. Writers in the UK generally have an income of about £12,000, well below the minimum wage for a full-time job. In contrast, James Patterson, one of the world's best-selling authors, reportedly earned over £65 million in 2018.

B Even writers who eventually rise to the top often suffer through the painful experience of rejection. Stephen King's first major novel, *Carrie*, was rejected thirty times, eventually leading him to give up hope and throw it in the bin. Luckily, his wife rescued it, and it went on to sell millions of copies. Judy Blume, winner of more than ninety literary awards, has sold over eighty million children's and young adult books which have been translated into thirty-two languages. She received nothing but rejections from publishers for two years straight. Thankfully for their readers, King and Blume didn't give up. Without a doubt, the publishers who rejected them must be sorry they did so now.

C It seems that writing or spotting best-selling novels is anything but easy. Is there a way to increase the chances of success? The authors of a book called *The Bestseller Code* believe that technology might be the answer. One of them, Jodie Archer, is a former commissioning editor whose job was to spot bestsellers. Having become fascinated by what makes large numbers of people want to read the same book, she decided to apply technology to the question. Archer and her co-author, Matthew Jockers, came up with an algorithm which they say can predict the likelihood of a book becoming a smash hit with eighty percent accuracy.

D According to the algorithm, best-selling novels tend to have a predictable combination of stylistic and structural elements. Firstly, there should be a strong opening sentence that gives a reader a taste of the story. The writing style should use shorter sentences and simple vocabulary. Authors with a background in journalism tend to do well because of their accessible and everyday style of writing. In terms of the plot, bestsellers usually have a clear emotional rhythm: an emotional high, followed by an emotional low, next another high, then another low. Archer and Jockers' algorithm also identified 500 important topics that are commonly found across a range of bestsellers. These include things like love, the law, and the most popular topic – human closeness and relationships. It showed that the most successful authors choose a limited number of topics to explore in each book. Archer says that less experienced authors tend to include too many topics in their books, resulting in a lack of clarity and focus.

E There are of course, plenty of people who are unconvinced by the algorithm. Some of them say that success is the result of everything that an author has experienced, read or written about in life. They doubt that anything as mechanical as an algorithm could accurately predict the potential of a complex thing like a novel. Other critics point out that appearing on a bestseller list is only one measure of success, and that bestsellers follow predictable patterns, which is why the algorithm is able to 'measure' them. Clearly, the lessons offered by Archer and Jockers' work are nothing new. Such advice has long been given out by authors and teachers of creative writing, so the algorithm does little more than confirm what we already knew about successful books. It has also had at least one spectacular failure. A book by a best-selling author was fed into the computer and given a 100 percent chance of becoming a bestseller. When it was released however, it was a complete flop in terms of sales.

F Despite these criticisms, there has been plenty of interest in the work of Archer and Jockers. They plan to offer writers a chance to have their books analysed by the algorithm, followed by a discussion of what they can do to improve their chances of becoming the next big thing in the publishing world.

10E VOCABULARY | Performance

1 ⭐ **Choose the correct words to complete the sentences.**

1 *Dead Poets Society* is definitely a *must-watch / stand-up*. It's an important film that will make you think.

2 I spent all day biting my nails on the *edge / side* of my seat, watching *A Quiet Place*. What a(n) *appalling / breathtaking* movie!

3 I'd like to *catch up / deliver* on episodes I missed. Fortunately, they are made available to stream and download once I've paid a fee.

4 My father advised me to pause before *delivering / heckling* the punchline. It is supposed to give the audience some suspense and surprise.

5 My brother is trying to become a comedian; he's already done his hilarious stand-up *leads / routines* in the local pubs.

6 He started the evening telling a few *offensive / worthwhile* gags about mothers-in-law. Nobody laughed.

2 ⭐⭐ **Choose the correct words to complete the sentences.**

1 Finding the comedian's racist jokes ___, several audience members walked out of the comedy club.
   a comical   **b** offensive   **c** cheesy

2 Critics have called the film ___, but audiences seem to love it nevertheless.
   a appalling   **b** magical   **c** exceptional

3 The jokes were so ___ it was embarrassing.
   a comical   **b** cheesy   **c** lively

4 An awful film; the acting was poor, the special effects terrible and the dialogue ___.
   a lively   **b** worthwhile   **c** unconvincing

5 This ___ performance by Julie Danch is sure to win her plenty more awards.
   a appalling   **b** offensive   **c** breathtaking

6 This film was made for the big screen, making a trip to the cinema extremely ___.
   a magical   **b** unconvincing   **c** worthwhile

7 This is the best version of *Macbeth* ever to hit the stage; truly ___ in every way.
   a exceptional   **b** comical   **c** cheesy

8 Smith gave a ___ performance as the Genie in this excellent stage production of *Aladdin*.
   a offensive   **b** unconvincing   **c** lively

3 ⭐⭐ **Complete the pairs of sentences with the words in bold.**

1 MAGIC / MAGICAL
   a Watching the paper lanterns float up into the sky was a truly *magical* experience.
   b The Great Gondino waved his _____ wand over the hat and produced a live white rabbit.

2 COMIC / COMICAL
   a Are you a _____ actor?
   b He looked _____ in that big hat.

3 HISTORIC / HISTORICAL
   a This is an excellent _____ play.
   b Today is a _____ day for the world's largest movie studios.

4 CLASSIC / CLASSICAL
   a Don't miss the _____ car show next week!
   b I quite like some _____ music.

5 TASTY / TASTEFUL
   a The way the opera house was decorated was very _____.
   b _____ snacks will be available during the break.

6 LIVELY / ALIVE
   a The concert was a _____ start to the city's cultural weekend.
   b If only the artist had been _____ to see his painting sell for 47 million dollars.

7 INVALUABLE / WORTHLESS
   a This wonderful book is full of _____ advice for drama students.
   b It seems the final week of rehearsals was _____ as the first night of the play was awful.

8 CHILDLIKE / CHILDISH
   a The artist's best work has a _____ innocence about it.
   b I found the director's reaction to the criticism of his film extremely _____ .

4 ⭐⭐⭐ USE OF ENGLISH **Complete the preview from a TV magazine with one word in each gap.**

Today's best television

[1]*Catch* up on the latest episode of *Folly-foot* on BBC2 at 7.00 tonight. It's a [2]_____ -watch for fans of gentle English comedy. If you're more of an action lover, *Mystery Mission 4* on Cloud TV at 9.00 will have you on the edge of your [3]_____. The lead, of course, is [4]_____ by Tim Cross.

For those that like their comedy a little more lively than *Folly-foot*, there's Bob Hicks doing a classic stand-up [5]_____ on UKTV at 11.00. Watch Bob [6]_____ the gags, [7]_____ the punchlines, and deal with audience members who are foolish enough to raise their voices to try and [8]_____ him.

5 ON A HIGH NOTE **Write a message to a friend recommending a TV show or film you love.**

1 🔊 73 **Listen and repeat the phrases. How do you say them in your language?**

SPEAKING | Negotiating informally

MAKING SUGGESTIONS

How would you feel about watching a documentary about New Orleans?

I thought perhaps we could watch the news.

Supposing we watched that quiz show.

Would it be OK if we watched the next episode of that detective series?

ASKING FOR CLARIFICATION

Isn't that a bit childish/silly/boring?

So, are you saying (that) going to the theatre is boring?

What kind of thing were you thinking of?

ACCEPTING A SUGGESTION

I could go along with that.

Fair enough.

I'm happy with that.

NOT ACCEPTING A SUGGESTION

I don't know if I would fancy that.

I can see what you're saying, but I don't agree that the theatre is a waste of time.

I don't want to be awkward, but that time isn't very convenient for me.

MAKING A FINAL DECISION

So how can we resolve this?

Is everyone happy with that?

2 **Complete the suggestions with the correct forms of the verbs in brackets to make them sound tentative.**

1 I thought perhaps we _could eat out_ (can/eat out).

2 Supposing we _____ (stay) at home tonight?

3 Would it be OK if we _____ (leave) early?

4 What if we _____ (go out) to dinner instead?

3 🔊 74 **Complete the mini-conversations with the phrases from the box. Listen and check.**

How would you feel about
Isn't that a bit childish?
OK, fair enough.
~~What kind of thing were you thinking of?~~

Liam So what are we doing on Saturday night?

Corey No plans yet. ¹_What kind of thing were you thinking of?_

Liam ²_____ seeing a play? _The Diary of Anne Frank_ is on at Broadend Theatre.

Corey Er, I think I'd rather go see the new Marvel film.

Liam Cheesy superheroes, Corey? ³_____

Corey Plenty of people our age are into superheroes.

Liam Well, not me – sorry. I'll ask someone else then.

Corey ⁴_____

I could go along with that.
I thought maybe we could
Supposing we
Would it be OK if I

Elsa I think we should buy Kate an experience for her birthday. ⁵_____ get her tickets to the music festival at the weekend. She's into mellow stuff, so she'll like _The Remedy_ and _The Jones Boy_. It's pretty soulful stuff.

Jim ⁶_____ We could go to the festival too. ⁷_____ bought tickets for the three of us?

Elsa ⁸_____ brought another friend?

Jim Why not? It'll be fun with more people.

I don't want to be awkward, but
I'm happy with that.
Is everyone happy with that?
So are you saying
So how can we resolve this?

Astrid So, are we going to the 7 p.m. showing of the film or the 10 p.m. one?

Dolph 7 p.m.

Jan 10 p.m.

Astrid Ah. ⁹_____

Dolph 10 p.m. is too late. We'll get home after midnight.

Jan So? It's Friday.

Dolph ¹⁰_____ I've got a football match tomorrow.

Jan What time?

Dolph Er ... midday.

Jan ¹¹_____ you need – like – ten hours' sleep or something?

Astrid Wait! It's on at Filmhouse at ... half eight. ¹²_____

Dolph Yes, ¹³_____

Jan OK – whatever.

4 **Find and correct one mistake in each sentence.**

1 I can't see what you're saying, but I'm not sure I agree with you completely. _can_

2 Imagine you were an actor, how will you feel about playing Romeo in the school production of _Romeo and Juliet_? _____

3 Supposing we meeting outside the theatre twenty minutes before the play starts? _____

4 I could go away with the plan as long as we all stick together at the concert. _____

5 I thought perhaps we can go and see some stand-up comedy at the weekend. _____

6 So are you say that you don't like any kind of electronic music whatsoever? _____

5 ON A HIGH NOTE **Write a short dialogue between two friends who are trying to decide which film to see.**

10G **WRITING** | An article

Give your article an eye-catching title.

Grab the reader's attention from the start; outline what the article is about.

Describe the show in more detail: give key information and summarise the plot.

Give more detail, talk about the major themes or the plot.

Describe one or more of the lead actors' performance(s).

Give your opinion on the second part of the question: make connections between the performance(s) you described and the second part of the question.

Summarise the main points. You may refer back to the opening paragraph.

A LIVELY LIVE PERFORMANCE KEEPS ENTERTAINMENT ALIVE!

Is it more entertaining to watch a live performance than a TV show or film? Having recently seen an adaptation of the hit film *School of Rock* at the New London Theatre, I think the answer is that, in some cases, it is.

Set in a privileged US school, *School of Rock* tells the story of Dewey Finn, a scruffy rock music fan who gets a job as a teacher by pretending to be someone else. As the story unfolds, Finn bonds with his students, teaches **[1]**them about life and the history of rock music, and struggles to keep his true identity a secret. On stage, the plot remains much the same and includes all the funny moments from the film plus many hilarious new **[2]**ones. One of the great strengths of the adaptation is the number of wonderful new original songs that have been added. The young actors that play Finn's pupils are required to dance, sing and play instruments and they give a truly mesmerising performance as they **[3]**do so. I was blown away by the talent on display.

I would argue that the live version of *School of Rock* supports the suggestion that **[4]**such performances are the most rewarding to watch. Firstly, there is the matter of immediacy. Playing to a camera, actors may have taken many attempts to perfect a scene, and performances can be edited to polish them. In the theatre on the other hand, there is 'nowhere to hide', and seeing actors get everything right just metres away from you is a unique thrill. Secondly, the physical aspect of performances is much better appreciated when you are watching live. This is particularly true of a performance which involves dancing, playing instruments and singing.

Without taking anything away from the talents of film and TV actors, I think there is some truth in the suggestion that live performances can be more entertaining to watch. If you don't believe me, go and see *School of Rock*.

1 Read the article and complete the advice with *Do* or *Don't*.

1 *Do* give personal opinions.
2 _____ give concrete examples.
3 _____ repeat the same words or phrases often.
4 _____ use emphatic structures.
5 _____ use contracted forms, informal language.

2 The underlined parts in the model text are used to avoid repetition. Match them with these words and phrases which they replace.

a ☐ funny moments   c ☐ Finn's students
b ☐ live   d ☐ dance, sing and play

3 WRITING TASK Write your article.

A recent online review of a film that was adapted from a best-selling book suggested that watching an adaptation is never as rewarding as reading the original book. Write an article in which you review a film that was adapted from a book, and express your thoughts on the suggestion that was made in the online review.

ACTIVE WRITING | An article

1 Plan your article.
- To what extent do you agree with the suggestion made in the task?
- Make some notes in support of your opinion.
- Decide on a film adapted from a book to review in your article. Ideally, you should have read the book and seen the film.

2 Write the article.
- Grab attention with the title and the first paragraph.
- Ensure that you describe the performances in the film and give your opinion.
- Try to avoid repetition by using synonyms and reference devices.
- Use a variety of vocabulary and emphatic structures.

3 Check that ...
- you have answered both parts of the question.
- there are no spelling, grammar or punctuation mistakes.

UNIT VOCABULARY PRACTICE

1 10A GRAMMAR AND VOCABULARY **Complete the labels of the pictures with the words from the box.**

~~bone~~ circular curved geometric miniature pointed rectangular spherical wooden

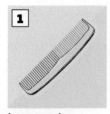 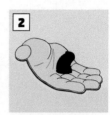 

bone comb   _____ cat   _____ spoon

 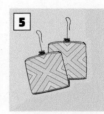 

_____ parcel   _____ pattern   _____ button

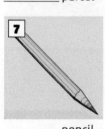 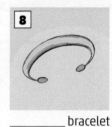 

_____ pencil   _____ bracelet   _____ necklace

2 10A GRAMMAR AND VOCABULARY **Complete the sentences with one word in each gap.**

1 What exactly is the difference between be_ige_ and cr_____? They're both a kind of dirty white.
2 This en_____ shield is made of br_____ and must have been carried by a strong man.
3 The ring has a go_____ colour, although it's not actually made of gold.
4 The hat was squashed fl_____ after our cat sat on it!
5 This piece is carved from so_____ iv_____, unfortunately for the poor elephant involved.

3 10B LISTENING AND VOCABULARY **Choose the correct words to complete the text.**

We've got a diverse and exciting line up on this evening's show. First to perform will be rapper MC Chin, who'll have you dancing and jumping to the ¹_mellow / rhythmic_ beats of his ²_soulful / upbeat_ summer dance hit 'Junk-store Hero'. It's got to be the ³_brassiest / catchiest_ tune I've heard for years. I can't stop singing it even though I always sing ⁴_off-key / soothing_. Then it's time to calm things right down and get ⁵_mellow / upbeat_ with the ⁶_exhilarating / soulful_ voice of Athena J. Rain singing her heartbreaking hit 'Alone Again'. So here we go ... give it up for MC Chin!

4 10D READING AND VOCABULARY **Complete the mini-conversations with one preposition in each gap.**

Clyde I wish they wouldn't keep me ¹_in_ suspense. I'm sure they're doing it ²_____ purpose!

Oona Well, ³_____ all likelihood they'll be in touch today. You said the interview went well.

Clyde Yes, ⁴_____ fact, it went really well. They seemed to like me.

Oona ⁵_____ a doubt, they'll offer you a place. Just be patient for a little longer.

Verity I was ⁶_____ the impression that you were going to pay for the tickets, Raj.

Raj Well, ⁷_____ the sake of equality, Verity, I think we should each pay for our own tickets.

Verity Oh, ⁸_____ that case, I guess we should.

5 10D READING AND VOCABULARY **Find and correct one mistake with a prepositional phrase in each sentence.**

1 It's a bit of a boring film, but ~~at last~~ the seats are comfortable! _at least_
2 On addition to the usual programme of entertainment, there will also be a poetry reading. _____
3 I threw away the tickets for accident and now I've no idea what to do! _____
4 With contrast to the unconvincing first season, the second season is exceptional. _____
5 They whispered to each other in the cinema under fear of disturbing the other people in the audience. _____
6 If we are going to be ready for the opening night of this play, I need more effort in everyone's part. _____

6 10E VOCABULARY **Choose the correct words to complete the sentences.**

1 The new season of _Darker Days_ is an absolute ___ for horror fans everywhere.
   a stand-up   b feature-length   c must-watch
2 The stand-up comedian dealt amusingly with the member of the audience who tried to ___.
   a play him   b catch him up   c heckle him
3 The review said that the movie was 'edge of the ___ stuff', but I found it really boring.
   a routine   b seat   c stage
4 The new lead singer has a(n) ___ voice and is a worthy replacement for Kelly Simmons.
   a exceptional   b appalling   c unconvincing
5 The video for this song was made in the ___ hills that look down on Beirut.
   a lively   b breathtaking   c worthwhile
6 After being damaged by fire, the once-valuable collection of film costumes is now ___.
   a worthwhile   b invaluable   c worthless

7 ON A HIGH NOTE **Do you think that some subjects are unsuitable for humour? Write a short paragraph and give your opinion.**

1 For each learning objective, write 1–5 to assess your ability.

1 = I don't feel confident. 5 = I feel confident.

	Learning objective	Course material	How confident I am (1–5)
10A	I can use past modals to talk about hypothetical situations in the past.	Student's Book pp. 138–139	
10B	I can understand standard British and American accents and talk about music.	Student's Book p. 140	
10C	I can use reduced adverbial clauses in written texts.	Student's Book p. 141	
10D	I can identify specific details in a text and talk about spoilers.	Student's Book pp. 142–143	
10E	I can talk about performances.	Student's Book p. 144	
10F	I can negotiate informally.	Student's Book p. 145	
10G	I can write an article.	Student's Book pp. 146–147	

2 Which of the skills above would you like to improve in? How?

Skill I want to improve in	How I can improve

3 What can you remember from this unit?

New words I learned and most want to remember	Expressions and phrases I liked	English I heard or read outside class

GRAMMAR AND VOCABULARY

1 Choose the correct words to complete the sentences.

1 This *mellow / rhythmic* music is very pleasant, but it's no good for dancing to.
2 I didn't mean to hurt you; I'd never do anything like that by *accident / on purpose*.
3 This is a *historic / historical* moment for our country.
4 Conrad's *cheesy / exceptional* performance will go down as one of the greatest of all time.
5 Le Dearn *delivers / plays* the lead for the first time and proves she is a name to remember.

/ 5

2 Complete the sentences with one word in each gap.

1 I'm afraid we'll have to keep you *in* suspense until all the votes have been counted.
2 I'm staying in and _____ up on a few episodes of *Horseforth* tonight.
3 The tennis finals were so exciting that we spent the entire afternoon on the _____ of our seats.
4 _____ the sake of security, we will need to see identification from every single one of you.
5 _____ fact, I love the Sun but I'm staying out of the Sun _____ fear of getting sunburnt.

/ 5

3 Complete the sentences with suitable past modals and the correct forms of the verbs in brackets. Sometimes more than one answer is possible.

1 Someone *must have been sitting* (sit) here recently because the chair is still warm.
2 These jeans _____ (wash) properly because they are still dirty at the bottom of the legs.
3 That _____ (be) the same actor that was in *True Life*, but I'm not completely sure.
4 It seems logical to conclude that these glasses _____ (wear) by a very young child.
5 Yes, I agree that it's very likely. I think these gloves _____ (belong) to Queen Beatrice.
6 The Romans _____ (construct) those buildings – they aren't that old.

/ 5

4 Combine the two sentences using a participle clause.

1 They walked into the room. They saw that they'd been burgled.
Walking into the room, they saw that they'd been burgled.
2 I lost my wallet. I had to cancel all my cards.
_____
3 She saw two men arguing outside the shop. She crossed the street to avoid them.
_____
4 I had been lying in the sun for an hour. I decided it was time for a swim.
_____
5 He didn't hear his alarm. He overslept by two hours.
_____
6 Corey changed his degree course. He felt a lot happier at university.
_____

/ 5

USE OF ENGLISH

5 Complete the text with one word in each gap.

[1]*Having* done stand-up comedy routines for many years, I can report that it may [2]_____ be the scariest profession there is. My life would have [3]_____ so much easier if I'd chosen a different career. I regularly have nightmares where I'm on stage [4]_____ a gag and I get to the end, [5]_____ the punchline and it's followed by absolute silence from the audience. They stare at me; I stare at them.
In fact, at this point I usually wake up, stressed and sweaty but relieved [6]_____ least, that it was only a dream.

/ 5

6 Choose the correct words a–d to complete the text.

[1]___ into the antiques market, I approached the first stall with a sense of excitement. This lovely little [2]___ music box caught my eye immediately. It is a classic design with a [3]___ ballerina that spins when the lid is open. In all [4]___, it was made and sold in Geneva in the 1920s and would have been a [5]___ possession for a very lucky child.

1 **a** Have walked **b** Walking **c** To walk **d** Walked
2 **a** pointed **b** cheesy **c** wooden **d** enormous
3 **a** spherical **b** miniature **c** childish **d** geometric
4 **a** likelihood **b** doubt **c** fear **d** contrast
5 **a** magically **b** magic **c** magician **d** magical

/ 5

/ 30

PHRASAL VERBS

be blown away: I was blown away by the performance of the actress.

be fed up with: I'm completely fed up with people gossiping about me.

be off: We're all off to the coast for a few days for half-term.

break down: The freezer broke down.

break off: We can break off at any time and go back to our normal lives, whereas the people whose lives we're experiencing can't.

bring about: Climate change could bring about the end of the world.

bump into: I bumped into an old friend yesterday.

calm down: I need to calm down, but a wave of anxiety overcomes me.

catch up on: Tonight we'll catch up on the latest episode of the show.

chop down: Two cherry trees commemorating WWII heroes were chopped down with no warning.

clean up: Aliens might treat us the same way we would treat bacteria – as a nuisance to be cleaned up.

clear up: I joined a group that wanted to clear up the town where I live.

come across: I happened to come across this gem of a museum last week on a family trip to Prague.

come across as: People are more likely to take to you if you come across as a warm and approachable person.

come off: The door handle has come off.

come up against: While we can experience the sounds and sights of a refugee camp, we don't come up against the same difficulties.

come up with: It's a good idea to come up with different arguments.

curl up: Curled up on every piece of furniture were a dozen or so cats, just hoping for us to make a fuss of them.

cut down on: Cut down on fatty foods if you want to lose weight.

do up: The worst thing was that the kitchen had only recently been done up and the walls were freshly painted.

drive off: He saw the man get into the car and drive off.

drop out: When she went to university, she was still immature and dropped out after her first year.

eat away at: The stress might eat away at you inside.

end up: Each year, over £140 million worth of clothing is thrown away and ends up in landfill.

fade away: It is a passing fashion that will fade away.

fall out with: Carrie's always falling out with people.

fight back against: Local people are fighting back against the council's decision to close the park.

figure out: After an hour, we figured out how to turn it off.

fit in: Desperate to fit in, she did all she could to hide her blindness.

get sth across: But how can you possibly get across to an alien civilisation what it means to be human?

get ahead: She has always been determined to get ahead, so she quickly got a new job.

get away with: I thought I'd got away with it, as I had many times before. But not this time. This time I was going to prison.

get by on: When I was at uni, I used to be able to get by on £100 a week.

get on with: How well do you get on with your family?

get rid of: Living in a small space means that you have to get rid of your excess possessions.

go out: I was watching a film when the lights suddenly went out.

go with: OK, so will we go with banning single-use bottles then?

hang up: I never knew that we say 'hang up the phone' because phones used to be hung on the wall.

hold down: People with autism might have problems at school or with holding down a job.

keep up with: Malcolm found it difficult to keep up with the other students in his class.

laugh off: Locals living on the street at the centre of the police investigation laughed off the accusation.

leave out: They leave out details which they think are unnecessary.

look down on: Mr Garcia looks down on anyone who hasn't had a university education.

look up to: I've always looked up to Bill because of his determination.

lose out: Unless you make an effort, you're going to lose out on the job.

make out: She had once been able to make out faces, colours and landscapes, but by the age of twelve she was totally blind.

make up with: Have you made up with Patty yet?

mess about: I was quite naughty and messed about from time to time.

mess up: It doesn't matter if you mess it up, you can always try again.

pass on: I can pass on a message to him if you like.

pay off: It hasn't worked yet, but I'm sure our persistence will pay off in the end.

pick up: The world's largest radio dish can pick up signals from even the very deepest realms of space.

pick up: Dad's picking up his new electric car tonight at 7 p.m.

pick up: As children do, I picked up the new language quite quickly.

play out: We've seen this scenario played out many times in films.

point out: He pointed out that we won't be able to process what the aliens are trying to tell us.

put aside: If you don't put aside some money, you will never buy a car.

put away: Bedding can be folded and put away every day.

put in: Concerned individuals put in a Freedom of Information request, which revealed a secret operation to cut down a lot of trees.

put off: She discovered that the Braille writing system did not exist in Tibetan, but she didn't let that put her off.

put off: I have a bad habit of putting things off.

put on: I've been rehearsing for a musical we're putting on next week.

put up with: I don't know how you put up with all this noise while you're trying to do your homework.

run out of: We know that Amelia Earhart had just run out of fuel when she disappeared.

send out: And might it be actually hazardous to send out signals to attract the attention of these superior beings?

set (sb) apart: At school she was patronised by her teachers in a way that set her apart from the other children.

set out: Five years later, she set out to fly around the globe.

set up: I set up a small business recycling and customising denim.

settle down: Simon has settled down in Seattle with his wife and two children in a three-bedroom house.

shrug off: He knew that people sometimes mocked him for being overweight, and he was usually able to shrug it off.

show off: My brother is always showing off.

speak up for: He is willing to speak up for the rights of women.

speak out against: People need to speak out against discrimination.

spell out: You must spell out your idea very clearly so he understands.

splash out: It's worth thinking twice before you splash out on that shiny new gadget.

split up with: I thought she'd split up with her boyfriend.

stay out: I'm not allowed to stay out after 10 p.m.

stay up: Are you really planning to stay up that long?

step out: I'm sure I'll be terrified when I actually have to step out in front of an audience.

strike up: Often the best way to strike up a conversation is simply to say something funny about what's happening around you.

take in: It is highly likely that, even if we do make contact, we won't be able to take in or process what the aliens are trying to tell us.

take on: She was more than ready to take on this challenge.

take to (sb): People are more likely to take to you if you come across as a warm and approachable person.

teem with: The Indian subcontinent was a place teeming with cities and towns, with deserts and mountains, rivers and forests.

tell apart: Rhinoceroses are so short-sighted that they are unable to tell a person and a tree apart from a distance of five metres.

tell off: When I was little, my parents were forever telling me off about the things I'd done.

throw away: How much rubbish do you throw away every day?

trick (sb) into: It is relatively easy to trick people into doing something.

turn out: It turned out that the girl had a rare disease.

wind (sb) up: Everyone makes a big fuss of him. It really winds me up.

wipe down: I wiped down the wall with a damp cloth.

wipe off: Hilary wiped the spilt milk off the table.

wipe out: In this film, the aliens' one goal is to wipe out humanity.

work out: If things don't work out, try to make the best of the situation.

work out: Aliens would be intelligent enough to work out a means of communication.

PREPOSITIONS

PREPOSITIONS IN PHRASES

AGAINST
against the rules: Her bosses told her that this was against the rules.

AT
at a distance: People use many ways of communicating at a distance.
at stake: There was a lot at stake, but he did it anyway.
at the age of: I can't imagine children starting work at the age of eight.
at the end: It's a bit sad when he dies at the end though.
at the moment: Where is he working at the moment?
at the time: We didn't know about the hoax at the time.
at that time: At that time, he was working for a different company.
at the turn of the century: At the turn of the twenty-first century, the world population was just under seven billion people.
at your convenience: I would be glad to attend an interview at your convenience.

BY
by accident: She found the book by accident.
by chance: I met an old friend by chance yesterday.
by law: Endangered species are now protected by law.

FOR
except for: There was no noise except for the rustling of paper.
for fear of: They don't use social media for fear of getting addicted.
(take sth) for granted: He took it for granted that sooner or later his boss would come and rescue him.
for instance: For instance, they can make fruit look and taste like meat!
for safety reasons: For safety reasons, toxic waste must be stored in sealed containers underground.
for the better: The Internet has changed my life for the better.
for the sake of: I'm doing this for the sake of my parents.

FROM
from time to time: I used to mess about from time to time.

IN
in addition: In addition to providing entertainment, the Students' Union organises societies which any student can join.
in all likelihood: In all likelihood, we enjoy it more the second or third time because we are now free to notice more of the detail.
in charge of: He had been in charge of a big company for many years.
in conclusion: In conclusion, the priority is to install a fridge.
in contrast: In contrast to Christenfeld's research, the stories that had been 'spoiled' were considered to be less moving.
in danger of: One in four mammals is in danger of extinction.
in fact: In fact, his younger brother is now quite a bit taller than him.
in general /particular: Fluency in a foreign language in general and English in particular is very important for a student's future.
in many ways: In many ways, human life on this planet is better than ever.
in no way: In no way should we abandon our logical conscious mind.
in order to: Then there is the fact that in order to travel to our planet, the aliens would have to be far more advanced than we are.
in principle: It's a good idea in principle, but I need to think it over.
in sb's power: Do everything in your power to stop using plastic.
in suspense: I was in suspense right through the film.
in that case: In that case, you should tell him the truth.
in the end: Dad said that secrets always come out in the end.
in the hands of: Are mobile phones a threat or a blessing when in the hands of children?
in the long run: Even when things don't immediately go my way, they usually turn out to be positive in the long run.
in the middle of: I was woken in the middle of the night to move my car.
in the public eye: As an actor, he was used to being in the public eye.
in the wild: He taught children about how to survive in the wild.
in touch with: It's getting easier and easier to stay in touch with people.
in recent years: In recent years, text messaging has become popular.
in those days: In those days, mobile phones did not have keyboards.

OFF
off the record: This news is off the record. Don't tell anyone.

ON
on average: Most people's concentration span is 14 minutes on average.
on board: The video shows the moment when he was taken on board.
on foot: She rarely goes into the local village on foot.
on horseback: She usually goes into the local village on horseback.
on your own: I was an only child and I felt bored at home on my own.
on your way: The creatures captured the child on his way to school.
on purpose: Did the paparazzi cause the crash on purpose?
on stage: Stand-up comedians tell a series of jokes on stage.
on the edge of your seat: I watched the film on the edge of my seat.
on the fence: I'm on the fence, really. I can't decide what to do.
on the loose: A lion escaped from the zoo and was on the loose.
on the news: The speaker doesn't enjoy watching violence on the news.
on the safe side: Buy your own ticket, just to be on the safe side.
on the shore: I love listening to waves crashing on the shore.
on the spot: Think ahead. It's hard to think of good examples on the spot.
on the way out: Plastic cutlery and straws are on the way out.
on the whole: On the whole, I thought the film was pretty good.
on time: Most of my friends who were invited to the party arrived on time.

OUT OF
out of breath: I stopped, completely out of breath, and glanced around.
out of place: He looked out of place among the young couples.
out of the ordinary: We were probably malnourished, but then so were poor children all across India, so it was nothing out of the ordinary.

TO
face-to-face: Would you rather speak to her on the phone or face-to-face?
to my mind: People sometimes think that stressful or upsetting events shape us negatively, but to my mind, the opposite can also be true.
to some extent: Most of us experience synesthesia to some extent.

UNDER
under threat: Condors are now under threat once more.
under no circumstances: Under no circumstances should you be here.

UP
up to date: They brought circus up to date with motorbike stunt men.

WITH
with any luck: With any luck, he won't be living in this way in a few years.
with regard to: I am writing with regard to your advertisement.

WITHOUT
without a (shadow of a) doubt: Without a doubt, the majority of us do our best to avoid seeing spoilers.

PREPOSITIONS AFTER NOUNS

advances in: Advances in robotics will eliminate semi-skilled jobs.
advantage of: What is the advantage of changing the clocks?
advice for: Have you got any advice for me?
alternative to: Scientists are already working on alternatives to meat.
campaign against: It's a campaign against climate change.
concerns about: Dak Kopec, of the University of Las Vegas, has concerns about the number of vast mansions being built in the area.
connection with: We need to open our minds to the possibilities that greater connection with others could bring.
difference to: Becoming a 'befriender' is a direct way to make a difference to someone's life.
disadvantage of: What are the disadvantages of the new system?
downside of/to: There are some downsides to working as a lawyer.
drawback of/to: The main drawback of travelling by bus to college is that it takes a long time.
experience of: I have experience of this kind of work.
impact on: Watching crime on TV has a negative impact on our emotions.
increase in: There was a gradual increase in the numbers of IoT devices.
interaction between: He fears that such arrangements could limit social interaction between parents and children.
key to: For her the key to happiness was being in the natural world.
preference for: Regarding wall colour, a few students expressed a preference for bright colour.

rally against: We're going to be at the rally against gun violence.

reason for: Harry felt that there was a good reason for what he did.

research on: He's done research on the impact of space on relationships.

respect for: When you share space, you learn respect for others.

solution to: They weren't able to find a solution to the problem.

taste in: You have a really great taste in music.

threat to: Habitat loss is the greatest threat to endangered species.

PREPOSITIONS AFTER ADJECTIVES

anxious about: He felt anxious about his sister.

ashamed of: Why are many Tibetans ashamed of blindness?

aware of: Sean was not aware of the hurtful comments.

based on: The report is based on a survey of fifty students.

bound to: Technology is bound to make our lives easier.

capable of: Despite her disability, she was capable of doing many things.

careful with: Most people are careful with online banking details.

concerned about: I'm extremely concerned about my ill cat.

conscious of: Were you conscious of any change in her behaviour?

different from: Trying out something for a few minutes is very different from experiencing it over several months, years or a lifetime.

distressed by: Many people were distressed by these painful scenes.

due to: His success is due to excellent education.

embedded in: I hope you know that cookies are embedded in websites.

entitled to: You're entitled to your opinion.

envious of: It's a way of making people envious of your popularity.

excited about: Are you excited about the Internet of Things?

happy for: She was happy for them to join her if they wanted.

inaccessible to: The thick vegetation was inaccessible to walkers.

inclined to do sth: I'm inclined to think that we should make a new plan.

intrigued by: Why was the author so intrigued by the map of India?

likely/unlikely to: Males are more likely to be colour-blind than females.

passionate about: These young people are passionate about music.

prejudiced against: Some employers are prejudiced against old people.

prior to: Prior to the invention of the washing machine, it was usual to spend an entire day doing laundry.

related to: They receive 50 calls an hour related to domestic violence.

successful in: He can help you be successful in your career.

sure to: Driving is sure to become safer in the future.

suspicious of: Many of the local people are suspicious of strangers.

superior to: Some TV series are superior to many big-budget films.

surprised at: The woman was surprised at her friend's behaviour.

vital to: It is vital to be honest with your children.

PREPOSITIONS AFTER VERBS

account for: Recent pressure at work may account for his behaviour.

accuse sb of: Smith accused her of lying.

adapt to: After living in a house, it's hard to adapt to living in a flat.

adjust to: It may not be easy to adjust to the results of climate change.

apologise for: They apologised for not listening to her.

appeal to: This programme appeals to people's emotions.

attribute sth to: This was attributed to a mixture of cultural reasons.

ban/bar sb from: This gym banned thin people from entering.

be into sth: They are into experiences rather than material possessions.

beg for: The children begged for food and money on the streets.

blame sb/sth for sth: In those days, TV was blamed for the breakdown in communication between parents and kids.

bother about: I'm not really bothered about my personal appearance.

campaign against: They were campaigning against gun violence.

comment on: You can comment on the weather to start a conversation.

compete for: Do you need to compete for space with your sister?

compete in: The company competes in the international marketplace.

congratulate on: She congratulated me warmly on my exam results.

connect to: Forums connected to our interests make us feel we belong.

connect with: Does this wire connect your computer with the telephone?

contribute to: This can contribute to the breakdown of the family.

cope with: Some people with ASD can't cope with noisy environments.

cram into: He shared a house with twenty-four others and people would often just cram into one room.

criticise sb for: Shelley's manager criticised her for being late to work.

decide on: How did you decide on the order of the paragraphs?

defend against: The new pupil defended Ben against the bullies.

demonstrate against: They're demonstrating against police violence.

depend on: A positive body image shouldn't depend on your size.

discourage from: People need to be discouraged from throwing litter.

empathise with: Manage your emotions and empathise with other people.

engage in: The campaigners never engage in any illegal activities.

experiment with: Early cinema pioneers experimented with silent movies.

favour sth/sb over sth/sb: I favour savoury over sweet food.

feed on: The condor plays an important role by feeding on dead animals.

gaze at: For centuries people have gazed at the stars.

go on about: Please stop going on about your job – it's boring.

hope for: We were hoping for an improvement in the weather today.

insist on: He always insists on having the last word.

integrate sb into sth: Her vision integrated people into their communities.

interfere in: Don't interfere in someone else's relationship.

intervene in: So far the high court has refused to intervene in the case.

lead to: Global warming is certain to lead to water shortages.

link sth to sth: This part of the brain is linked to memory.

live on: She doesn't earn enough money to live on.

lobby for: The Students' Union lobbies the university for real change.

negotiate for: Staff are negotiating for better working conditions.

object to: Robson strongly objected to the terms of the contract.

participate in: They want to participate in the life of the village.

persist with: Why are you persisting with this ridiculous plan?

plead for: Civil rights groups pleaded for help from the government.

praise sb for sth: I praised her for working so hard on the campaign.

prevent (sb) from: What prevented Dan from doing well at school?

proceed with: The government proceeded with the election.

prohibit (sb) from: He was prohibited from entering the building.

protect sb/sth against: The shelters protect cats against the weather.

push for: Local businesses have been pushing for this development.

react to: She reacted angrily to what someone said during the meeting.

rebel against: Pupils rebelled against the new uniform regulations.

rehearse for: I've been rehearsing for a musical.

relate to: The growth in organised crime is related to increased poverty.

rely on: If you rely on solar power, you can consider yourself green.

remind sb of sth: The landscape reminded her of Scotland.

report on: Can the media report on the private lives of famous people?

restrict sb from: The protesters were restricted from entering the city.

result in: Below average rainfall can result in water shortages.

result from: We're still dealing with problems resulting from your errors.

retreat to: People in confined spaces get on better when they don't retreat to their own private space.

run for: She is planning to run for president.

slip on sth: My brother slipped on the wet floor in the kitchen.

spy on sb: She was spying on Japan for the US government.

stare at: She stared at me as if she had seen a ghost.

stick at: It's taught me the value of sticking at something.

survive on: The pay is so bad now that we can't survive on it.

suspect sb of: He had suspected her of lying for some time.

switch to: Many people are switching to online news sites.

think of: He was the first person to think of sending a short message.

warn sb against: They warned tourists against leaving the tourist centres.

WORD BUILDING

PREFIXES

Prefix	Examples
anti- (=against)	anti-bullying, anti-hacking
co- (= with, together)	co-working, co-pilot
extra- (= more than normal)	extra-special, extra-large
inter- (= between)	international, Internet
multi- (= many)	multi-sensory, multi-talented
over- (= more than expected)	overweight, overload
re- (= again)	re-establish, re-read
self- (= me)	self-confident, self-aware

Prefixes that give an opposite meaning

Prefix	Examples
dis-	disabled, disagree
il-/ir-	illegal, irregular
im-/in-	immature, insecurity
mis-	misjudged, misbehave
non-/un-	nonsense, unacceptable

SUFFIXES

Noun suffixes

Suffix	Examples
-age	marriage, package
-al	proposal
-ant/-ent	assistant, president
-ation/-ion/-ition	communication, rebellion, definition
-cian/-ian	musician, librarian
-dom	freedom
-ence/-ance	appearance, defence
-er/-or/-ist	sailor, voyager, artist
-hood	childhood
-ice	practice, notice
-ing	meaning, revising
-ism	sexism, mechanism
-ment	government, improvement
-ness	weakness, goodness
-ship	relationship, friendship
-sis	analysis, emphasis
-tion/-sion/-cion	obstruction, suspension, suspicion
-ty/-ity	activity, reality
-ure	pressure, culture

Adjective suffixes

Suffix	Examples
-able/-ible	habitable, horrible
-al	informal, social
-ed	exhausted, relaxed
-ic	artistic, ecstatic
-ing	interesting, matching
-ive	active, productive
-ful/-less	useful, useless
-ous	generous, nervous
-ory/-y	contradictory, chatty
-ly	curly, likely

Adverb suffixes

Suffix	Examples
-ly	effectively, probably

Verb suffixes

Suffix	Examples
-ate	complicate, congratulate
-en	shorten
-ify	clarify, identify
-ise/-ize	victimise, realise
-ute	commute

PRONUNCIATION TABLE

Consonants

p	pair, complete, appear
b	box, abbreviation, job
t	tennis, waiting, attend
d	degree, wedding, word
k	kiss, school, think, section
g	girl, again, luggage, ghost
tʃ	check, match, future
dʒ	judge, page, soldier
f	feel, difficult, laugh, physical
v	verb, nervous, move
θ	third, author, bath
ð	this, father, with
s	saw, notice, sister
z	zone, amazing, choose, quiz
ʃ	ship, sure, station, ocean
ʒ	pleasure, occasion
h	habit, whole, chocoholic
m	meaning, common, sum
n	neat, knee, channel, sun
ŋ	cooking, strong, thanks, sung
l	lifestyle, really, article
r	respect, correct, arrival
j	year, use, beautiful
w	window, one, where

Vowels

ɪ	information, invite
e	sentence, belt
æ	add, match, can
ɒ	not, documentary, wash
ʌ	love, but, luck
ʊ	footwear, look, put
iː	reading, three, magazine
eɪ	race, grey, break
aɪ	advice, might, try
ɔɪ	boy, join
uː	two, blue, school
əʊ	coat, show, phone
aʊ	about, now
ɪə	appear, here
eə	pair, various, square
ɑː	dark, father
ɔː	bought, draw, author
ʊə	tour, pure
ɜː	hurt, third
i	happy, pronunciation, serious
ə	accessory, actor, picture
u	situation, visual, influence

SELF-CHECK ANSWER KEY

Unit 1
Exercise 1
1 establish 2 lost 3 pass on 4 point 5 wiped
Exercise 2
1 terrified 2 took 3 bond 4 hit 5 ecstatic 6 doubt
Exercise 3
1b 2b 3c 4c 5a
Exercise 4
1 shall we 2 will you 3 aren't I 4 was it 5 won't you 6 isn't it
Exercise 5
1 currently 2 conversation 3 favourable 4 weight 5 devastated 6 unbearable
Exercise 6
1 made 2 were 3 out 4 hit 5 on 6 have

Unit 2
Exercise 1
1 bring about 2 resulted in 3 habitat loss 4 endangered species 5 pours, rain 6 lead to
Exercise 2
1 heavy 2 claws 3 nocturnal 4 skeletons 5 poachers
Exercise 3
1a 2c 3b 4b 5a
Exercise 4
1 Hmm ... I think I'll have a California roll, please. 2 We're planning to go home as soon as this class finishes. 3 Are you meeting Lara tomorrow? 4 I'm about to put dinner on the table. 5 At the moment, Rachel is thinking of helping a charitable institution. 6 Samuel's train leaves at 10 a.m.
Exercise 5
1 been 2 to 3 be 4 will 5 second 6 such
Exercise 6
1b 2c 3b 4c 5b

Unit 3
Exercise 1
1 behind 2 down 3 off 4 with 5 of 6 up
Exercise 2
1 defensive 2 flunked 3 decent 4 pushy 5 clash
Exercise 3
1 is forever asking 2 will leave 3 used to order 4 didn't use to like it 5 would always remember 6 will play the drums
Exercise 4
1 Ø 2 ,which 3 Ø 4 whom 5 ,where (and comma after 'grew up') 6 whom
Exercise 5
1c 2b 3a 4b 5c
Exercise 6
1 to look up to 2 to whom Agata usually goes 3 tends to bark 4 is constantly biting 5 trust people who 6 put up with

Unit 4
Exercise 1
1 hoax 2 enigma 3 abducted 4 light 5 hit
Exercise 2
1 sensational 2 muttering 3 suspicion 4 neighbourhood 5 quirky 6 corruption
Exercise 3
1 had/'d been waiting 2 had already started 3 went 4 hadn't checked 5 were waiting 6 did you do
Exercise 4
1 Scarcely had we arrived 2 At no time did I believe 3 In no way is she saying 4 Little did they think 5 Seldom do you see 6 Never have so many people

Exercise 5
1 awareness 2 topical 3 workers 4 newsworthy 5 information 6 attention
Exercise 6
1 Hardly had 2 it had already 3 had been queuing 4 went viral 5 Under no circumstances did 6 do for a living

Unit 5
Exercise 1
1 eyesight 2 tell the two houses apart 3 mouth-watering 4 stink 5 silky
Exercise 2
1 colour-blind 2 Immediate 3 runny 4 spicy 5 sense 6 fluffy
Exercise 3
1 thinking 2 to apply 3 borrow 4 having 5 eat 6 going
Exercise 4
1 stopped to chat 2 saw someone fall over 3 needs cleaning 4 regrets promising 5 go on burning 6 tried to give up
Exercise 5
1 sensitive 2 sticky 3 crunchy 4 hearing 5 interested 6 overpowering
Exercise 6
1 rather you didn't hum 2 doesn't let anyone/anybody 3 tried calling your parents 4 tends not to eat 5 would/'d sooner stay 6 stop doing

Unit 6
Exercise 1
1 significantly 2 decorating 3 repair 4 replace 5 a lot 6 spacious
Exercise 2
1 like 2 medium 3 down 4 up 5 move 6 rid
Exercise 3
1 was able to 2 need to 3 may not 4 forbidden 5 supposed
Exercise 4
1 the 2 a 3 the 4 The 5 Ø 6 the
Exercise 5
1 nowhere near as difficult 2 What you do is pour 3 Are we obliged to attend 4 are not allowed to eat 5 don't have to keep 6 managed to sell
Exercise 6
1c 2d 3b 4a 5d

Unit 7
Exercise 1
1 placards 2 stance 3 streets 4 slogans 5 delinquency 6 oppressing
Exercise 2
1 for 2 off 3 on 4 against 5 from 6 against
Exercise 3
1 (that) he and his wife are trying to eat fewer calories 2 what time they/I had arrived there the day before 3 to be quiet and pay attention 4 (that) they had been preparing for the party all week 5 (that) the weather is always great on their island. 6 (that) direct action can/could make governments change their plans
Exercise 4
1 agreed that black doesn't/didn't suit me. 2 offered to give me/us a lift in his new car. 3 objected to sharing a tent with Paulo. 4 refused to walk in the rain. 5 congratulated Carmen on passing her test. 6 advised Kelly to come up with a different solution.
Exercise 5
1 organisation 2 institutional 3 inequality 4 slavery 5 poverty 6 victimised

Exercise 6
1b 2a 3c 4d 5a

Unit 8
Exercise 1
1 backed up 2 break off 3 flaws 4 overwhelming 5 malfunction
Exercise 2
1 embedded 2 obsolete 3 latest 4 wave 5 flattering 6 dated
Exercise 3
1 to be 2 being 3 be 4 were 5 been 6 to be
Exercise 4
1 is thought that the device exploded during the flight 2 was reported that the killer was innocent 3 has been claimed to have caused the accident when it flew into the engine 4 were revealed to have accessed the bank's security system 5 are known to be safely back at school 6 was thought that cinema would never become popular
Exercise 5
1 in 2 being 3 It 4 down 5 away 6 needs
Exercise 6
1 facial 2 upgraded 3 latest 4 functionality 5 outdated 6 dramatically

Unit 9
Exercise 1
1 mind 2 got 3 out 4 choose 5 did 6 surely
Exercise 2
1 inside – aside 2 on – in 3 of – and 4 concerned – considered 5 waiting – to wait 6 masterstrokes – setbacks
Exercise 3
1 had backed up 2 shouldn't 3 didn't need to make 4 would wash 5 had done
Exercise 4
1a 2c 3a 4b 5c
Exercise 5
1 vain 2 himself 3 clue 4 through 5 wait 6 would
Exercise 6
1 needn't have bought 2 unless you go 3 wish I had 4 only I hadn't sent 5 shouldn't have told him 6 had no choice

Unit 10
Exercise 1
1 mellow 2 on purpose 3 historic 4 exceptional 5 plays
Exercise 2
1 in 2 catching 3 edge 4 For 5 in, for
Exercise 3
1 must have/must've been sitting 2 cannot/can't have been washed 3 might/may/could have been 4 would have/would've been worn 5 may/might/could (well) have belonged 6 can't have constructed
Exercise 4
1 Walking into the room, they saw that they'd been burgled. 2 Having lost my wallet, I had to cancel all my cards. 3 Seeing two men arguing outside the shop, she crossed the street to avoid them. 4 Having been lying in the sun for an hour, I decided it was time for a swim. 5 Not hearing his alarm, he overslept by two hours. 6 Having changed his degree course, Corey felt a lot happier at university.
Exercise 5
1 Having 2 well 3 been 4 telling 5 deliver 6 at
Exercise 6
1b 2c 3b 4a 5d